The Design Directory of
Window Treatments

The Design Directory of
Window Treatments

Written and Illustrated by

Jackie Von Tobel

Gibbs Smith, Publisher
TO ENRICH AND INSPIRE HUMANKIND
Salt Lake City | Charleston | Santa Fe | Santa Barbara

First Edition
12 11 10 09 08   6 5 4 3 2

Published by
Gibbs Smith, Publisher
P.O. Box 667
Layton, Utah 84041

Orders: 1.800.835.4993
www.gibbs-smith.com

Designed by TTA Design
Printed and bound in China
Cover background fabric "Vicarious Color," Desert, courtesy Robert Allen:
Pattern in Color. www.robertallendesign.com; 800-333-3777; To the Trade

Library of Congress Cataloging-in-Publication Data

Von Tobel, Jackie.
  The design directory of window treatments / written and illustrated by
Jackie Von Tobel.—1st ed.
     p. cm.
  ISBN-13: 978-1-4236-0216-3
  ISBN-10: 1-4236-0216-1
  1. Draperies—Handbooks, manuals, etc. 2. Draperies—Pictorial works. 3.
Window shades—Pictorial works. 4. Cornices—Pictorial works. 5. Valances
(Windows)—Pictorial works. 6. Draperies in interior decoration—Themes,
motives—Dictionaries. 7. House furnishings industry and
trade—Directories. I. Title.

TT390.V66 2007
645'.32—dc22
                          2007009579

Contents

✤

Acknowledgements

MY LOVE OF FABRICS and all of the beautiful things that can be made with them began at a young age. My sister Julie and I spent countless hours as small children sewing doll clothes and making dollhouses complete with little draperies and bed sets. I still feel that same passion today when a new shipment of fabric books or trims arrive. I open every new box as if it is a long-awaited birthday present and eagerly flip through the swatches, envisioning all of the wonderful possibilities they present.

A long and sometimes bumpy road has led me to writing this book and along the way there have been many important people in my life that I wish to thank.

Thanks to my always-supportive and inspiring husband, Arnie, who never questioned my ability or desire to write this book and who ate a lot of takeout dinners while I spent what seemed like thousands of hours drawing drapery.

To my beautiful daughter, Angelica, who spent so many hours copying pages and organizing binders; I couldn't have done it without you. Thanks to my boys, JT and Geordie, who were always there to lend a helping hand.

I would like to thank my wonderful sisters, Julie, Vickie, Trudi, and Valorie, for their constant support and encouragement in this and all of the other endeavors of my life.

Thanks to my inspirational drafting teacher, Al Forster, who taught me my most important lesson in design school.

I would like to impart my gratitude and admiration to the many design professionals who have shared their knowledge and expertise so openly with others, especially Deb Barrett and Joan Willis.

To Dannette, Meka, and Jacquelyn, thanks for always being there for me.

Finally, thank you to Suzanne and Madge and the wonderful staff at Gibbs Smith, Publisher, who made me feel so at home. From my first visit to your wonderful barn on salad day, I knew I had made the right choice.

Introduction

I HAVE WORKED AS AN INTERIOR DESIGNER for almost twenty years and I still love to design window treatments.

Over the years, as many designers do, I have conducted a never-ending search for ideas and inspiration. I have attended numerous trade shows and seminars around the world, and I've eagerly searched through every magazine I received and every book I bought for anything fresh, new, and different. This book is the culmination of that search. From basic design fundamentals to intricate multilayered designs, it contains the most complete directory of window treatments ever assembled.

The *Design Directory of Window Treatments* is the "must have" resource for designers, workroom professionals, and do-it-yourselfers. Concise, straight-to-the-point lists, definitions, and descriptions of design fundamentals and components provide a comprehensive education on window treatments.

Over 1,500 individual components and complete designs illustrated in this book are meant to provide you with the guidance and inspiration needed to encourage your creativity and enable you to stretch your design boundaries. It is an indispensable tool of the trade that no designer or workroom should be without.

Standardized definitions of industry terminology developed by the Window Coverings Association of America (WCAA) will help you communicate effectively within the industry.

Black-and-white line drawings of every color illustration in this book are available on the enclosed CD-Rom. They can be downloaded to your computer or you can print them and personalize them with color for your project. Also included on the CD-Rom are printable resource directories, workroom worksheets, and service request forms.

While I have made every effort to include all the pertinent information and current design options I could find, I am sure I have forgotten a few things. If you would like to post pictures of your original designs, if you have comments or suggestions for information you think should have been included, or if you would like to submit a picture or sketch of a unique design or a new idea for future revised editions of this book, please e-mail me at: ideas@designdirectory4u.com

Jackie VonVolel

Window Treatments

are made up of various pieces and parts that, when combined properly, produce a beautiful window dressing.

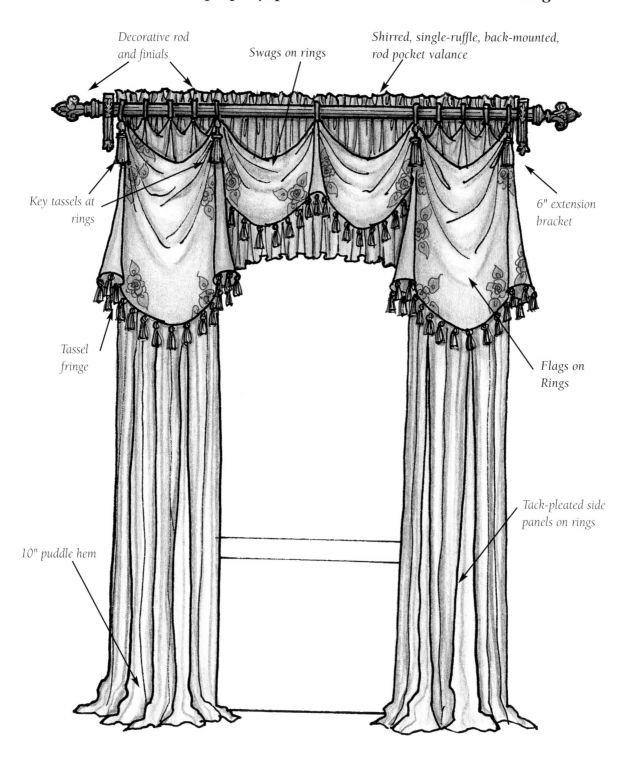

Decorative rod and finials

Swags on rings

Shirred, single-ruffle, back-mounted, rod pocket valance

Key tassels at rings

6" extension bracket

Tassel fringe

Flags on Rings

10" puddle hem

Tack-pleated side panels on rings

How to Use This Book

CREATING A BEAUTIFUL WINDOW treatment that meets the specifications of your project is all about making the right choices.

Too many times the wrong decisions are made due to lack of knowledge or exposure to the many options that are available to you. This directory breaks down thousands of current window treatment designs into over 350 individual components that can be used alone or in combination with each other to create unique designs that will expand your options and allow you to express your creativity.

Each section of the directory will assist you in making decisions critical to your design success.

Design: Using the fundamentals and calculations outlined in the first chapter, measure your window, analyze your space, and calculate the basic proportions, lay out, and construction of your design.

Fabric: Choose the fiber, weave, pattern, hand, and color of the fabrics you will use.

Heading: Plot your heading style and variations if you are designing panels, a valance, or a shade.

Style: Choose one of the finished treatments in the book or use a combination of the individual components shown to create a new look.

*Patterns are available for many of the designs. Look for the pattern maker listed below the design description. Find their contact information in the resource directory.

Embellishments: Apply the finishing touches that will personalize your design.

Hardware: Choose the appropriate type and style of hardware or mounting technique for your treatment.

Workroom: Communicate your designs effectively and accurately to your workroom to ensure that your treatments are made properly.

Design
Fundamentals

❧

Window Treatment Design Fundamentals

WHEN DESIGNING YOUR WINDOW treatments, basic design fundamentals should always be used as a guide to assist you in making the right choices. By combining your knowledge of these principles with your knowledge of the products available, you will be able to create designs that will meet your needs.

The design fundamentals are separated into five categories:

Features and Functions: The features and functions of soft treatments are the beneficial attributes that can be achieved with the application of window treatments.

Principles: The design you choose for each window should meet its functional needs in an appropriate, attractive manner. The principles of design are used to evaluate the functional and aesthetic needs of the window, as well as the finished window treatment.

Elements: The elements of design are the set of physical tools or raw materials with which the principles of design can be applied.

Rules of Thumb: The rules of thumb are a set of tools that help you calculate correct proportions for your treatments.

Specifications: The specifications for soft treatments are a list of rules and guidelines that should be applied during the fabrication of your window treatments to insure quality in construction.

The Features and Functions of Window Treatments

Design

- Create a sense of style and visual interest
- Add softness and warmth
- Complement the architectural style, line, and scale of the room
- Establish, continue, or reinforce a decorative theme
- Create a focal point
- Accentuate a good view or a specialty window
- Bring focus to architectural details

Function

- Light control
- Privacy
- Exterior noise control
- Interior noise reduction
- Reduce glare

Camouflage

- Hide architectural flaws
- Obscure a bad view
- Soften hard lines

Illusion

- Create balance between windows of different sizes and styles
- Add the illusion of added height to low windows
- Manipulate the appearance of the size of the window
- Balance the proportions of the room

Energy Efficiency

- Insulate the window from outside temperatures
- Help to maintain the interior temperature

The Principles of Window Treatment Design

The design you choose for each window should meet its functional needs in an appropriate, attractive manner. The principles of design are used to evaluate the functional and aesthetic needs of the window, as well as the finished window treatment.

Proportion: Proportion is the relationship of the individual parts to the whole window treatment when comparing sizes and shapes. The proportions must be manipulated to create a harmonious balance between all of the components used and the overall size and scale of the treatment.

Scale: Scale is the relative size of an element, whether it refers to the scale of the entire window treatment or the scale of the pattern on the fabric. You must consider the relationship of the scale of the room to the window treatment to be used in it. You must also consider the scale of the patterns of different fabrics to be used on the treatment in order to produce a harmonious balance between them.

Balance: Balance is the state of evenness, stability, or equilibrium among the design elements used in the treatment. There are three types of balance:

Symmetrical: Both sides of the treatment are the same or mirrored.

Asymmetrical: The two sides are somewhat different yet they are balanced by a central element or equilibrium.

Radial: The elements radiate from a central point outward in spokes or concentric circles, such as a fanlight window.

Rhythm: Rhythm is the connection of elements within the design scheme used to create balance and harmony. There are three types of rhythm:

Transition: The use of elements such as trim, color, or lines to create visual movement.

Gradation: Shapes are made to decrease and increase in size or colors and are made to darken or lighten in a specific order to create visual movement.

Repetition: A color, texture, or element is used repeatedly.

Emphasis: Emphasis is the use of colors, pattern, or elements to create a focal point in the treatment.

Harmony: Harmony is composed of unity and variety. Design elements should be applied to the treatment to create a sense of unity among the components; however, it must also be imparted with enough variety within those components to create a pleasing balance or harmony.

The Elements of Window Treatment Design

The elements of design are the set of physical tools or raw materials with which the principles of design can be applied.

Space: Space sets the limits on the functional and decorative boundaries of your designs. Use pattern, color, line, and opacity to manipulate the visual interpretation of the treatment.

Light: Light enables the visual alteration and manipulates the intensity of the light at the window through fabric choice, color, and texture.

Line: Line is used to create movement, expand or contract space, and define mood.

Color: Use the choice of color to manipulate the visual impact of the treatment.

Texture: The surface smoothness or roughness of the elements used can affect the visual interpretation of the treatment. Smooth and shiny surfaces can be more formal and sophisticated while rough surfaces can impart a casual, comfortable feel.

Pattern and Ornamental Decoration: The inclusion or omission of a specific pattern and ornamentation can create or reduce drama, excitement, or visual attention to the treatment.

Form and Shape: The overall form and shape of the treatment can be altered and adjusted to create the balance needed to develop harmony within the treatment.

Rules of Thumb

While good design sometimes calls upon us to think out of the box, there are certain rules of thumb that can help calculate the proper proportions to use as a starting point.

The Rule of Halves: Equal vertical halves are not pleasing to the eye. Never cut the window in half by designing any element to be exactly half of the length of the treatment.

The Rule of Three: The human eye finds objects grouped together in threes or multiples of threes to be the most visually pleasing. In design, using three elements allows for one to be used as a statement, the second as a contrast, and the third as a complement. This rule can be used in choosing the placement and number of individual elements to be used in a window treatment.

The Rule of Fifths and Sixths: When calculating the dimensions of a treatment, ratios of 5 and 6 are the most visually pleasing. By using these ratios mathematically, you can calculate good starting points for the lengths of your treatment.

For example
If you have a treatment that will be 96" finished length mounted at the ceiling and you want to calculate the proper length for the valance.

Finished length of the treatment = 96"

$$96" \div 5 = 19 \ 1/4"$$
$$96" \div 6 = 16"$$

The finished length of the valance according to this rule of thumb should be somewhere between 16" and 19" in order to insure that it is in good proportion. This range of measurements can also be used to determine the long and short points of hems or tails.

To calculate swags and cascades using this rule:
Swag drop = 1/5 total length of the treatment
Cascade = 3/5 of the total length of the treatment

Specification for Soft Treatments

Fabric

- Don't skimp on fabric! It is better to use a less expensive fabric to construct your treatment at the correct fullness than to sacrifice volume for a more expensive fabric.
- Match the fabric repeat and plot the pattern placement to best complement the treatment and the room.
- Always match pattern repeats on multiple treatments.
- Plot the fabric's pattern placement on the treatment before construction.
- On textured fabrics like velvet, specify the direction of the nap as it will affect the color of the finished treatment. Make sure the nap falls in the same direction on all pieces.
- Use drapery weights or string weights to control the hang of your drapery panels. They can also be used in top treatments, swags, cascades, jabots, and tails.

Construction

- All seams should be serged and finished with an overlock stitch. If using an open pressed seam, the selvages should be overlocked for a finished look and to prevent raveling.
- Where possible, plan for seams to be hidden at the back of the pleat.
- Always match patterns exactly at seams.
- Avoid topstitching unless it is an integral part of your design. It makes treatments look unprofessional, and it interferes with the hang of the fabric.
- Coordinate the color of thread to be used with the fabric on the treatment. Use several colors, if necessary. Clear monofilament thread should be used only as a second choice.
- All corners should be mitered and hand stitched.
- Hems should be blind stitched.
- Bottom hems should be at least 4" to 6" long and double turned. Wider hems allow for adjustment if the fabric shrinks.
- Side hems should be 1" to 3" wide and double turned.
- Trim should be topstitched through the face fabric only, never through the lining.

Hems

✦ Insert shade cord in a casing sewn in the bottom hem of puddled panels. This allows you to cinch the hem and control the puddle so it falls the same way all the time.

✦ Increase the width of the bottom and leading edge hems, or self-line tieback panels so the lining does not show.

✦ Request steamed edges as opposed to pressed. A soft edge is usually superior to a hard, crisp fold.

✦ Self-line the entire excess portion of the hem in puddle panels so the white lining does not show.

✦ Spray the puddle section of the hem with a fabric protector to help keep the area clean.

✦ If necessary, attach side hems to the wall to avoid light gaps and to prevent the panel from blowing in the wind.

Pleats

✦ Don't rely on the "standard" size and spacing of pleats. Plan their size, placement, and spacing to best complement the treatment.

✦ Self- or contrast line the heading of goblet pleats so the white lining does not show in the open goblet. Use French seams on shear or unlined panels for a finished couture look.

✦ Insert stuffing in open pleats or horns where needed to help maintain their shape.

Linings

✦ Always line treatments unless they are meant to be sheer or the design specifically requires no lining.

✦ Think about your lining choices before settling on the "standard" lining. Find out which linings your workroom stocks and ask for samples to keep on hand.

✦ Always test the effect your lining choice has on the face fabric. Hold your fabric and lining up to a light source and check for color or texture changes.

✦ To eliminate light seepage at the sides of blackout panels, increase your overall width by several inches or add a 1" pocket to the return and insert a stiffener. Fold the extra inch inward and attach directly to the wall.

Standard Drapery Measurements

Rod face width = window width + side extension width

Rod face with full-glass clearance = window width + 1.5"

Return = bracket projection + 1/2"

Overlap = 7' per pair—3 1/2" per panel

Stackback = 1/3" of the rod face width

Stackback for full-glass clearance = rod face x 1.5"

Finished length minimum = top of the window to the floor + 6"

Fullness minimum for pleated draperies = 2.5x to 1

Fullness minimum for sheer draperies = 3x to 1

Fullness for stationary side panels = minimum of 2x fullness of the

finished panel width

Bishop's sleeve panels minimum length = add 15" to 20" per pouf

Puddled panels = add 6" to 18" to the length

Drapery Yardage Calculator

Use these easy steps to calculate accurate plain yardage for your treatment.

Step 1—Calculate the Finished Width

Rod Face Width (RFW) + Overlaps (OL) $RFW + OL + RT = FW$

Step 2—Calculate the Number of Fabric Widths or Cuts

Multiply Finished Width (FW) x Fullness (F),
and then divide by the Fabric Width. $(FW \times F) \div Fabric\ Width = W$

Step 3—Determine the Finished Length (FL)

Add allowances for hems, headings, take up, puddle, etc.
(H/H) to figure the Cut Length $(CL)\ FL + H/H = CL$

Step 4—Determine the Total Yardage

Multiply the Cut Length (CL) by the number of
widths or cuts (W) and divide by 36 to determine the
total yardage. $(TY)\ (CL \times W) \div 36 = TY$

Round up the yardage to the next full yard.

Step 5—Determine Additional Yardage for Repeat Allowance

Divide the Cut Length (CL) by the Repeat (R) and
round up the sum to the next whole number. $(CL) \div (R) = (X)$

Multiply that number by the repeat to determine the
new Cut Length (CL) with allowance for the repeat. $(X) \times (R) = (CL)$

*   *As a rule of thumb, it is always a good idea to order 1 to 2 extra yards of fabric
when working with medium to large patterns to allow for pattern variations.*

Fabric

Fabric is a manufactured product that is constructed of fiber, weave, color, pattern, and finish.

Fiber

Fibers are natural, such as silk, linen, or cotton, or man made, such as polyester, nylon, or rayon. Fabric can be made exclusively of natural or man-made fibers or a combination of the two, such as polyester and cotton. The qualities of the individual fiber are integral to the performance of the finished fabric. Those qualities should be taken into consideration when choosing the right fabric for your application.

Fiber Characteristics

Fabric	Special	Resistance characteristics	Resistance to deterioration	Soil resistance to fading by sun	Flammability	Care
COTTON	Drapes well	Poor to fair	Good to very good	Fair unless treated	High unless treated	Washable
Acetate	Drapes well	Poor to fair	Fair to good	Fair to good	Burns quickly unless treated	Dry clean
Acrylic	Drapes well, may stretch	Very good	Very good	Good	Melts or burns	Washable
Modacrylic	Drapes well, may stretch	Very good	Very good	Good	Will not flame	Washable
Nylon	Builds up static	Fair to good	Fair to good	Good to very good	Melts	Washable, press on low
Polyester	Wrinkle resistant, may stretch	Good to very good	Good	Good	Melts & drops off in flame	Washable
Rayon	Drapes well, tends to stretch unless modified	Poor to fair	Fair to good	Fair to good	Burns like paper unless treated	Washable or dry clean depending on label

Weave

The fibers or threads of a fabric are woven together in a specific manner in order to achieve the desired pattern for that fabric.

Fabric Weave
Each filling yarn passes over and under each warp yarn with each row alternating.

Satin Weave: The face of the fabric consists of only the warp or the weft threads, giving the fabric a very smooth and lustrous surface.

Twill Weave: It is similar to plain weave. The warp yarns skip at regular predetermined intervals, creating a diagonal rib in the weave.

Basket Weave: Two or more warp yarns cross alternately side-by-side with two or more filling yarns. It resembles a plaited basket.

Jacquard Weave: Fabrics woven on a Jacquard loom have intricate patterns.

Rib Weave: It is a plain weave type formed with heavy yarns in the warp or the filling direction.

Dobby Weave: It is a decorative weave, which is characterized by small designs or geometric figures being woven in the fabric structure.

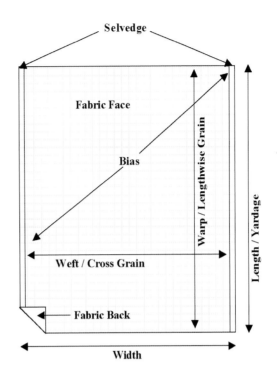

Leno Weave: The warp yarns are arranged in pairs. One yarn is twisted around the other between picks of the filling yarn.

Oxford Weave: A group of fabrics made with modified plain weave or basket weave. Usually made for shirting materials.

Cut Pile: The face of the fabric is composed of cut ends of pile yarn such as in a velvet or velveteen.

Uncut Pile: This is a pile of yarns consisting of loops as in terry cloth.

Chenille Fabric: A soft wool, silk, cotton, or rayon yarn with protruding pile.

Coloring

Coloring is the process of applying pigments or dyes to fibers or finished fabrics using dyeing or printing processes.

Dyeing Methods

Piece Dyeing: The dyeing of woven lengths of finished fabrics.

Solution Dyeing: The addition of dyes or pigments to the viscose solution that forms the extruded fiber. This process locks the color into the fiber, making it resistant to sun fading.

Stock or Fiber Dyeing: The dyeing of natural fibers before they are spun into yarn.

Yarn Dyeing: The application of dye to a finished length of yarn.

Printing Methods

Hand Printing: Batik, Silk Screen, Stenciling, Hand Painting, Block Printing

Semi-automated and Rotary Screen Printing: Multiple semi-automated screens are used to apply multiple colors and patterns to the fabric face.

Roller Printing: A series of engraved copper rollers apply the color and pattern to the fabric.

Pattern

The pattern can be woven into the fabric as with a jacquard weave or it can be printed onto it. In the case of a combination print, a woven jacquard pattern in the fabric is covered with a printed pattern on top.

Pattern Repeat: The repeat denotes the size of the print and the repetition and should be appropriate for the scale of the length of the treatment. Avoid using large repeats on small treatments. They should be used on long panels with a wide exposure.

Pattern Match: The pattern ends and begins at the selvedge edge of the fabric, usually cut in half. Make sure that all patterns match across the widths of the treatment, at the leading edges of panels, as well as in all other applications of the fabric in the room.

Pattern Direction: The pattern is woven into or printed onto the fabric. The standard direction is parallel to the length of the fabric. If the pattern is "railroaded," it runs perpendicular to the length of the fabric.

Finish

Fabric finishes are treatments or processes that complete a textile. The average fabric used in interior design has a combination of six finishes. Finishes that are applied to the fabric after it has been colored fall into two categories: standard and decorative.

Standard: Standard finishes add to the fabrics durability or lend it the ability to perform in a certain way. The most common of these finishes are:

Antibacterial: Suppress mold and mildew and delay decay—applicable in health care.

Antistatic: Inhibit static.

Flame retardant: Slow the rate of ignition and flame spread and help the fabric to self-extinguish.

Insulating: Usually a foam product that is sprayed onto the back of the fabric to insulate from temperature or noise; i.e., insulated blackout lining.

Fabric care: Make the fabric easier to care for, such as permanent press or wrinkle resistance.

Laminating: The process of joining two fabrics together; i.e., vinyl laminated with a knit backing in upholstery fabric.

Mothproofing: Protects from insect infestation.

Soil repellent: Protects the surface of the fabric from dirt and stains.

Water repellent: Makes the fabric less water absorbing; i.e., patio furniture upholstery fabric.

Water absorbent: Improves the absorbent qualities of the fabric.

Decorative: Decorative finishes create a specific decorative look or improve the feel or appearance of fabric. The most common of these finishes are:

Brightening: Brighten the colors in the fabric and make them last longer.

Calendaring: Starches, glazes, or resins are forced deep into the fabric with a heavy roller to achieve a specific effect.

Chintz: A calendared finished that uses a glaze to add shine to the fabric.

De-lustering: Removes the shiny finish from fabrics in which it would not be appropriate.

Antiwrinkling: Makes the fabric more wrinkle resistant and helps it retain its shape.

Embossing: Uses an engraved roller to calendar the fabric, producing a permanent three-dimensional design.

Etching or Burn-out: Uses an acid compound that burns or etches the fiber to reveal a sheer pattern.

Flocking: A decorative pattern is made with small fibers bonded to the fabric.

French Wax: The shiniest, highest-gloss finish.

Moiré: Embossing that leaves a watermark pattern on the fabric.

Napping: The fabric fibers are brushed to create a fuzzy finish or short pile.

Panné: An embossing technique that presses down the fibers of a velour or velvet in a particular direction to create a pattern.

Plisse: An acid is applied to cause the yarns to pucker into a plaid or all-over wrinkle.

Resin: Applied as a glaze or as a base for waterproofing or soil repellent.

Lustering: A method which produces a luster to the fabric without the addition of resins or starches.

Post Finishing: Some specialty finishes can be applied to fabrics after they have been manufactured such as flame-retardant, lamination, paper, foam, or latex backing.

Pattern

Types of Pattern

Small Patterns: Tiny all-over motifs are often seen by the eye as texture rather than pattern. They can be used to blend colors and give the illusion of tactile dimension.

Large Patterns: Large motifs will cause a space to look smaller. They create a focal point and command attention. Large patterns appear to advance visually.

Directional Patterns: Stripes, checks, and plaids create a directional flow. They can be manipulated to provide horizontal, vertical, and diagonal emphasis. These patterns must be matched precisely and can be subject to pattern drifting or weave warping.

Optical Patterns: Patterns such as moirés, geometrics, and dots can create the illusion of movement. These patterns can imitate depth, projection, and three-dimensional texture.

Random Pattern: A pattern that has an asymmetrical or unbalanced configuration. This can range from a large-scale floral bouquet to a contemporary squiggle pattern. These patterns create excitement and energy. Although they appear random, they do possess a horizontal repeat that must be matched.

Regulated Pattern: A pattern is considered regulated when it repeats on a regular basis horizontally or vertically. This can include stripes, plaids, checks, or geometrics. These patterns provide structure and formality to a design.

Pattern Direction

Railroaded Pattern: The pattern runs horizontally from selvedge to selvedge. Railroaded patterns are used primarily for upholstery and can make pattern matching a challenge.

Typical Pattern: The pattern runs vertically along the length of the fabric. This is typical for most drapery and upholstery fabrics.

Typical

Railroaded

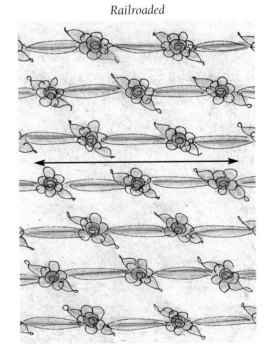

Pattern Dominance

Many fabrics have a motif that includes a primary and secondary pattern. It is important to choose which one you want to highlight when plotting your pattern placement.

Pattern Repeats and Pattern Matching

Vertical and Horizontal Repeats: The distance between the full repeat of the pattern on the face of the fabric going in either horizontal or vertical direction.

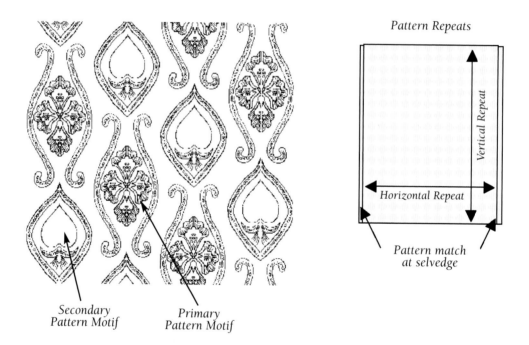

Secondary Pattern Motif

Primary Pattern Motif

Pattern Repeats

Vertical Repeat

Horizontal Repeat

Pattern match at selvedge

Print on Print Repeats: In fabric such as woven damasks that have a printed pattern on the face, there are two patterns that must be matched. the base pattern of the damasks as well as the printed pattern. Failing to match the ground pattern as well as the printed pattern will result in an off matched ground pattern, which will be obvious when hung.

Small Pattern Repeat: Very often a fabric with a small pattern that seems to have little or no repeat will have a larger full-length repeat. This can result in a striping effect when it is used in length. The only way to check for this patterning is to inspect a generous length of the fabric.

Balanced Pattern Match: The pattern that is repeated is a whole motif that is balanced on both selvedge edges of the fabric. In this case the seam runs through the field of the fabric or a secondary pattern when joining cuts and there are no seams running through the primary motif.

Halved Pattern Match: The pattern that is to be repeated is cut in half at each selvedge edge of the fabric. In this case the seam will run through the center of the primary motif when joining cuts.

Half Drop Repeat or Drop Match Pattern: The pattern on one selvedge edge of the fabric panel will not match straight across the other edge. The pattern on the right edge of the fabric will be one half its height up or down from the left edge. Therefore, additional fabric is needed to match the pattern as one half of the repeat is wasted in making matching cuts.

Straight Repeat or Straight Match Pattern: The pattern is positioned in a straight line across the width of the fabric and is the same on the right side of the fabric as on the left.

Half Drop Pattern Repeat

Straight Match Pattern Repeat

Fabric Widths

Knowing the accurate bolt width and usable width of the fabric you are using is key to estimating the correct amount of yardage you will need.

Bolt Width: The measure of the fabric from selvedge edge to selvedge edge.

Usable Width: The measure of the fabric from selvedge allowance to selvedge allowance.

Selvedge Allowance: The portion of the fabric from the selvedge edge inward to the line on which the pattern match is centered. This line is where the seam must be placed in order to match the pattern properly. The fabric past that line to the selvedge edge is rough and is not meant to be seen.

While the majority of home decor fabrics are woven at 54" wide, there are many exceptions. The selvedge allowance or unusable edge of the fabric can also vary in width as much as 1/2" to 1 1/2" as with some woven fabrics such as rayon and silk velvets. It is important to know what the "usable" width of your fabric is after selvedge and seam allowances are deducted.

Typical Widths

Standard drapery and upholstery fabric . . . . .54" wide

Drapery sheers . . . . .54"–60"–106" wide

Extra-wide drapery sheers . . . . .108"–118"–126" wide

Extra-wide jacquards . . . . .114"–116" wide

Some high-end silks and linens . . . . .42"–45" wide

Dress-making fabric . . . . .45"–58" and 60" wide

Quilting cottons . . . . .45" wide

Knits . . . . .60" wide

Drapery lining . . . . .48"–54"–60" wide

Extra-wide drapery lining . . . . .115"–126" wide

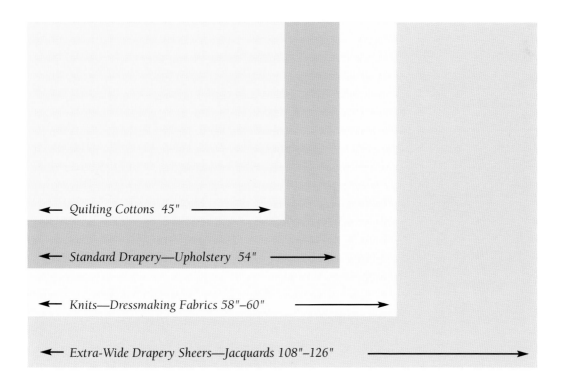

← Quilting Cottons 45" →

← Standard Drapery—Upholstery 54" →

← Knits—Dressmaking Fabrics 58"–60" →

← Extra-Wide Drapery Sheers—Jacquards 108"–126" →

Lining

Lining is a key component of any window treatment. It is what sets apart the professional treatment from the amateur. Lining is a tool that allows you to manipulate the fabric in your treatment and add performance.

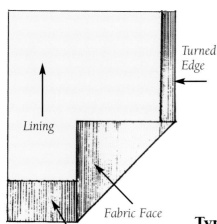

Lining

Turned Edge

Turned Hem

Fabric Face

- ✤ Lining adds body and volume to thin fabrics.
- ✤ It protects the face fabric from sun rot and fading.
- ✤ It provides a uniform look to the windows from the street.
- ✤ It stabilizes the panel and reduces droop.
- ✤ It reduces light and color bleed-through.
- ✤ It provides a clean, finished, professional look.
- ✤ It adds stability and strength to the heading.

Types of Lining

White polyester-cotton lining is standard in most workrooms unless otherwise specified. The degree of quality and pliability can change dramatically from vendor to vendor. Get a sample of your workrooms standard lining to see if it is acceptable to you. White lining keeps the color true on the face fabric.

Ivory Lining has a softer look than white and is more appealing when seen from the outside of the home. It can subtly change the color of face fabric.

Self-lining or colored lining is used when any part of the treatment lining can be seen. Remember to consider the view of the treatment from a sitting position, as well as from above in a two-story setting.

French or Black Lining can be used as a lining or interlining for a blackout look or to eliminate color and pattern bleed-through. When using a light-colored face fabric, black lining can turn the face fabric slightly gray.

Blackout lining is used to achieve maximum light blocking. Pin or needle holes can show through the treatment during daylight hours. Glue baste the widths of blackout lining together before sewing to avoid pin holes. In the past, blackout lining was stiff, heavy, and hard to work with. Many vendors are now offering a new breed of soft, pliable blackouts and thermal linings that have a wonderful hand and are easy to sew.

Thermal Suede is heavier than regular lining and has a rubber backing for insulation.

The lining color selected should be consistent in all of the front windows of the client's home.

Place linings behind the face fabric and hold up to a light source to check for color changes.

Interlining

Interlining is a layer of specialty fabric placed between the face fabric and the lining of the treatment. In recent years the practice of interlining has become very popular.

There are many reasons and ways to use an interlining:

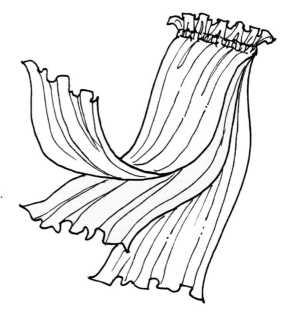

- ✤ To protect the face fabric from the sun.
- ✤ Add a thermal layer to the treatment to reduce cold or heat.
- ✤ Create a blackout effect without using stiff blackout lining.
- ✤ Add bulk and volume to a thin fabric.
- ✤ Stabilize a loosely woven fabric.
- ✤ Eliminate pattern or color bleed-through.
- ✤ Impart body, strength, and stability to silks.

Types of Interlining

- Most interlinings are 100 percent cotton goods that have been felted or flannelled.

- English Bump is a thick but soft interlining. It imparts a fluffy, heavy look to the fabric.

- Heavy Weight Flannel or Interlining Plus is heavier than regular interlining but not as heavy as table felt.

- Table Felt is a very thick, heavy interlining. It imparts a heavy, stiff look to the fabric.

- Lightweight interlining such as "Domette" are used in valances, swags, cascades, and tails.

- Double-sided interlinings combine thermal properties with blackout capability or a sueded interlining with a finished lining side. This eliminates the need for triple layering.

- Always interline silk treatments. Use bump for a thick, fluffy look or lightweight interlining for a crisper, lighter look.

- Let interlining rest for twenty-four hours after it is cut before you begin fabrication. Interlining stretches when it is rolled on the tube at the mill. It returns to original size when unrolled and allowed to rest.

- Interlining can be placed in face fabric hems of draperies, dust ruffles, and top treatments for a soft edge.

- Do not seam interlining. Join the selvedges by overlapping to reduce bulk.

- Allow the interlining to float free above the hem to avoid bunching.

Key Terms for Fabric

Bias cut: Fabric that is cut at a forty-five-degree angle of the fabric weave. This cut of fabric will allow swags to drape better, and better enable cording to hug curves. Prints should be checked before cutting on the bias. Some upright prints can be cut on the bias and look great, others won't.

C.O.M. (aka COM): Customer's own material.

Crinoline (aka buckram): A heavily sized or stiff fabric used as a foundation for pleats in draperies.

Crosswise grain (aka fillers, woof, weft): The threads of a woven fabric that run perpendicular to the selvedges. The fabric has a slight give in the crosswise grain.

Cuts: The number of widths of fabric needed to construct a window treatment.

Cut allowance: The amount of fabric added to finished measurements for hems and headings.

Cut width: The complete amount of fabric needed for treatment width, including hems and/or any other allowances.

Drapability: The ability of a certain fabric to hang in pleasing folds.

Drop match: A drop match is when the width is cut straight across by the print; the pattern will NOT line up perfectly to be seamed at the selvedge. The pattern repeat does not match until down 1/2 of the vertical pattern repeat. Therefore, additional yardage is required. Add 1/2 pattern repeat per cut. This is commonly found in fabrics that coordinate with wallpaper. It is usually designated in the sample books (but not always) as a drop match.

Dye lots: A batch of fabric printed at the same time. Each time a new printing is done, the fabric is classified with a new dye lot. Fabrics from different dye lots can vary in color. If color matching is important for your project, always get a cutting of the dye lot you will order from.

Fabrication: The process of manufacturing raw goods into a finished product.

Face fabric: The decorative fabric on a treatment that "faces" into the room. The lining is behind it.

Facing: A piece of fabric is stitched to a raw edge and turned to the backside to form a finished edge. The diagonals of jabots or cascades are sometimes faced to show a contrast in the angles.

Finish: Product applied to fabric as a protection against watermarks and fading.

Flame-retardant fabric: Fabric that will not burn. It can be inherently flame retardant, which means the actual fiber from which it was made is a flame-retardant fiber, e.g., polyester, or be treated to become flame retardant, which usually changes the fibers and makes the fabric stiff.

French seam: A way of stitching fabric together with the seam hidden from view. Used on sheer fabrics.

Grain: The direction of threads in a fabric. Can be crosswise or lengthwise.

Hand: The feel of the fabric.

Half-drop match: One in which the pattern itself drops down 1/2 the repeat on the horizontal but does match at the selvedge. It is a concern when planning cuts for horns, pelmets, empire swags, box pleats, etc., when the same design or motif is needed on each piece. It is usually designated in the sample books as a half drop.

Lengthwise grain (aka warp): The threads in a woven fabric that runs parallel to the selvedges. Fabrics are stronger along the lengthwise grain.

Nap: A texture or design that runs in one direction, such as in corduroy and velvet. A fabric with a nap will often look different when viewed from various directions. When using a fabric with a nap, all pieces must be cut and sewn together so the nap runs in only one direction.

Pattern repeat (aka repeat): The distance between any given point in a design and where that exact point first appears again. Repeats can be horizontal or vertical.

Pillowcase (aka pillowslip): The technique where face fabric and lining fabric are seamed together, usually with a 1/2-inch seam, then turned and pressed so the seam becomes the very edge of the item.

Poplin: Cotton fabric with corded surface.

Railroad: To turn fabric so the selvedge runs across the treatment instead of up and down. Sheer 118" is made to be used this way so that pinch pleats are put in across the selvedge end instead of across the cut end. This can eliminate seams on some treatments.

Right side: The printed side of the fabric that is used as the finished side of an item. The right side generally has the most color and the most finished look to it.

Seam: The join where two pieces of fabrics are sewn together.

Seam allowance: An extra amount of fabric used when joining fabric.

Selvedge: The tightly woven edge on the length of the fabric to hold the fabric together.

Straight grain: The lengthwise threads of the fabric, running parallel to the selvedges.

Tabling: Measuring a treatment and marking it to the finished length before the final finishing.

Turn of cloth: The minute ease of fabric that is lost from making a fold.

Warp and weft: Refers to the direction threads in a fabric. Warp threads run the length of the fabric. Warp threads are crossed by the weft threads that run from selvedge to selvedge across the width of the fabric.

Width: A word to describe a single width of fabric (from selvedge to selvedge). Several widths of fabric are sewn together to make a panel of drapery.

Wrong side: The back of the fabric. The less finished side that may have stray threads or a rough look to it.

Window Measurement Diagram

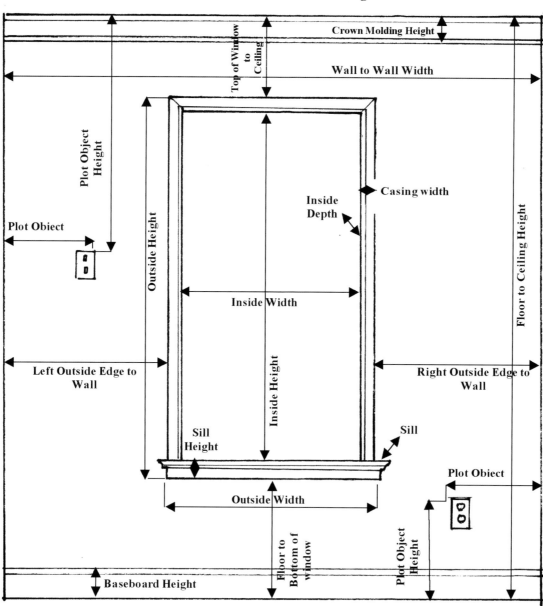

How to Measure a Window

🔹 Measure the entire window wall and all the elements contained within it. It may also be necessary to measure adjoining walls if they will affect the design of the treatment.

🔹 Always use a steel tape measure for accuracy.

🔹 List all measurements in total inches, not feet and inches.

🔹 Always measure left to right so you are reading the tape measure in the upright position.

🔹 Measure all windows width first, then length. Always list your measurements width first.

🔹 No two windows are exactly the same. Measure all windows individually.

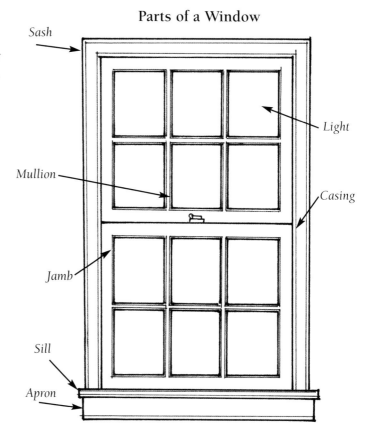

Parts of a Window

Sash

Light

Mullion

Casing

Jamb

Sill

Apron

🔹 Plot all switches, outlets, air registers, etc., and take their placement and usage into consideration when designing the treatment.

🔹 Measure the projection of the casing and other millwork and adjust the return of the treatment to accommodate their depth.

🔹 It is better to take all standard measurements, even if you don't think you will need them, rather than regret not having taken them later.

🔹 Identify the composition of the wall (cement block, wall board, steel beam construction, etc.). Calculate how it will effect the selection and placement of hardware. Can the wall hold the overall weight of the finished treatment? How should it be hung?

🔹 Measure twice, order once! Or better yet, have your installer measure to double check your accuracy. Two pairs of eyes are better than one.

Measuring for an Inside-Mounted Treatment

✦ Measure the width of the window at the top, middle, and bottom, and use the smallest figure.

✦ Give the fabricator the actual window dimensions. Do not make clearance allowances.

✦ Measure windows to the nearest 1/8". Deduct for clearance only if you are making the treatment yourself. It is standard for the workroom or fabricator to make the clearance adjustments for you. If you make those deductions yourself, your treatment will be too small.

✦ Measure for length of the window at the right, middle, and left, and use the longer figure for shades and blinds. Use the shorter figure for verticals.

✦ Measure the depth of the window recess to make sure it can accommodate your treatment's headrail. If it is too small, you must consider an outside-mounted treatment.

✦ Calculate the stacking space that your treatment will require. Will it interfere with the view? If you are using a top treatment, will it cover the stack?

✦ Always make templates of specialty-shaped windows for your fabricator. Butcher paper or wrapping paper works well. Tape it to the window and trace the outline.

✦ On operational treatments, plot the placement of the pull cord on the side where it is most accessible. Remember to specify toggles or cord wraps for shades.

✦ Always take safety measures into consideration when specifying shades and blinds in homes with small children.

Measuring for an Outside-Mounted Treatment

✤ Check to see if your treatment will require extension brackets to clear the window frame. If so, how much clearance is necessary?

✤ Make a template for any specialty shapes or arches.

✤ If measuring for a traversing drapery, you must calculate the stack back clearance and take into consideration the effect it will have on the view and the operation of the window or door. How much glass do you want to see when the treatment is open? Adjust your clearance to achieve the optimal effect.

✤ When calculating treatments for different-size windows in the same room, try to balance them by adjusting the dimensions of the treatments to be uniform, making the windows appear the same size.

✤ When measuring for rods with rings, remember that your panel will hang from the bottom of the ring, not the pole. Use this formula:

Ring Diameter + Finished Panel L. = Finished L. of the treatment.
Factor in the key measurements of your decorative hardware:

> *Pole:* Diameter, Width, Length, Extension before and past the Bracket.
> *Brackets:* Height, Width, Extension,
>   Minimum clearance to the ceiling.
> *Finials:* Height, Diameter, Length,
>   Minimum wall clearance.

✤ When specifying layered treatments, adjust all the measurements accordingly to avoid bunching or crowding.

✤ When measuring for hardware, remember to specify center or multiple support brackets on wide or heavy treatments.

✤ On traversing treatments, plot the placement of the pull cord on the side where it is most accessible. Always take safety into consideration when placing treatments with cords in homes with small children.

Key Window Terms

Allowance: A customary variation form an "exact" measurement, taken for the purpose of anticipated needs.

Apron: The wood trim molding below the windowsill.

Arch apex: The top point of the arch.

Arch window: A window in the shape of a half circle, often placed over a door or other windows for decoration and additional light.

Awning window: Windows that are hinged on top and swing outward to open; usually rectangular and wider than they are long.

Baton: A rod or wands used to hand draw traverse draperies.

Bay window: A group of windows set at angles to each other.

Bow window: A type of window that is curved or semicircular.

Bracket: A metal piece attached to the wall or casing to support a drapery or curtain rod, blinds, or shade.

Carriers (aka slides): Small runners installed in the traverse rod, which hold a drapery pin or hook.

Window casing: The wood trim placed around the outside edge of the window recess.

Cathedral window: Slanted window often found with cathedral ceilings; the top of the window follows the slope of the ceiling.

Center support bracket: Additional hidden drapery brackets placed at the center of a long drapery rod when additional support is needed for heavy drapery and to prevent sagging.

Clearance allowance: The amount of space needed between layers of hardware or mounted treatments in order to allow them to function properly.

Clerestory windows: A series of small windows that let in light and air, usually high up on the wall to allow privacy.

Cord cleat: A piece of hardware attached to the wall around which window treatment cords can be secured. (As a safety precaution, use these to keep the cords out of children's reach.)

Cord lock: A piece of hardware mounted to the headrail of a shade, through which the operating cords run. When the cords are pulled up, it secures the shade at the desired location.

Corner windows: Windows that meet at right angles at the corner of a room.

Crown molding: Decorative molding placed at a forty-five-degree angle at the ceiling.

Dormer window: An upright window that breaks the surface of a sloping roof.

Double-hung window: The most common style of window; two sashes move up and down.

Eyebrow window: Arched top window with elongated width. Not a true half circle.

Finished drop line: The place where the curtain stops.

Finished length: This is the length after draperies have been made.

Finished width: The actual width after the treatment is finished.

French doors: Usually used in pairs, the doors are made almost entirely of glass panes and open outward. They often open onto a porch or patio.

Front width: The width of the treatment board without returns.

Hopper windows: Hinged from the bottom of the window and open inward from the top. The reverse of awning windows.

Inside measurement: Measurement for a treatment so the window facing would be exposed after the treatment is installed.

Inside mount (aka ISM): Location of hardware and treatment are inside a structure, usually a window frame or cornice board. Mounting a treatment wall to wall is also treated as an inside mount.

Inside depth: The minimum depth of the window from the frame to the wall surface.

Inside width: The maximum width of the window recess as measured from the inside.

Mullion: The vertical wood or masonry sections between two window frames.

Muntin: The horizontal and vertical wood strips that separate panes of glass in windows.

Outside measurement: Measurements taken of the outside perimeter of the window frame so that the treatment will cover all window facings.

Outside mount (aka OSM): The hardware for treatment is mounted on the outside of the window on the frame or wall and the treatment is not against any structure on the ends.

Outside width: The measurement of the window from the outside edge of the casing including the window to the other outside casing edge.

Palladian window: A series of windows with an arch on top.

Picture window: A type of window with a large center glass area with usually two smaller glass areas on each side.

Plinth: A square of decorative wood installed at corners of window frames.

Projection (aka return): the distance from the front of the window treatment to the wall.

Pull cord: The cord on a shade or blind that is pulled to open or close it.

Return: The distance from the face of the rod to the wall or casing where the bracket or board is attached.

Sash: The part of a window that opens and closes. It includes a frame and one or more panes of glass. Also the frame and glass of an inoperable window.

Sidelight: A glass panel adjacent to a door, often used at entries for appearance and to provide more light.

Sill: The horizontal "ledge-like" portion of a window casing.

Skylight: A window in the roof that admits light from above. A skylight can be operable or not, some are flat while others are bubble-like.

Sliding glass doors: Large glass doors mounted on a track that bypass each other.

Template: A tracing made on butcher paper of a hard-to-measure window, arch, or other element in order to create a record of its exact shape.

Vertical stack up: The area taken up by the stack of a shade or blind when it is fully open.

Window recess: The depth of the setback of the window from the wall surface.

Drapery and Curtains

Full-length panel treatments are separated into two categories: draperies and curtains.

Draperies are full-length, lined, pleated or un-pleated panels that traverse open and closed on a drapery track or rod.

They can be hung from functional or decorative traversing rod carriers or rings using drapery hooks or pins attached to the heading or they can be attached to traversing rings with loops or ties.

Draperies are functional treatments that provide privacy and light control.

Curtains are mid- to full-length, lined or unlined, panels that are hung on stationary or hand-drawn hardware.

They can be hung by a straight heading, by tabs, ties, loops, or grommets using a wide variety of hardware options: decorative rods, continental rods, sash rods, café rods, swing arms, wall hooks, ceiling hooks, rings, knobs, medallions, tiebacks, or board mounted.

Curtains can be functional treatments but many times they are purely decorative. They can be used in combination with blinds, shades, shutters, or verticals to provide privacy and light control.

Anatomy of a Window Treatment

Each window treatment is constructed of certain standard elements that when combined creatively, make it unique.

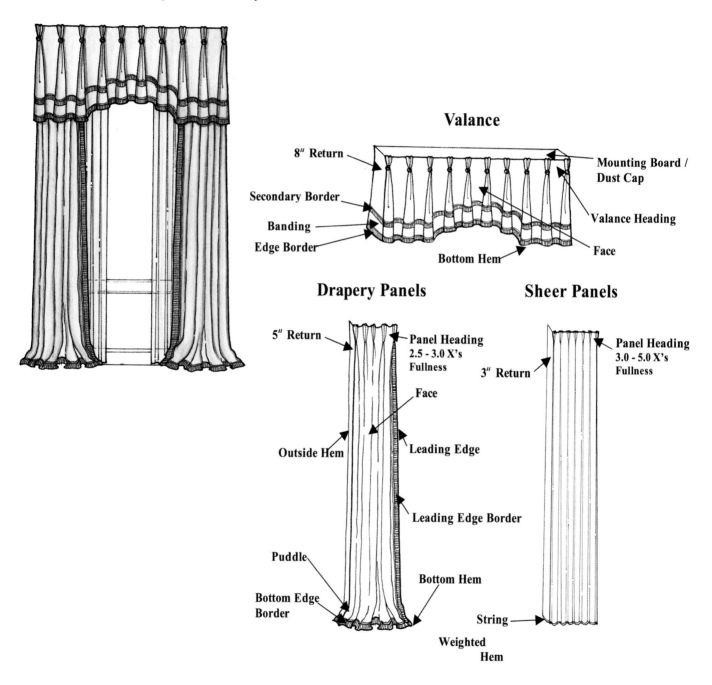

Valance

8″ Return

Mounting Board / Dust Cap

Secondary Border

Banding

Valance Heading

Edge Border

Bottom Hem

Face

Drapery Panels

Sheer Panels

5″ Return

Panel Heading 2.5 - 3.0 X's Fullness

Panel Heading 3.0 - 5.0 X's Fullness

3″ Return

Face

Outside Hem

Leading Edge

Leading Edge Border

Puddle

Bottom Hem

Bottom Edge Border

String

Weighted Hem

Specialty Stationary Side Panels

These side panels are great problem solvers developed by designers and workrooms to address specific obstacles that arise in designing window treatments.

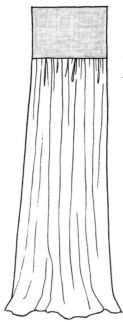

No-Bulk Flat Panel

Attach a flat panel of lining fabric to a shirred panel to eliminate bulk under top treatments. This panel also saves the cost of yardage hidden under the top treatment.

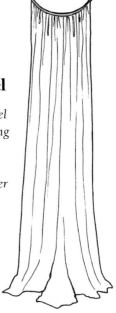

No-Show Flag Panel

A scalloped top, shirred panel bound at the top with banding and loops eliminates panel droop and allows the panel heading to hang hidden under the flag.

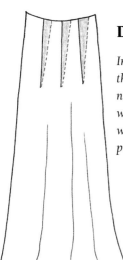

Dart Top Panel

Inserting dressmaker darts at the top of the panel will eliminate heading bulk and create a wide, flared bottom hem. This works well for a mermaid puddle effect.

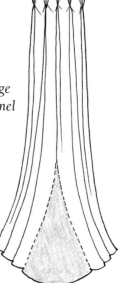

Ball Gown Panel

Inserting a "godet," or large dart, in the front of the panel to create a graceful flair allows the appearance of more yardage and volume with less cost and heading bulk.

Standard Hardware Configurations for Multiple Treatments

With the innovative drapery hardware available today, there are an infinite number of decorative and functional combinations possible. Always check the manufacturer's suggested installation guidelines for the product you are using, and make sure you adjust your clearance and returns for multiple treatments.

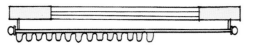

One-Way-Draw Traversing Drapery

Two-Way-Draw Traversing Drapery

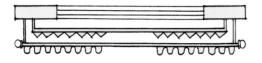

Two-Way-Draw Traversing Drapery with Two-Way-Draw Traversing Underdrape

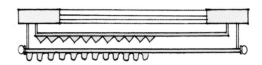

One-Way-Draw Traversing Drapery with One-Way-Draw Traversing Underdrape

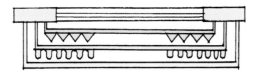

Two-Way-Draw Traversing Underdrape and Overdrape with Upholstered Cornice Top Treatment

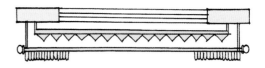

Decorative Stationary Side Panels with Stationary Underdrape

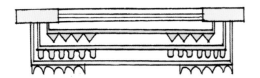

Two-Way-Draw Traversing Underdrape and Overdrape Decorative Stationary Side Panels

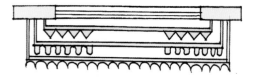

Two-Way-Draw Traversing Underdrape and Overdrape with Stationary Valance Top Treatment

Key Terms for Drapery

Banding: Long strips of fabric or flat trim applied to the edges or hems of drapery and curtains.

Bottom hem: The turned part forming a finished edge at the bottom of drapery.

Break: The appearance of the drapery panel when extra length is added to the hem so it rests on the floor usually just 1" to 2".

Buckram: A coarse cotton, hemp, or linen cloth stiffened with glue or a glue-like substance used in the curtain heading. Buckram gives a formal shape to the heading (aka crinoline).

Board mounted: Any portion of a treatment that is mounted on a board inside or out of the window.

Border: A decorative edging that runs along the panel edge or hems.

Casement: A cloth drapery that is an open-weave material but more opaque than a sheer.

Casing: A pocket made in fabric for a curtain rod, weight board, or drawstring.

Curtain drop: The total length of the curtain window treatment from the top of the hanging system to the bottom hem edge.

Clearance: The distance from the back of the rod, pole, or mounting board to the wall.

Curtain: A lined or unlined finished panel of fabric that is hung from a non-traversing rod at the top of a window.

Curtain drop: The length of a curtain window treatment from the hanging system to the bottom edge.

Cutout return: A buttonhole or rectangular cutout at the top return of the panel or top treatment to allow the return to go back to the wall in a pole-mounted treatment.

Double-hung draperies: Two sets of draperies, usually a sheer fabric under an opaque fabric, both operating separately.

Drapery: The proper name for a long traversing window covering, i.e., pinch-pleated drapery.

Draw drapery: A drapery treatment designed for use with a traverse rod, creating a window covering that can be drawn to open or close, either from both sides to the center (center draw) or from one side to the other (one-way draw).

Dressing: The process of folding and manipulating the fabric of a treatment, after it has been hung, to create the desired effect.

Drop length: The distance from the top of the object to where you want the fabric to end.

Face: The right side of the drapery treatment.

Fullness: The amount of fabric used in relation to the finished width of a drapery, usually between double (2x) and triple fullness (3x). 2x indicates the flat fabric is twice as wide as the finished drapery, 3x indicates it is three times as wide.

Heading: The heading refers to the top hem of the treatment. Its description refers to the type of construction used in the top hem, i.e., pinch-pleated heading, smocked heading, or tab-top heading.

Hem: To turn under and stitch a raw edge. Also refers to any finished edges of a treatment.

Header: The edge that extends above a heading such as a ruffle over a rod pocket or smocked heading.

Leading edge: The leading edges of a pair of draperies or curtains are the two edges that overlap at the center.

Memory stitch (aka flagging): A stitch usually done by hand in the back of the drapery used to keep the lining and face in even folds.

Multi-draw: A simultaneous opening and closing of several draperies on one rod at one time.

Mounting board: A wooden board installed inside or out of the window frame to which curtains, valances, or other treatments are attached.

Return edge: The outside hem of top treatments, drapery, or curtain panels that makes up the return of the treatment.

Outside mount: Any treatment mounted outside the frame of the window, on the casing or on the wall surrounding it.

Overdrape: The top layer of draperies in a double or combination drapery treatment.

Off-center-draw: Draperies that traverse to a non-centered point.

One-way-draw: One panel of drapery designed to draw one way.

Overlap: The portion of fabric that overlaps (crossover) in the middle of a pair of draperies when they are closed; when two swags crossover each other on a board or pole that is the crossover or overlap area. The standard overlap for Kirsch and Graber traverse rods is 3 1/2".

Pair width: Rod width plus one overlap and two returns. This is a measurement you would get if you took two panels of a pair of pinch-pleat draperies and you laid them down end to end widthwise, not overlapping. When closed, the draperies should hug the traverse rod.

Panel: One-half of a pair of draperies or curtains, even though it may consist of several widths of fabric.

Panel width: The pair width divided by 2. This is the finished width of a panel of draperies.

Pleat: A fold of cloth sewn into place to create fullness.

Pleat to: A finished width of the fabric after it has been pleated.

Pleat to pleat: The measurement from the first pleat to the last pleat.

Pleater tape: Pocketed heading material designed to be used with slip-in pleating hooks.

Projection (aka return): The distance from the front of the window treatment to the wall.

Puddle: Formed when drapery panels are long enough to literally lie on the floor. Extra length must be added from 1" to 18", depending upon the effect desired.

Return: The distance from the face of the rod to the wall or casing where the bracket or board is attached.

Side hem: The hem of the treatment has only 1/2" to 1" turned down inside to make a fold for sewing to the body fabric.

Sash curtain: Any sheer material hung close to the window glass. Usually hung from spring tension rods or sash rods mounted inside the window casing.

Sheers: Curtains or draperies made of translucent fabric to filter light and provide minimal privacy; often used under another drapery.

Stack back (aka stack up): The amount of space taken up by a drapery or shade when they are completely open.

Total width: The width of the board or rod, end to end, plus two returns.

Traverse: To draw across. A traverse drapery is one that opens and closes across a window by means of a traverse rod from which it is hung.

Under-draperies: A lightweight drapery, usually a sheer, closest to the window glass. It hangs beneath a heavier over-drapery.

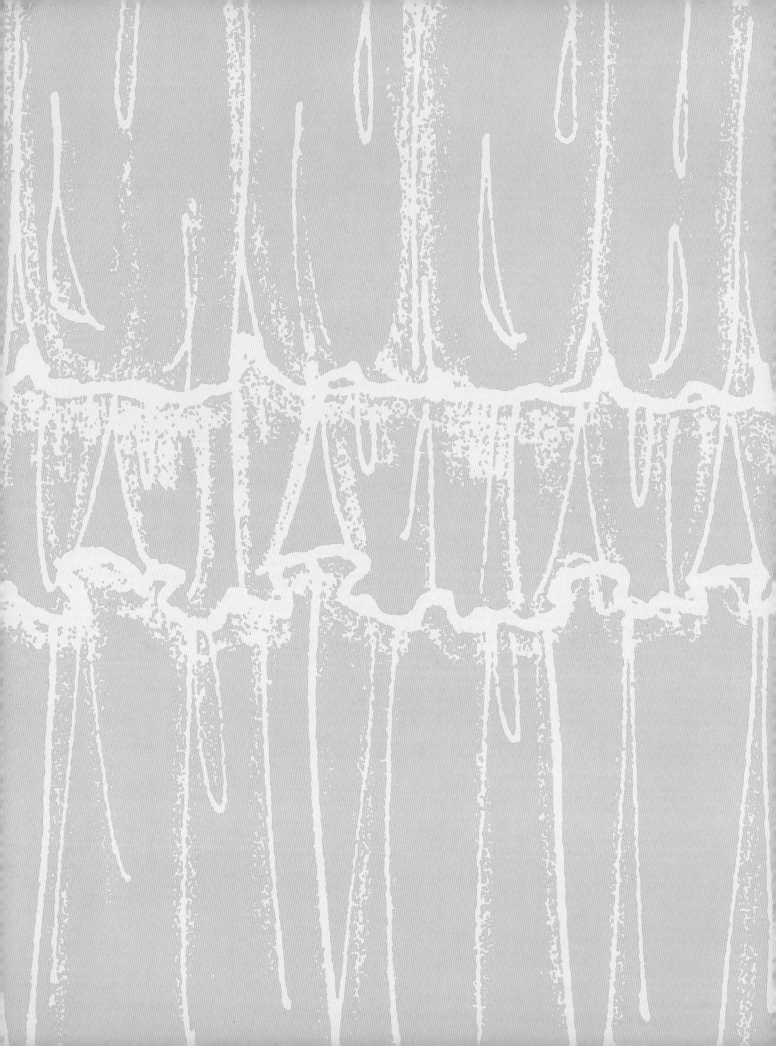

Headings

Headings

A heading is a combination of materials and design elements used to construct the top hem of a flat panel of fabric in a specific manner in order to create fullness and, or enable it to be hung as a window treatment. The style of the heading you choose imparts a personality to your treatment. It is one of the most critical decisions made in the design process.

Headings are used to create:

Drapery panels

Curtain panels

Valances

Shades

There are three types of headings:

Pleats

Rod pockets

Hanger headings

Pleated Headings

A pleat is a small section of fabric at the panel heading that has been folded and sewn in place to create fullness.

- Pleats create uniform proportion and spacing at the panel heading.

- Pleats allow the smooth operation of the panel while opening and closing on hardware.

- Pleats create a smaller, cleaner stack back than other types of headings.

- Pleats provide uniformly spaced draping.

- Fabric can be pleated by hand, by machine, or by using drapery pins or commercial pleating tapes.

- Fullness of the panel can be manipulated by adjusting the size of the pleats, the spacing between pleats, and the number of folds in each pleat.

- Pleats are cost effective due to the simplicity of design and construction.

- Pleats allow versatility for one panel to be used with multiple types of hardware. They can be pinned directly to a traverse rod, pinned to decorative rings, mounted on a board, or attached directly to a cornice or valance.

- Pleated panels cannot be laid flat for cleaning and pressing.

- When using fabrics with large patterns or repeats, take into consideration how the pattern will be affected by the pleat. Try to adjust the style and spacing to pleat to the pattern.

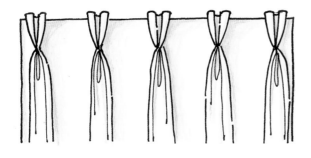

Double Pinch Pleat
Heading: Formal Stiffened
Fullness: 2.5–3.0
Hardware: Hooks, Rings

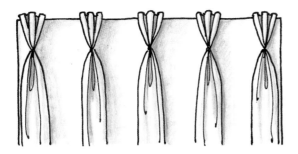

Triple Pinch–French Pleat
Heading: Formal Stiffened
Fullness: 2.5–3.0
Hardware: Hooks, Rings

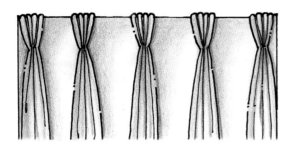

Four-Finger Pinch Pleat
Heading: Formal Stiffened
Fullness: 2.5–3.5
Hardware: Hooks, Rings

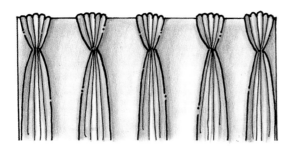

Five-Finger Pinch Pleat
Heading: Formal Stiffened
Fullness: 2.5–3.5
Hardware: Hooks, Rings

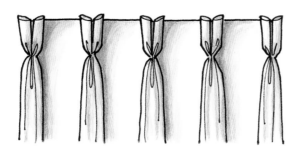

Butterfly Pleat
Heading: Formal Stiffened
Fullness: 2.5–3.0
Hardware: Hooks, Rings

Euro Pleat

Heading: Formal Stiffened

Fullness: 2.5–3.0

Hardware: Hooks, Rings

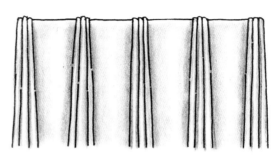

X Pleat

Heading: Formal Stiffened

Fullness: 2.5–3.0

Hardware: Hooks, Rings

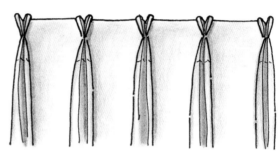

Goblet Pleat

Heading: Formal Stiffened

Fullness: 2.5–3.0

Hardware: Hooks, Rings

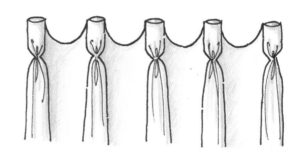

Fan Pleat

Heading: Formal Stiffened

Fullness: 2.5–3.0

Hardware: Hooks, Rings

Double Tack Pleat

Heading: Formal Stiffened

Fullness: 2.5–3.0

Hardware: Hooks, Rings

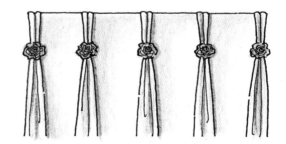

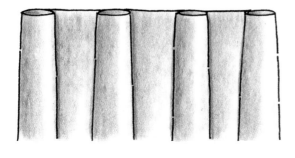

Bell Pleat

Heading: Formal Stiffened

Fullness: 2.5

Hardware: Hooks, Rings

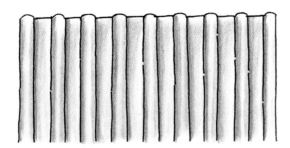

Cartridge Pleat

Heading: Formal Stiffened

Fullness: 2.5

Hardware: Hooks, Rings

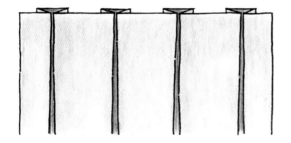

Inverted Box Pleat

Heading: Formal Stiffened

Fullness: 2.0–2.5

Hardware: Hooks, Rings

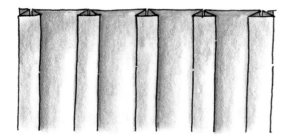

Box Pleat

Heading: Formal Stiffened

Fullness: 2.0–2.5

Hardware: Hooks, Rings

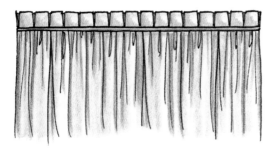

Box Pleat Heading with Shirred Panel

Heading: Soft

Fullness: 2.5–3.5

Hardware: Hooks, Rings

Swagged Fan Pleat
Heading: Slouched
Fullness: 2.5–3.0
Hardware: Hooks, Rings

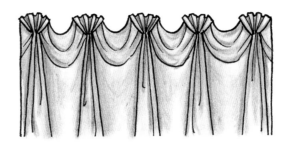

Knife Pleat
Heading: Formal Stiffened
Fullness: 2.0–2.5
Hardware: Hooks, Rings

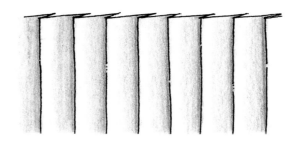

Top-Tacked French Pleat
Heading: Formal Stiffened
Fullness: 2.5–3.0
Hardware: Hooks, Rings

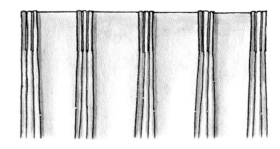

Pencil Pleat
Heading: Formal Stiffened
Fullness: 2.5–3.5
Hardware: Hooks, Rings

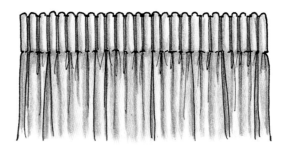

Accordion Pleat
Heading: Formal Stiffened
Fullness: 2.5–3.5
Hardware: Hooks, Rings

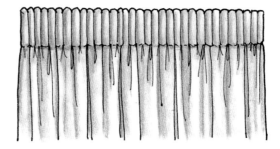

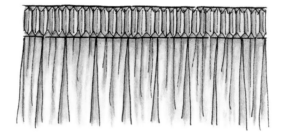

Single Diamond Smocked Pleat

Heading: Smocking Tape

Fullness: 2.5–4.0

Hardware: Hooks, Rings

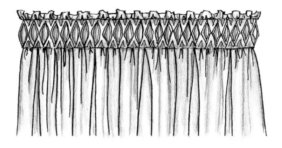

Double Diamond Smocked Pleat

Heading: Smocking Tape

Fullness: 2.5–4.0

Hardware: Hooks, Rings

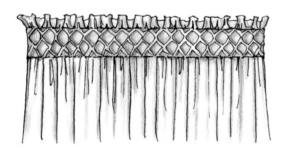

Triple Diamond Smocked Pleat

Heading: Smocking Tape

Fullness: 2.5–4.0

Hardware: Hooks, Rings

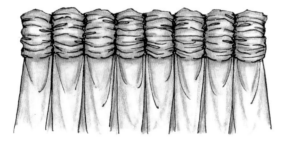

Shirred Cuff

Heading: Shirring Tape

Fullness: 2.5–3.0

Hardware: Hooks, Rings

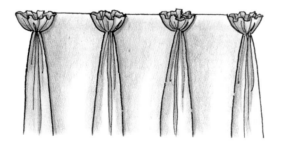

Cupped Pleat

Heading: Soft

Fullness: 2.5–3.0

Hardware: Hooks, Rings

Ruched Cuff
Heading: Gathered
Fullness: 2.5–3.5
Hardware: Hooks, Rings

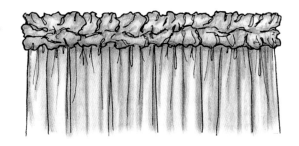

Rolled Cuff
Heading: Soft
Fullness: 2.0–3.0
Hardware: Hooks, Rings

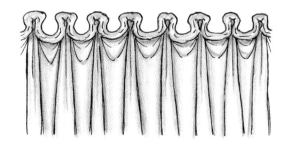

Wired Flounce
Heading: Soft
Fullness: 2.0–3.0
Hardware: Hooks, Rings

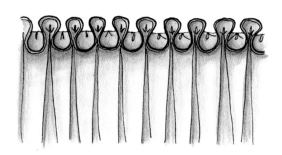

Raised Tack Pleat
Heading: Formal
Fullness: 2.0–2.5
Hardware: Hooks, Rings

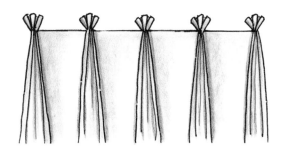

Pleated Heading Variations

The materials used in the construction of the heading and the design of the heading itself can be varied to create an infinite number of styles.

Some of the many options available are:

- Formal heading
- Informal heading
- Scalloped heading
- Scooped heading
- Swagged heading
- Tacked heading
- Flagged heading
- Integrated valance heading
- Raised heading
- Double heading
- Cuffed heading
- Ruched heading

Most of the variations shown on the following pages can be used with many different styles of pleats. Use your imagination to create the perfect heading for your project.

Formal Heading

Traditional heading stiffened
with buckram or crinoline.

Informal Heading

No buckram or stiffener is
used in the heading.

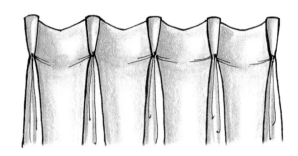

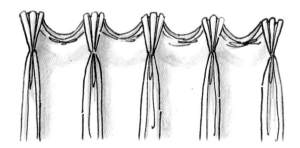

Tack Pleated Heading

The heading between pleats is
tack pleated down, creating a set
of horizontal pleats.

Scalloped Heading

The sections of the heading between
pleats are cut in a scalloped shape.

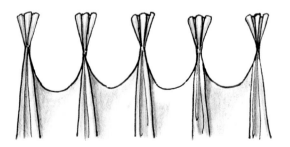

Scooped Heading

The sections of the heading between
the pleats are scooped down to
below the base of the pleat.

Integrated Valance
The valance is integrated into the heading panel and they are pleated together as one piece.

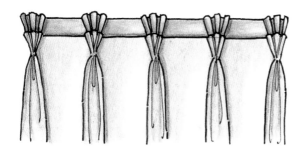

Raised Double Heading
A border heading is placed behind the main panel heading and they are pleated together as one piece.

Embellished Heading
Use decorative trim to highlight the pleat point of the heading.

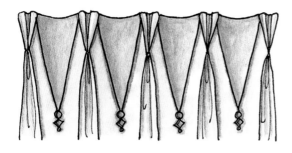

Flagged Heading
Flags are integrated into a soft heading between pleats.

Necktie Heading
A necktie flounce is attached to the main panel at the pleat and it is pleated together as one piece.

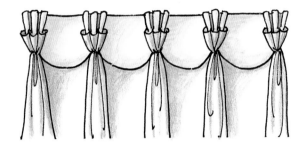

Raised Scalloped Double Heading

A straight border heading is placed behind the main scalloped panel heading. They are pleated together.

Closed Goblet Pleat

The pleat section of the panel is extended and tied close at each pleat.

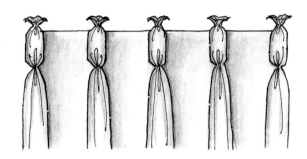

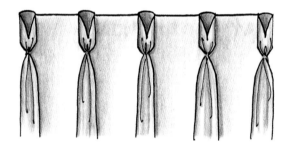

Open-Throat Goblet Pleat

The front of the goblet has a cutout section to expose the lined interior of the goblet.

Tuxedo Goblet Pleat

The front of the goblet is split and folded back to expose the contrast lining of the interior.

Rosebud Goblet Pleat

The heading has a raised border. The goblet is short and has an open throat. The upper goblet is stuffed.

Laced Scarf Heading
A fabric scarf is threaded through buttonholes between the pleats.

Goblet Pleats with Knotted Ties
Contrasting ties are threaded through buttonholes in the panel at the pleat base.

Ruffled Insert with Goblet Pleats
A ruffle is inset in the panel at the pleat base before pleating.

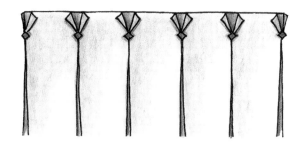

Tuxedo Box Pleat
The throat of the box pleat is folded back and tacked or pressed in place.

Inverted Box Pleat with Buttons
Buttons embellish the face of the panel at the pleat.

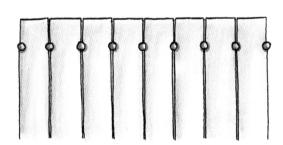

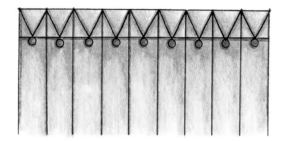

Tuxedo Pleats with Buttons

Open tuxedo pleats with contrast lining and interlining are trimmed with buttons.

Flap-Top Box Pleat

The box pleat has an integrated scalloped tab in the heading that is folded over the top of the panel.

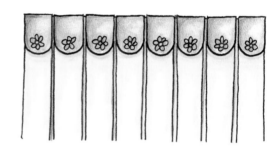

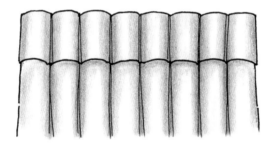

Cuffed Cartridge Pleat

The panel heading is folded over to create a single cuff at the heading.

Double Cuffed Heading

The heading has a double valance pleated together as one piece.

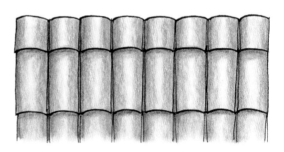

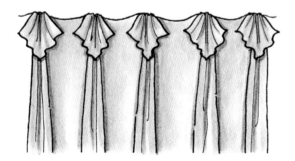

Pinch Pleats with Fanned Flags

Triple-point flags are added to the top of the heading before pleating to create gathered fans.

Flag-Top Box Pleat

The box pleat has an integrated flag in the heading that is folded over the top of the panel.

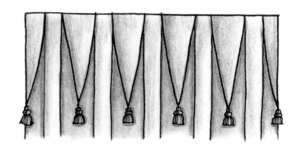

Euro Pleats with Swagged Heading

Pleated swags are placed between each pleat at the heading.

Ruched Cartridge Pleats

A gathered section of fabric is added at the base of each pleat.

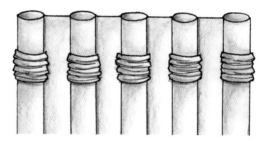

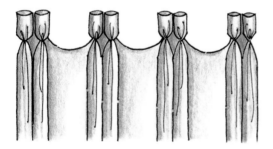

Double Pleats with Scalloped Heading

Group pleats together for an interesting heading.

Pleated Treatments

A pair of panels with **Ruched cartridge pleats** are rolled outward at the leading edge to expose the **contrast lining**. Extra-large **formal tiebacks** are use to keep the panels in place.

These **euro-pleated** side panels have a contrasting border that grows in width from top to bottom. An **empire swag** with a matching border is centered at the top.

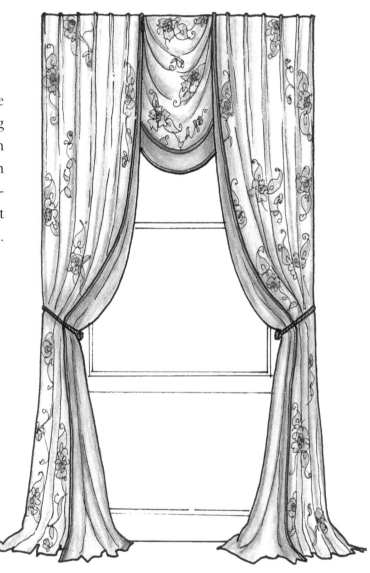

Simple **goblet pleated** panels
are embellished with a series
of **contrasting borders and
trims** to achieve a rich eclectic
look. The complementary
roman shade provides balance
to the treatment by carrying
the border pattern to the top
of the treatment.

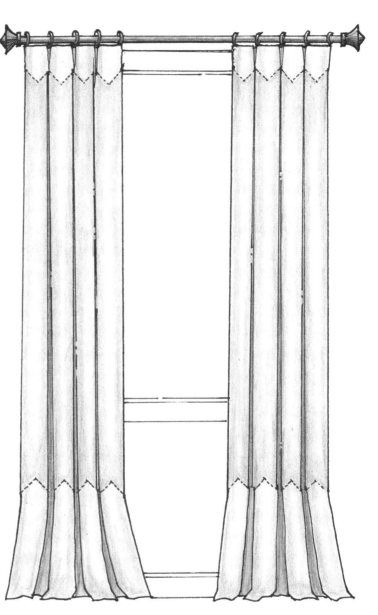

An attention to detail and **fine tailoring** turn these simple inverted **box-pleated** panels into a couture treatment. The pleats are tacked down in a **top-stitched** V at the heading and at the lower quarter of the panel, creating a graceful flair at the hem.

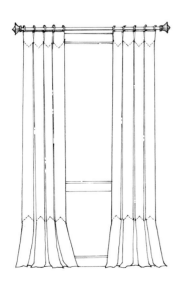

A matching **arched bottom valance** and panels are **pinch pleated** and embellished with **contrasting welting** and **banding**. Buttons covered in the contrasting fabric are applied at the base of the pleats to balance the treatment.

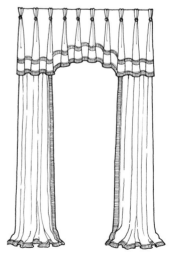

This beautiful **triple-layer** treatment consists of **dual-layer under panels** with an **attached valance**. The top layer of the under panel begins at the second pleat, exposing a large section of the bottom layer. The valance has a **scalloped top** that is attached at the pleat base. The three layers are then pinch pleated together. Buttons embellish the pleats and beaded trim finishes the hem of the valance.

A **deeply scalloped heading** is bordered with **short-looped fringe** before it is pinch pleated to create these unique panels.
Pattern: Pate Meadows— Julie Anne Panels

This tailored treatment is achieved by using **knife pleats** in the heading. The pleats are folded in opposite directions on each panel and are held together at the tieback by sewing a button on each side. **Decorative buttons** accentuate each crisp pleat at the heading. The **slouched roman shade** under treatment provides a soft contrast to the sharp lines of the over treatment.

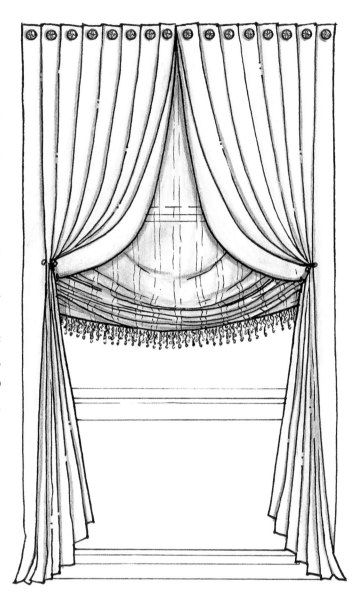

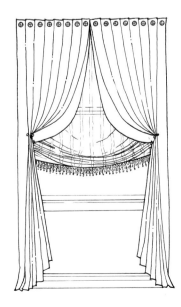

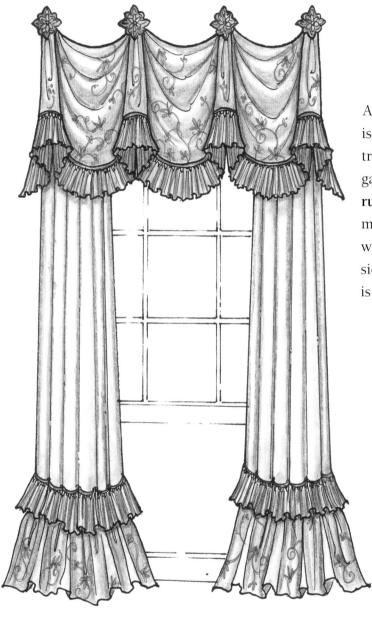

A graceful **empire valance** is box pleated and trimmed with an extravagant **accordion-pleated ruffle**. Hung from formal medallions and finished with matching stationary side panels, this treatment is the belle of the ball.

The strong **vertical lines** created by the border fabric and trim in this treatment are balanced by the **horizontal lines** of the hardware. A gently swagged, pleated **balloon valance** is mounted behind the side panels to soften the design and provide **light control** and **privacy**.

A **deep stiffened heading** with a double-pinch pleat pressed flat and tacked down at the top and base is then trimmed with a graceful **scalloped border**, creating a feminine yet tailored look. **Decorative braid** is used to create a border at the heading with **silk flowers** highlighting the individual pleats. Decorative braid tiebacks with silk flowers complete the treatment.

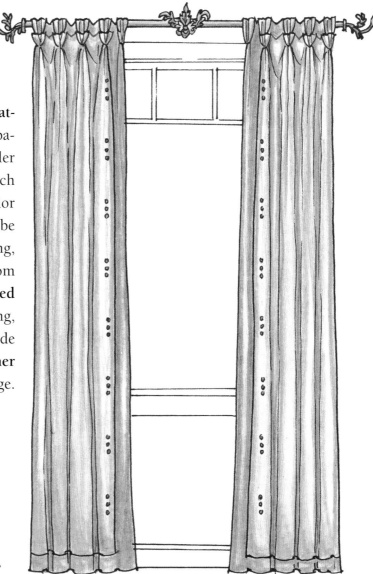

This **double-layered treatment** is topped with a separate panel that is smaller than the under panel, which allows the contrasting color of the bottom panel to be exposed at the heading, leading edge, and bottom hem. The layers are **pleated together** at the heading, sewn together at the outside edge, and **buttoned together** at the leading edge.

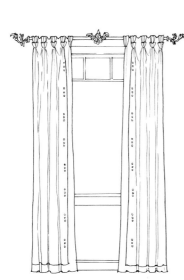

This flowing treatment is appropriate for a soft, lightweight fabric. The panels are **overlapped** the full width of the heading, and the extra-deep **back-folded pinch pleats** are stretched taught and board mounted. A designer touch is added to the treatment by making the panels different lengths for an **asymmetric balance** and casually knotting them at the tieback.

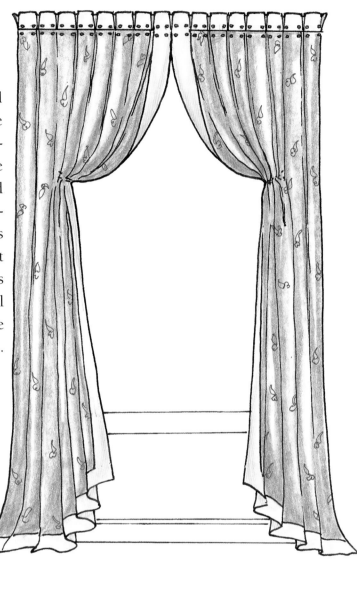

A simple pair of **inverted box-pleated** panels is made dramatic by adding a **contrasting border** at the heading, leading edge, and bottom hem. The **decorative buttons** at the pleats provide additional interest at the heading. The panels are **Italian strung** to pull back high in order to create a long, thin profile.

Formal **goblet pleats** arranged in an **eyebrow arch** and banded with a contrasting fabric are embellished with **chandelier crystals** at the base. Matching tiebacks complete this sophisticated look.

A **deep stiffened heading** of inverted box pleats is bordered with contrasting bands of fabric and trimmed with tiny bows at the top and base of the pleats. **Matching tiebacks** finish the treatment.

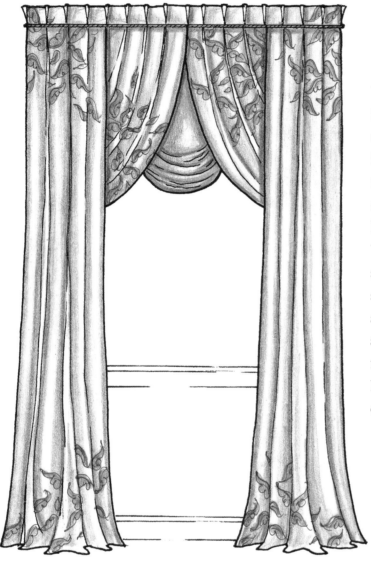

Three distinct layers in this treatment add dimension to a simple style. The first layer is a casual **contrasting swag**, which softens the strong vertical lines of the **pleated panels**. The second layer is **swagged back behind the side panels** and mounted at the sides on legs attached underneath to the mounting board. **Decorative braid** adds continuity to the heading.

These **ring-top panels** have a small **cowled flag** in a contrasting fabric between each pleat. The **contrasting bottom border** repeats the color at the heading.

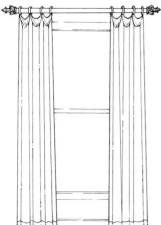

Flat panels become **exotic** when a **variety of fabrics** are mixed and matched in an attached multi-fabric valance and **bias-cut hem border**. Opulent **beaded trims** and **bullion fringe** separate the borders and complement the eclectic look.

The graceful flair at the bottom of these panels is achieved by using a **circular cut** for the hem section. The pinch-pleated panels are lined only to just above the first layer of lace trim, allowing light to filter through the lace. The borders are self-lined.

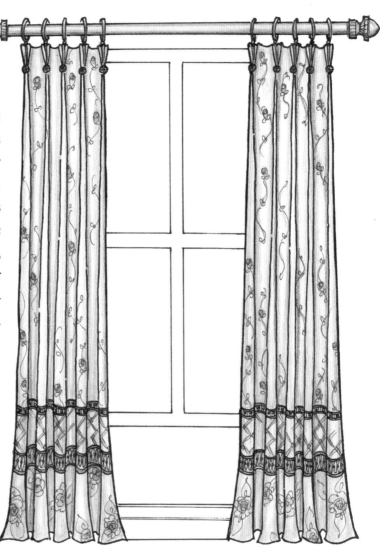

Deep pencil pleats head a
pair of panels that are board
mounted with a generous
return to accommodate the
voluminous under-mounted
balloon shade. The panels
are pulled back at the top 1/3
mark of the treatment and
trimmed with bullion fringe
to that point only. The fringe
is then repeated at the bottom hem.

Hanger Headings

Hanger headings are made using elements such as rings, tabs, ties, loops, and grommets to hang the panel.

- Tie, tab, and ring headings allow the versatile use of many different types of traditional and nontraditional hardware.

- They can be lightweight and casual, as well as luxurious and formal.

- Flat panels can be easily removed for cleaning or pressing.

- They can use less fabric and require simple construction, making them cost effective.

- They can be easy to construct for the beginner.

- Always self-line the full heading on flat panels to avoid seeing exposed lining as the panel droops between hangers.

- Tab, tie, and loop headings will not operate smoothly on a rod.

- Ring and grommet headings will operate smoothly on a rod.

- Consider using a drapery wand with ring and grommet headings to help open and close panels and reduce stress on the heading.

Hanger headings provide the opportunity to use a
wide variety of traditional and alternative hardware options.

Cabinet Hardware

Tiebacks

Drapery Rings

Ceiling Hooks

Tassels

Wall Hooks

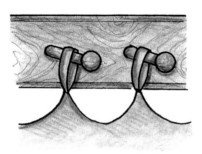

Peg Boards

Medallions

Basic Ring Top
Flat panel with soft or
formal heading.
Fullness: 1.0–2.0

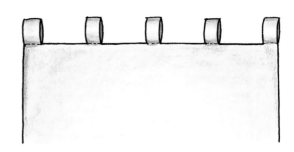

Basic Ring Top
Flat panel with soft or
formal heading.
Fullness: 1.0–2.5

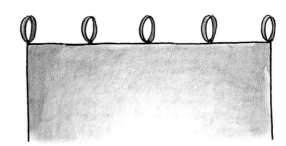

Basic Tie Top
Flat panel with soft or
formal heading.
Fullness: 1.0–2.5

Grommet
Flat panel with soft or
formal heading.
Fullness: 1.0–2.5

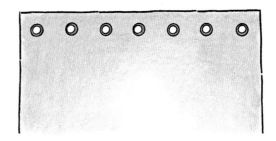

Long Ribbon Loop with Bow
Flat scalloped panel with ribbon on
all edges leading to long bows.
Fullness: 1.0–2.5

Switchback Loop
Flat panel with switchback loops
inserted at the heading.
Fullness: 1.0–2.0

Loop & Buttonhole
The loop is threaded through the
buttonhole and knotted.
Fullness: 1.0–2.5

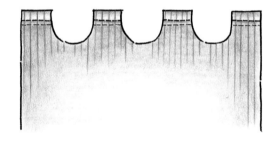

Rod Pocket Tab
Flat scalloped panel with the
tab folded over to create a rod
pocket.
Fullness: 1.0–2.5

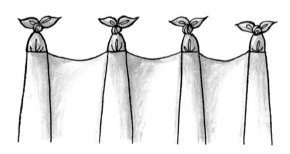

Front & Back Pleated Tab
Box-pleated panel with a pleated
knotted tie.
Fullness 2.0–2.5

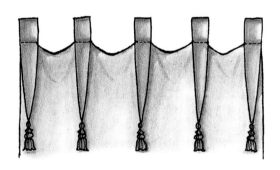

Tab with Flag
An elongated tab is folded over to
create a flag.
Fullness: 1.0–2.5

Scalloped Tab

Flat scalloped panel. Can be hung
by rings or hooks.
Fullness: 1.0–2.0

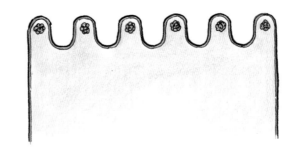

Double V Loop

Flat zigzag panel with contrast
loops and trim.
Fullness: 1.0–2.0

Double Loop Top

Long double loops are sewn into the
heading between scallops.
Fullness: 1.0–2.0

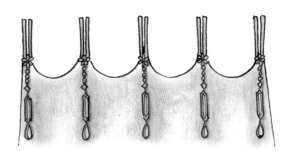

Stirrup Tab with Ring

Stirrups with rope rings can be hung
flat on knobs or hooks.
Fullness: 1.0–20

Fold-Over Tab

Tabs are folded over the face of the
panel and secured in place with decorative topstitching.
Fullness: 1.0–2.0

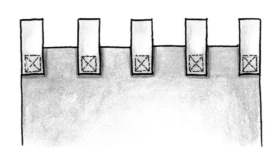

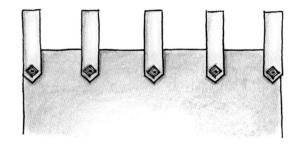

Fold-Over Tab with Button
Long tabs are folded over and secured with buttons.
Fullness: 1.0–2.0

Gathered Tab & Swag Heading
Swagged panel sections are placed between wide tabs that are shirred into columns.
Fullness: 2.5

Over-the-Rod Jabot Tabs
Over-the-rod jabots are used as tabs for a box-pleated panel.
Fullness: 2.0

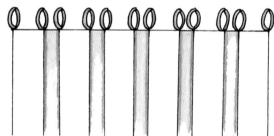

Double Ring
Box-pleated panel with rings at both sides of the pleat.
Fullness: 2.0–2.5

Raised Boxed Tab Heading
Box pleats are extended above the heading to create integrated tabs.
Fullness: 2.0–2.5

Long Loop with Rosette

A tack-pleated panel is hung with very long ribbon loops with a rosette at the base.
Fullness: 2.0–3.0

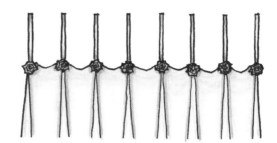

Gathered Tab

A box-pleated panel is hung with gathered tabs at the top of each pleat.
Fullness: 1.0–2.0

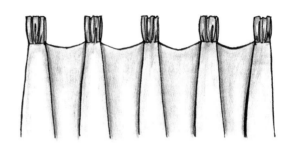

Pleated Tab

Inverted box pleats are set into a scalloped panel and topped with tabs.
Fullness: 1.0–2.0

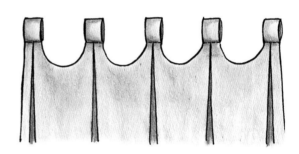

Gathered Tabs with Scrunched Sleeves

A sleeve of fabric is threaded over a wide tab and scrunched down below the pole line.
Fullness: 2.0–3.0

Ruched Pleat Heading

The pleats are Ruched at the top and a tail is added to enhance the panel.
Fullness: 2.0-3.0

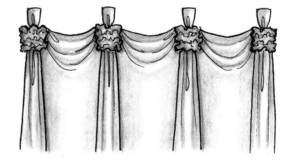

Flag Heading
A pinch-pleated panel is topped with swagged single-point flags and hung with tabs.
Fullness: 2.0–2.5

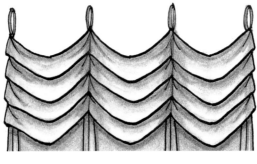

Step-Pleated Cuff Heading
This heading is pleated down the face to create a tiered cuff.
Fullness: 2.0–2.5

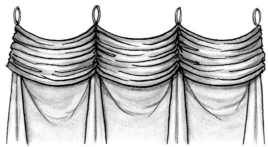

Accordion Pleat Cuff Heading
Accordion pleats pull the heading of this panel into a tightly pleated cuff.
Fullness: 2.0–2.5

Zigzag Flounce Heading
A short zigzag valance is added to this box-pleated panel.
Fullness: 2.0–3.0

Cone Flounce Heading
The valance of this pleated panel is gathered into cones at the tabs.
Fullness: 2.0–3.0

Clover Leaf Flag Heading
Pinch-pleated flip-over clover-
leafed flagged panel with
reverse-knotted loops.
Fullness: 2.0–2.5

Tiered Flag Heading
Box-pleated panel with tiered
flip-over flags and long tab.
Fullness: 2.0–2.5

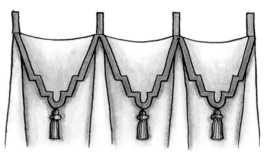

Accordion-Pleated Heading
Accordion-pleated heading with ties.
Fullness: 3.0–3.5

Shirred Ruffled Heading
Long bow ties support a single
ruffle-shirred heading.
Fullness: 3.0–3.5

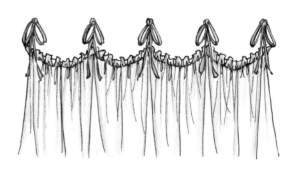

*Scallop Heading with
Box Pleats*
Box pleats are cinched at the
top and embellished with
buttoned bows.
Fullness: 2.5

Gathered Tab with Ruched Sleeve

A scalloped panel has wide box pleats and tabs that are cinched in by a Ruched sleeve threaded over the tab.
Fullness: 2.0

Tabs with Bow Loops

Inverted box-pleated panel with tabs has loops with bows threaded through the tabs. Hang flat with knobs or hooks.
Fullness: 2.0–2.5

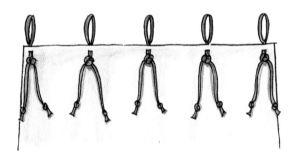

Looped Ties through Buttonholes

A flat panel with buttonholes or grommets to support long reversed looped ties.
Fullness: 1.0–2.0

Tabbed Long Ties with Buttons
Tabs with extended lengths folded to
the front are cinched at the base and
topped with a button.
Fullness: 1.5–2.5

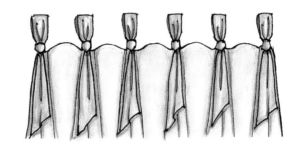

Knotted Raised Pleats
Extended box-pleated tabs are
knotted at the base. Hang with
hooks or rings.
Fullness: 2.0–3.0

Gathered Tabs with Flounces
Wide extra-long tabs folded over
the face of the panel and cinched
at the base with cording.
Fullness: 2.0–3.0

Hanger Treatments

This treatment looks best using soft, lightweight fabrics. The simple inverted box pleat panels are given a fairy tale appearance by using **alternating hangers** at the pleats, which shift between a **classic tab** embellished with a **large rosette** to a **long bow tied to a decorative ring**. The tabs should be secured at the rod to prevent shifting. The finishing touch is the **long ribbon** and **bows** embellished with **matching rosettes** attached at the rod and used to tie back the panels in a graceful sag.

Rich **bullion fringe** edges the **cuffed heading** and the bottom hem of these side panels, which are hung with decorative rings. A single **deep swag** is embellished with matching bullion at the hem and hung from the two leading edge rings, creating a central focal point.

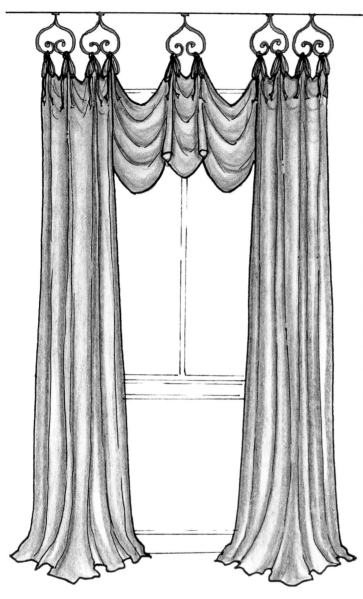

Decorative **ceiling hooks** are shown at their best with their application on this treatment. Flat tie-top panels are tied to the hooks in **long bows.** The **center swag** is a separate section attached to hooks at the tie base of the side panels and tied with matching long bows at the center hook. Tack pleats at the center ties finish the swag.

These deep **open-swagged** panels are draped over the rod and are self-lined. **Ruched sleeve cording** is used to tie back the panels with matching **decorative cord** embellished with large beads flanking each side panel.

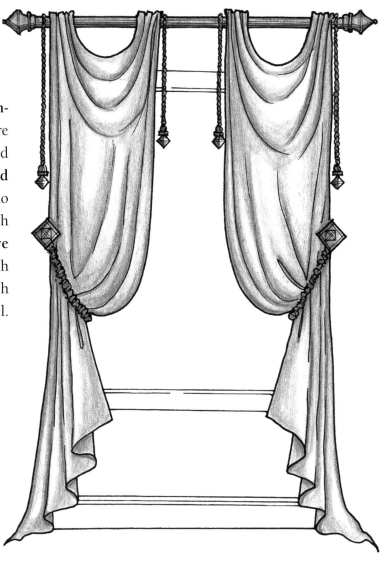

Ring-top panels with a small **inverted box pleat** at each ring and a **scalloped heading** are lined in a contrast fabric and pulled back tuxedo style. The unique tieback is a **single tassel threaded through a grommet** in the panel.

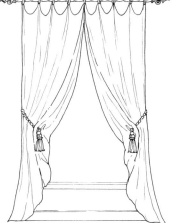

Tack-pleated side panels with attached loops are hung from this **wooden peg board strip**, which has been topped with crown molding. This is a versatile design that can be made **reversible**. Just add a **contrast lining** and use **pillowcase seams**. The panels can be easily slipped off the pegs and turned to the other side for a whole new look anytime.

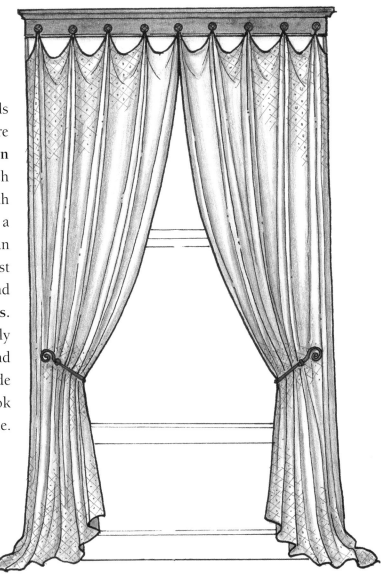

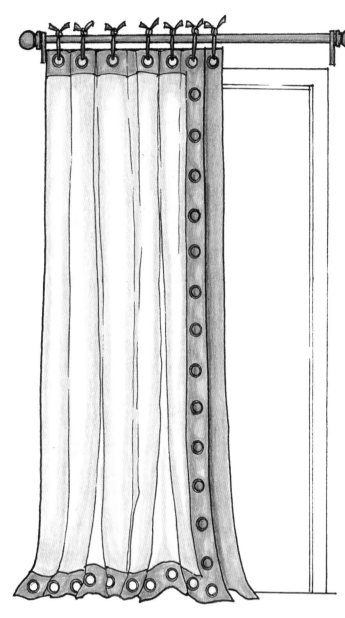

This treatment is a great example of how to use grommets creatively. The top panel shows a self-lined **contrasting border** at the heading, leading edge, and bottom hem with large **grommets** evenly spaced along the length of the leading edge and bottom. The two panels are attached at the heading only with the bottom panel extending beyond the top panel a distance equal to the width of the border. Grommets are then placed in the heading with **long ties** looped through to hang the treatment.

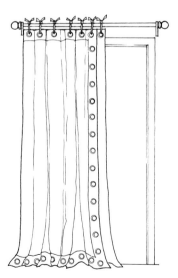

An extra-**deep smocked heading** tops these full panels. Long ties are sewn to the heading and tied in knots around the rod. The panels are pulled back using **Italian stringing**, which ends in knotted ties at the leading edge.

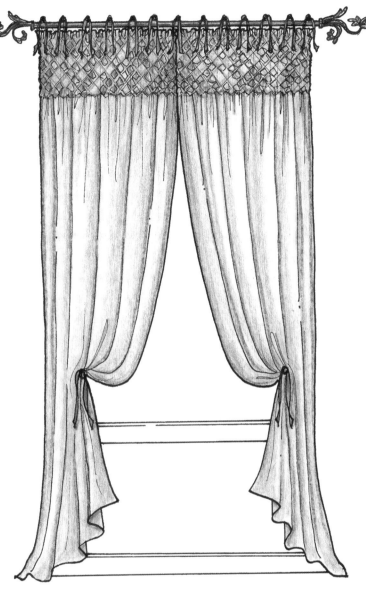

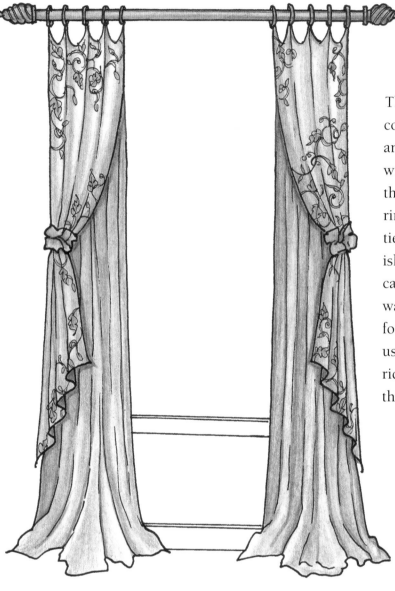

This stationary treatment is comprised of **side panels** and **self-lined top panels** with a scalloped heading that are sewn to drapery rings. A simple **casual knot** tied in the top panels finishes the look by creating a cascade at the hem. If you want to produce a crisp formal cascade, you can use a separate piece of fabric to tie the knot around the top panel.

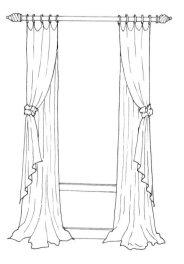

This very feminine look is achieved by inserting **ribbon loop fringe** between the main panel and the panel border. The entire border is **self-lined** and the heading is scalloped. Gathered tabs are embellished with **ribbon rosettes** as are the long **ribbon tiebacks**.

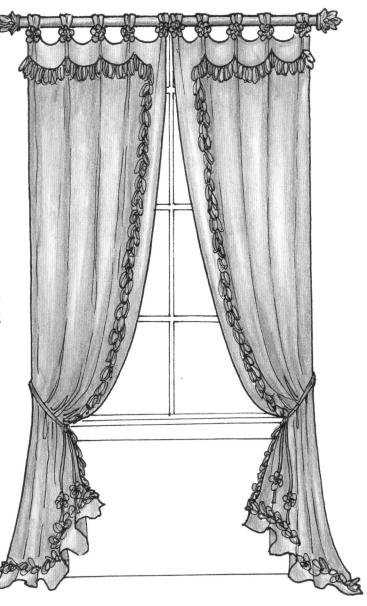

A **Ruched cuff heading**
with an **integrated valance**
tops off simple side panels.
Opulent contrasting wooden
tassel fringe and formal
tiebacks used as **tab holders**
impart a graceful elegance
to the treatment.

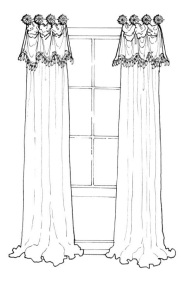

Flat panels are given a striking look by adding an **angular attached valance** and corresponding **hem border.** The contrasting fabric used at the valance and hem borders accentuate the sharp angles.

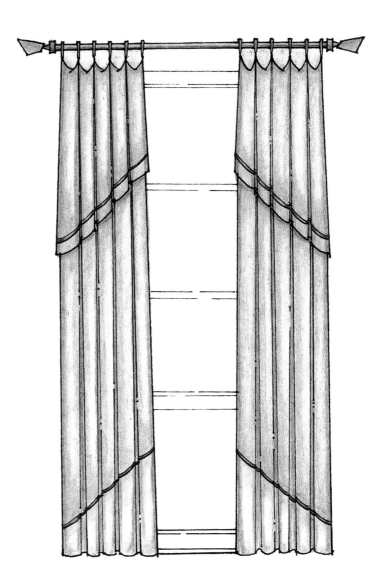

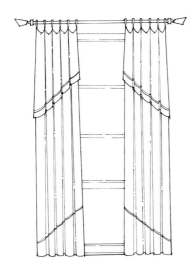

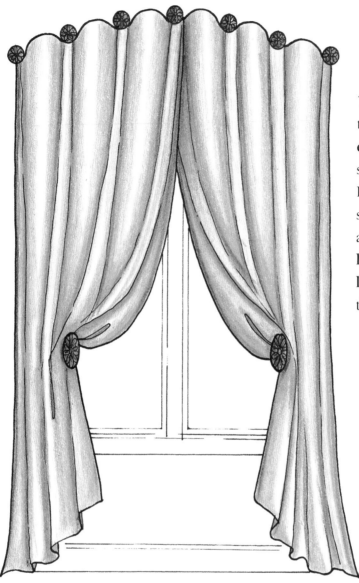

This simple yet striking treatment shows a **flat stiff-ened, formal heading** in the shape of an eyebrow arch. **Fabric loops** are evenly spaced along the heading to attach the panels to **medal-lions**. The panels are **self-lined** in and rolled back at the hold-back medallion.

This set of panels are constructed with **scalloped headings** attached to decorative rings. The top panel is interlined and lined to create fullness. The rings are embellished with **key tassels** and the leading edge, bottom, and outside edge are trimmed with **tassel fringe**. The second panel is **self-lined** and is made extra long so that it can be **wrapped around the main panel**. It should be secured in place with a hidden tieback bracket.

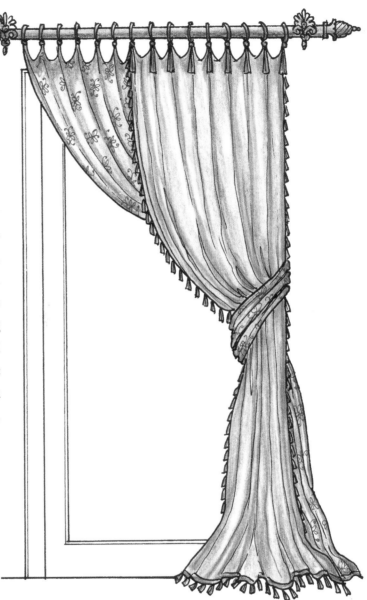

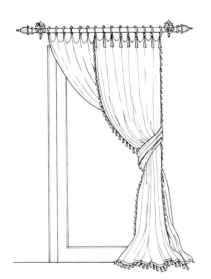

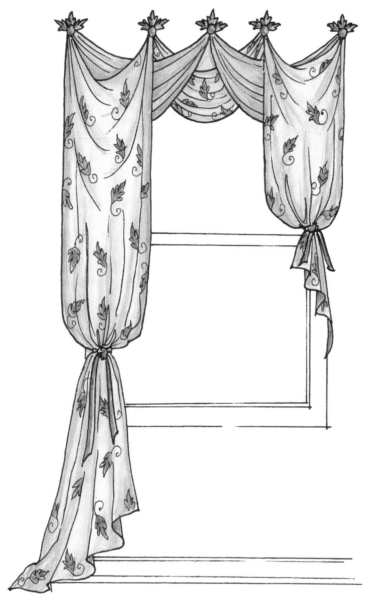

A series of **self-lined**, independent swags are **layered** to create a lovely treatment that interlaces complementary patterns and colors. The **open swags** alternate between the main fabric and the complementary fabric and are hung from decorative medallions. The top swag panels are lined in the complementary fabric and hemmed at different lengths to create an **asymmetrical balance**. They are tied into a **bishop's sleeve** with long ties of complementary fabric. A lightweight fabric should be used to avoid too much bulk at the top of the treatment.

Short valances with flip-over cuffs at the medallions are attached to full-length side panels. Small inverted tack pleats in the valance and the panel at each medallion add dimension to the treatment.

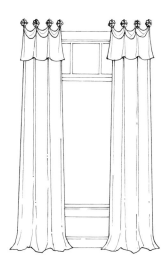

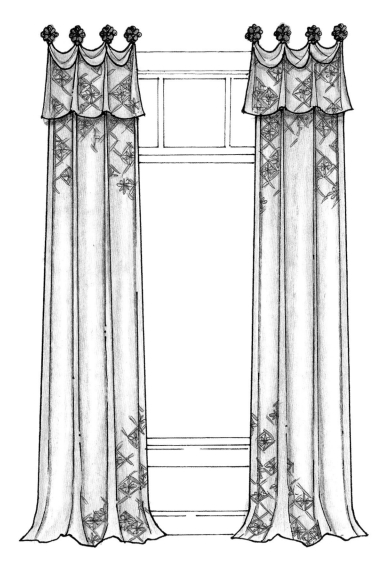

An identical treatment to the one shown on the opposite page is **simplified** by eliminating the bottom border and contrasting fabrics, using only **one pattern** to achieve a beautiful **unified design**.

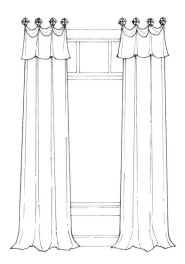

Swagged panels are interlined and lined in a contrasting fabric. The hem is cut at an angle to achieve a **steep cascade** at the tieback. The leading edge is tacked back at the hold back to expose the lining and to create an **opposite angle to the hem**. Tassels are tacked to the rod and draped over it at the swag heading, accentuating the waterfall effect of the swags.

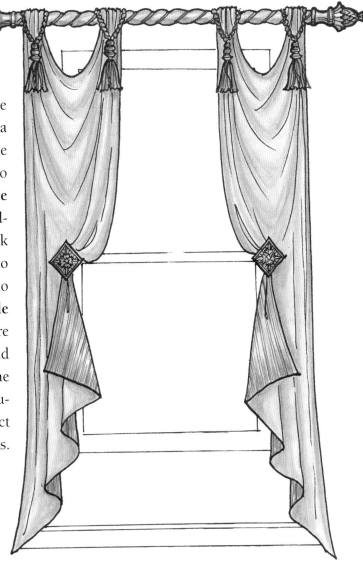

Flat **tie-top panels** are **self-lined** to avoid exposing white lining at the **heading droop** and the tieback. The hardware consists of metal **holdbacks** turned upward and mounted as drapery hooks. The panels are tied to the holdbacks with the extra-long ties, which are embellished with a **crystal bead** knotted at the end. When specifying holdbacks for this use, ask your vendor if they can be modified to have a narrower return such as 2". This eliminates creating a projection that appears too large for a single panel.

This treatment shows a creative use of **gathered tabs**. The panel heading is angled away from the center with the tabs **graduating in length** to allow the treatment to appear to hang at an angle. **Ruched sleeves** cover the seam between the panel and the tabs and cinch the extra-wide tabs inward to create fullness in the panel. The flair of the **circle-cut hem border** and the striping created by decorative tape at the bottom of the panels echoes the flair of the tabs and the vertical folds of the sleeves.

Ring-top side panels are mounted on top of the **under-mounted flat pelmet valance.** It is centered with a **necktie jabot,** which has been embellished with glass beads and an iron leaf that matches the decorative drapery rings. The pelmet is hung from the same rings as the side panels.

Scallops in the heading and the hem of this **classic tab-top valance** create a sophisticated surface perfect for displaying a **bold pattern**. The contrasting beaded fringe adds emphasis to the **graduated peaks** of the hemline.

Rod Pocket Headings

A rod pocket is a fabric panel in which the top hem is folded to the back and topstitched through the face to create an open "pocket" through which a drapery rod can be inserted.

- Pocket headings allow the use of economical hardware options.

- They are cost effective due to their simplicity of construction.

- The same panel can be used with straight or specialty shaped drapery rods.

- Panels can be easily removed and laid flat for cleaning or pressing.

- Pockets can be placed at both the top and the bottom of the panel.

- The rod pocket should be made 2 to 2 1/2 times the size of the diameter of the drapery rod to be used for easy insertion of the rod and to prevent bunching.

- Always use color-coordinated heavy-duty thread to stitch the seam for the rod pocket.

- Pocket headings can be both casual and formal.

- Pocket headings are simple and easy to construct for the home seamstress.

- Simple one-pocket panels shirred on a sash rod make great, cost-effective stationary side panels for most top treatments.

- Rod pocket panels are not appropriate for a functional drape and will not open and close on a rod.

- You must allow for a take up allowance in the length of the panel due to shortening that occurs once the panel is shirred on the rod.

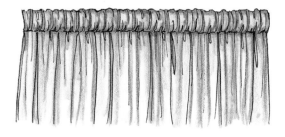

Single Rod Pocket
Fullness: 2.5–3.0

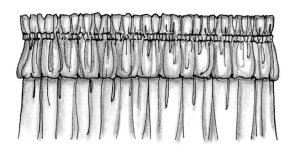

*Rod Pocket with Top and
Bottom Balloon Ruffle*
Fullness: 2.5–3.0

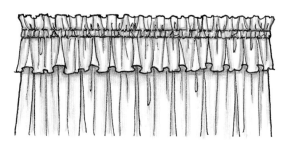

*Rod Pocket with Top and
Bottom Ruffle*
Fullness: 2.5–3.0

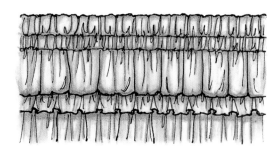

*Rod Pocket with Top and
Bottom Balloon Ruffle and
Bottom Ruffle*
Fullness: 2.5–3.0

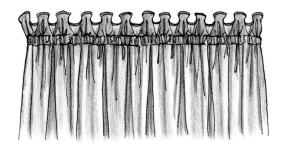

*Rod Pocket with Wired
Top Ruffle*
Fullness: 2.5–3.0

*Rod Pocket with
Top Ruffle*
Fullness: 2.5–3.0

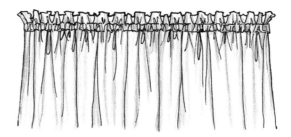

*Rod Pocket with
Balloon Ruffle*
Fullness: 2.5–3.0

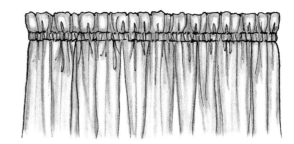

*Double Rod Pocket
with Top Ruffle*
Fullness: 2.5–3.0

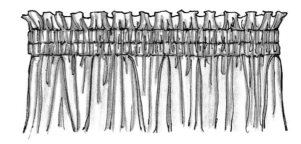

Rod Pocket with Flounce
Fullness: 2.5–3.0

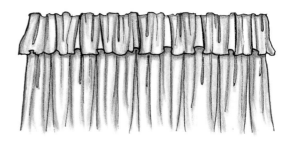

*Rod Pocket with Top
Ruffle and Bottom Flags*
Fullness: 2.5–3.0

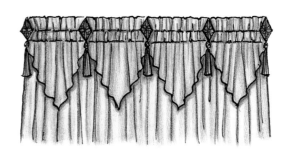

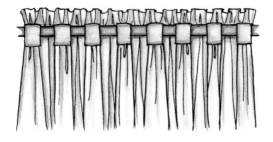

Rod Pocket with Top Ruffle and Flat Belt Loops
Fullness: 2.5–3.0

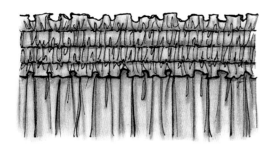

Double Rod Pocket with Top and Bottom Ruffle
Fullness: 2.5–3.0

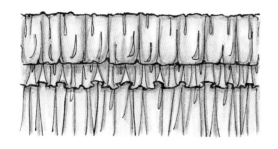

Rod Pocket with Top Balloon Flounce and Bottom Ruffle
Fullness: 2.5–3.0

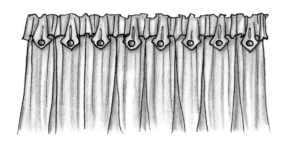

Rod Pocket with Button-Down Scalloped Flounce
Fullness: 2.5–3.0

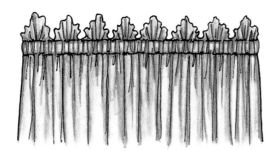

Rod Pocket with Top Zigzag Ruffle
Fullness: 2.5–3.0

*Rod Pocket with Top Ruffle
and Gathered Belt Loops*
Fullness: 2.5–3.0

Rod Pocket Take Up

When shirring the fabric on the rod, a small amount of the length of the panel is "taken up" by the diameter of the rod. Additional length must be added to the treatment to achieve the desired finished length after the treatment is hung.

ROD POCKET TAKE-UP ALLOWANCES

Rod Size	Rod Pocket Size	Take Up
Oval Rods	1 1/2"	1/2"
3/4" Curtain Rod	1 1/4"	1/2"
1 3/8" Pole	3"	1 1/2"
2" Pole	4"–4 1/2"	2"
2 1/2" Flat Rod	3 1/2"	1/2"
4 1/2" Flat Rod	5 1/2"	1/2"
Pinnacle/ Continental Plus	7"–8 1/2"	2"–3"

Remember to calculate individual take-up allowances for each rod used in multiple rod treatments.

Rod Pocket Treatments

A billowing **cloud valance** with a **lowered center swag** is flanked by two thin puddled side panels. The three sections of the treatment are gathered with a rod pocket with a single tall ruffle.

This rich set of rod pocket panels are pulled up at two separate points by **Italian stringing**. A heavy **interlining** should be used to add volume to the treatment.

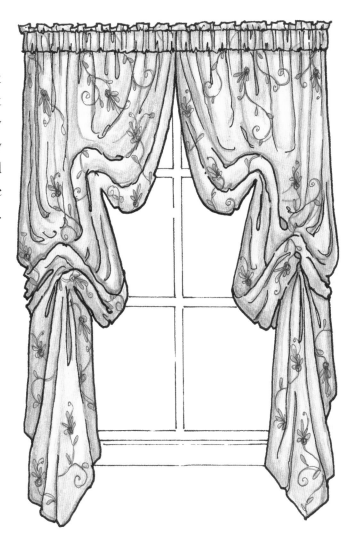

Luxurious **knotted tassel fringe** embellishes the heading of this pair of **single-ruffle rod pocket panels**. The knotted fringe is bordered with ribbon and used to tie back the panels.

This innovative heading is formed using a series of large scallops into which a **casing** has been sewn. **Buttonholes** at the center of each scallop allow **ribbons** to be inserted and the fabric **shirred** into the desired width. The ribbon is then tied into a long bow.

The treatment is finished with a ruched tieback embellished with a rosette and long ribbon bow. Use **lightweight or sheer fabrics only** at three times the fullness. Line with a solid sheer using a pillowcase hem.

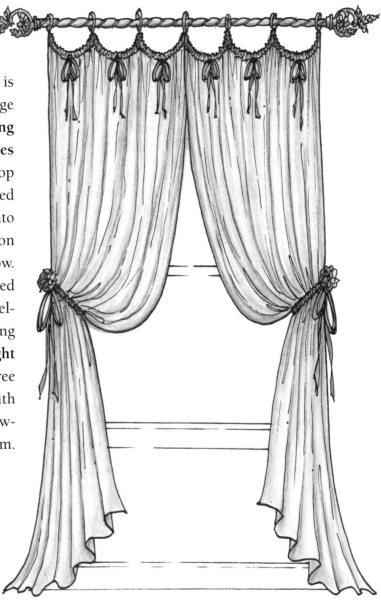

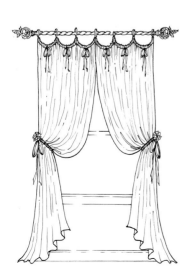

A single **pencil-pleated** panel is interlined and lined in a contrasting fabric and trimmed in a **flat ribbon fringe**. The panel is constructed with a pillowcase seam at the leading edge and bottom hem so the layers can be poufed open at the tieback to create a voluminous appearance. The panel is board mounted, and beautiful decorative **asymmetrical medallions** are added to finish the treatment. The panel is tied back with decorative rope hung from the long medallion.

A pair of **contrasting scarf swags** are pulled across the face of this rod pocket treatment and tied in place with long ribbon bows. They are trimmed with a **single contrasting ruffle**.

Two separate rod pocket panels are mounted independently to create a graceful **layered design**. The under panel is mounted just below the **decorative rod** of the top panel on a **curtain rod**. Both panels are held back by a matching **decorative medallion**.

A single panel with a **rod pocket with a ruffle** heading is lined in a complementary fabric that is exposed by rolling the panel outward and creating a **cascade** at the holdback. Tacking the cascade in place and creating a loop to attach it to the holdback ensures that the treatment will retain its style over time. **Rosettes** made from the complementary fabric bring visual interest to the heading.

The bottom layer of this treatment is composed of simple **rod pocket side panels** hung at the wall with sash rods. The contrasting top treatment is a continental rod pocket **zigzag ruffle valance** with a **zigzag hem**. Casual **swags** and **jabots** done in the panel fabric and lined in the contrast fabric adorn the valance. The design is finished by adding a velvet **rosette** with leaves at the apex of each swag.

This single rod pocket panel with a top ruffle is transformed into a couture treatment with the addition of a swooping **handkerchief swag** and **long puddled scarf**. The points of the self-lined handkerchief elements become leaves for the **double choux** at each side of the swag. The design is repeated in the holdback. The cascading hem of the panel should have at least a 12" self-facing to ensure that the lining does not show to the front.

This design is made with a rod pocket **inverted V-shaped valance** that is shirred onto a continental rod upside down. The valance is then flipped over the rod to create a **waterfall** look. The pocket should be secured to the rod to prevent it from slipping to the front. The swags are suspended from **medallions** mounted to the face of the valance. Side panels are hung from a separate rod underneath. This style can also be achieved by mounting the valance on a board.

Rod pocket panels are enhanced by adding an **attached valance** with a **contrasting border** at the leading edge and bottom hem. The valance has a gentle **rounded corner** at the bottom of the leading edge. The border is repeated along the leading edge and bottom hem of the panel with the rounded corner at the inside corner of the border. The border fabric is used again as **knotted ties** attached directly to the pole with a bow in the center to link the two separate panels together as one unified treatment.

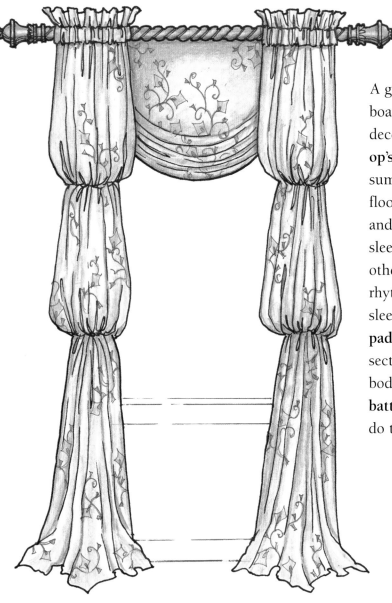

A graceful **swagged pelmet** is board mounted behind the decorative rod. **Double bishop's sleeve panels** fall into sumptuous puddles on the floor. The swag of the pelmet and the shape of the bishop's sleeves complement each other and create a balanced rhythm. Many times bishop's sleeve treatments need some **padding** inside the poufed section of the sleeve to add body and volume. **Upholstery batting** or **tissue paper** will do the trick.

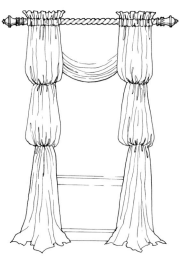

The stationary side panels of this treatment have a **single-poof heading with a ruffle** that has been gathered with **shirring tape**. The **open swag** at the back is mounted on a board and hung below the decorative rod. A second contrasting **scarf swag** is hung behind the side panels and tied up at the rod by a matching bow. **Fabric-covered finials** add the finishing touch to this design.

Tuxedo Panels

⁓

Tuxedo Panels

Tuxedo panels are pleated, shirred, or flat panels whose leading edge is folded back at one or more points, creating a tuxedo collar or tent flap effect.

- ❖ Tuxedo panels must be self-lined or lined with a contrasting or complementary fabric.

- ❖ They must be constructed with pillowcase seams.

- ❖ They are stationary and cannot traverse open or closed.

- ❖ Tuxedo panels are not suitable for a window with a great view as they can cover almost half of the glass surface.

- ❖ They can have a large area of flat surface and are suitable for fabrics with large patterns.

- ❖ They can be an economical solution because of their minimal fabric requirements.

- ❖ Tuxedo panels should always be interlined to add body to the flat or slightly gathered fabric.

Tuxedo Treatments

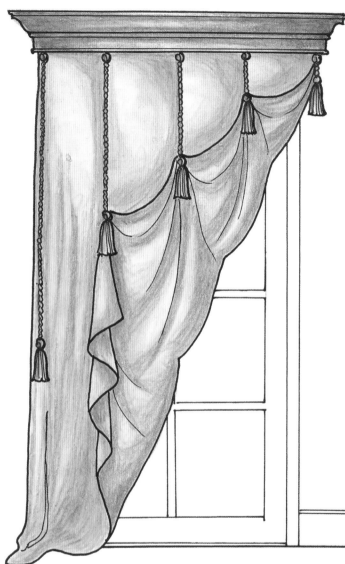

This single panel is topped with a formal **wooden cornice** and lined in a complementary fabric. Five lengths of **braid graduating in length** are knotted and attached to the bottom of the cornice. The other end of the braid is threaded through **buttonholes** in the leading edge of the panel and secured by attaching a **key tassel**. The last length of braid is not needed to hold back the panel but it is included to complete the repetitive **vertical element** created by the other lengths of braid.

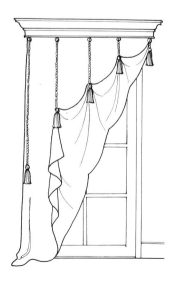

This cheerful design is a study in **versatility**. The rod pocket panels are lined in a contrasting fabric and are bordered on both sides, making them **reversible**. Decorative buttons placed down the outside border allow the panels to be **buttoned back** in a **tuxedo fold**. The higher the panel is buttoned back, the more sunlight is allowed into the space.

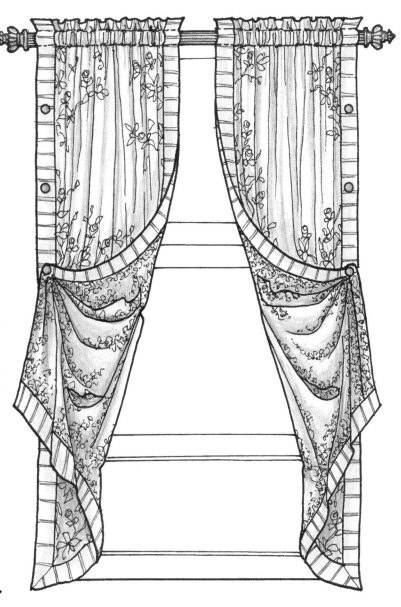

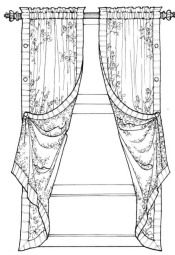

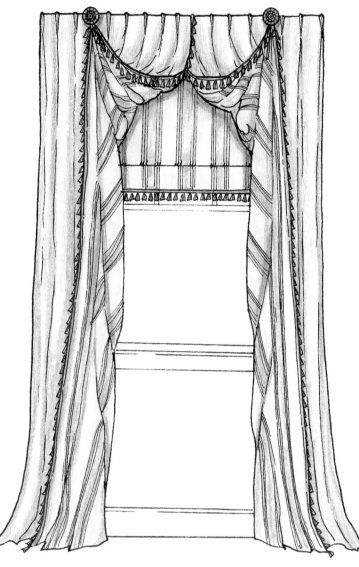

A pair of **pinch-pleated panels** is board mounted and lined in a dramatic stripe. **Medallions** are attached to the dust cap of the board so that they project beyond the face of the treatment. Loops are sewn into the leading edge border at the top 1/3 mark of the panel. The loops are picked up and hung on the medallions, creating a very **high tuxedo flap**. The **matching roller shade** provides light control and privacy.

Tailored **box pleats** with loops at each side of the pleat are designed specifically to work with this unique hardware. Each peat is the same width as the medallions, and the **double ties** look as if they are an extension of them. The pleats at the leading edge are overlapped to avoid a double pleat at the center. **Contrast lining** is exposed when the panels are pulled back.

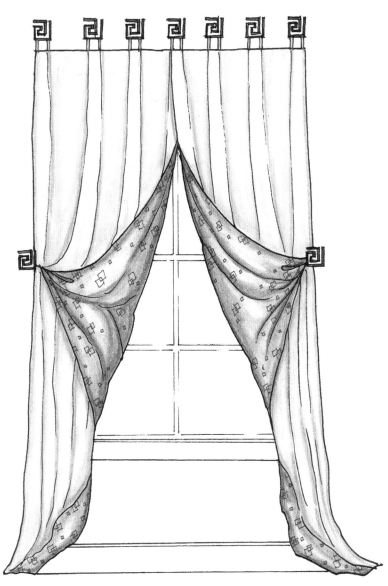

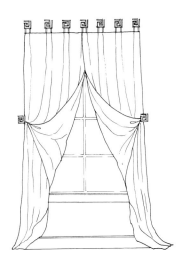

Many tuxedo designs can look tailored or masculine. Such is not the case with this one. The **rod pocket heading** with a single ruffle adds **volume** to the panel while long **ribbons and bows** hold up the tuxedo flap in a flowing cascade of fabric.

A flat panel is pulled up at the center into a **casual swag**, creating a focal point for this treatment. The **goblet-pleated top panels** have a **contrast-lined** extension added to the leading edge at the bottom half of the panel, which creates a **swagged tuxedo flap** across the face of the panel. This swag is hung from a medallion at the side of the panel.

Tailored flat tuxedo **panels** are usually reserved for masculine spaces. Here they are given a **feminine** flair by using **soft-colored** coordinating fabrics and **floral motifs.**

Many times, less can be more, as with this simple **inside-mounted flat panel** that has been lined in a contrasting fabric. It has been lifted up by an attached loop and held in place with a **decorative hook** exposing the lining.

Arched Treatments

Arched Treatments

Arched treatments have their own unique set of design opportunities and challenges.

The two most common types of arches are:

Full arch: A full half-circle forms an arch that can be extended at the sides.

Eyebrow arch: A slightly raised arch resembling the curve of an eyebrow.

When measuring an arched window or opening for an inside- or outside-mounted treatment, always make a template to ensure accuracy.

The choice of drapery hardware that can be used on an arched treatment is limited.

- Most arched treatments are board mounted.
- Traversing rods cannot be used on arches.
- Most swag treatments will not accommodate traversing under treatment.
- Rods with rings cannot be used.
- Custom arched iron rods with hooks that are welded in place to hold tab or tie panels are available.
- Full-length panels must usually be hung from the swag board or on separate boards or sash rods.

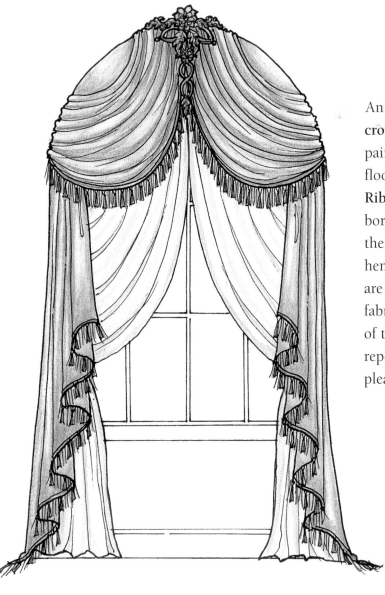

An intricate **custom iron crown** tops this beautiful pair of **turban swags** and floor-length cascades. **Ribbon and tassel fringe** borders the leading edge of the swags and the bottom hem of the cascades, which are lined in a contrasting fabric. The swooping lines of the turban swags are repeated by tying back the pleated **under panels**.

A beautiful pair of **self-lined turban swags** with a **pointed pelmet** at the center frames this arched window. They are trimmed with a rich fringe and are accentuated with a pair of **floor-length self-lined reversed cascades** pleated at the top and trimmed with fringe at the bottom hem. A focal point is created by mounting an **embroidered medallion** at the center of the pelmet.

Overlapped arched panels headed with deep **goblet pleats** are held back with brackets embellished with **double choux.** The tied-back panels form long, thin **cascades** at each side.

This elaborate treatment is remarkably simple in its construction. Two **scarf swags**, each in a different fabric and one longer than the other, are **self-lined** and hemmed at an angle to form a **steep cascade** at the bottom. To create the necessary width at the top of the treatment, the scarves should be mounted on a small board under the crown. The tails of the scarves are then draped over the swag holders. **Florist wire** or colored embroidery thread can be used to secure the tails in place.

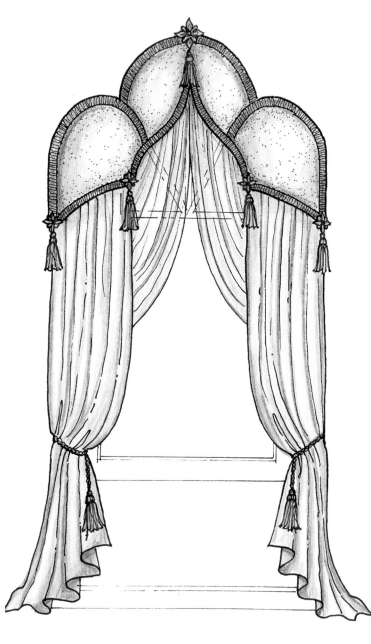

This whimsical **Ali Baba-inspired cornice** transforms the shape of the window beneath it. It is trimmed in contrasting **decorative tape** that is embellished with **medallions** and **key tassels**. The center sections of the trimmed cornice are heavily padded, creating soft mounds within each section. The **sheer panels** have a rod pocket heading and are mounted on separate angled sash rods on the wall. The side panels are shirred and mounted directly to the back of the cornice.

This **scarf swag** design imparts a decidedly Scottish feel to this pair of French doors. It is the utmost in ease of construction consisting of two **straight scarves** casually draped over large **medallions**. The top scarf is bordered with **onion fringe** between the **medallions** in order to add visual weight to the top of the treatment. The bottom scarf is done in a contrasting sheer fabric that adds an airy touch to the design. **Tassel tiebacks** are draped over the two bottom medallions.

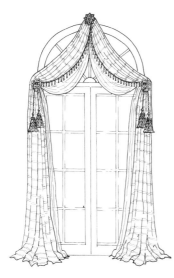

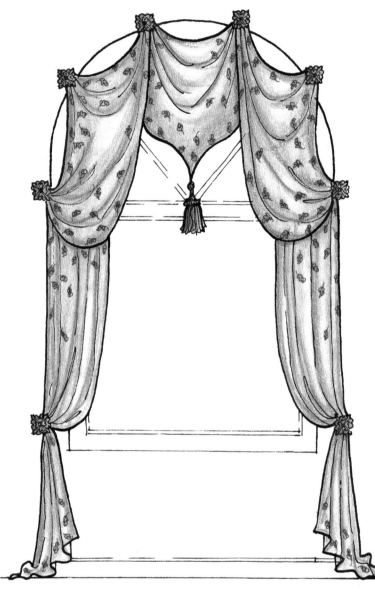

Pick-up swags are layered over one another to create this design. The center swag has a **Moroccan point**, which is embellished with a large **key tassel**. It is hung by loops threaded over **medallion swag holders**. The swagged side panels and the top two **pick-up swags** are hung together on each side of the center swag. Alternating contrasting fabrics on the swags and panels highlight their unique, individual shapes. Matching medallions are used as hold-backs to complete the design.

This complicated multilayer design is not for the novice. It is anchored by a heavily **padded half-circle cornice** embellished with iron ornaments. A **formal pleated swag** fills the arch ending at the tips of the cornice. Extra-long almost-to-the-floor **shirred cascades** provide the vertical emphasis of the treatment. The under panels are tied back behind the cascades. **Tassel fringe** trims the bottom hem of the swag as well as the bottom hem of the cascades.

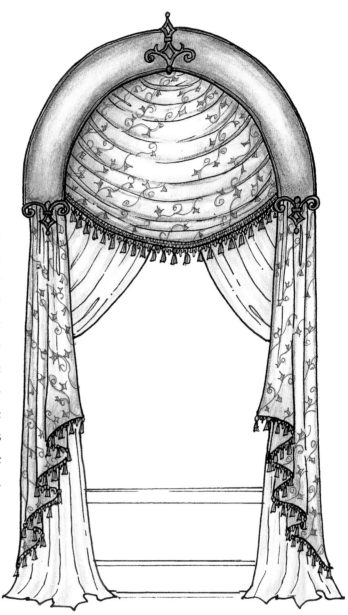

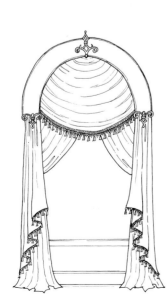

A pair of **raised swags** and **shirred double cascades** is hung from decorative medallions to create this simple yet sophisticated design. **Onion fringe** finishes the bottom hem of the swags and cascades. The **puddled** side panels have a rod pocket heading and are hung on sash rods attached to the window casing. This design is equally attractive without the side panels.

Deep **turban swags** are
draped over a half-circle
arched cornice. The center
of the cornice is topped
with a **horn jabot** that has
been bordered in a contrasting fabric and weighted with
beads. A pair of matching
jabots is mounted under-
neath the swag at each side
of the cornice.

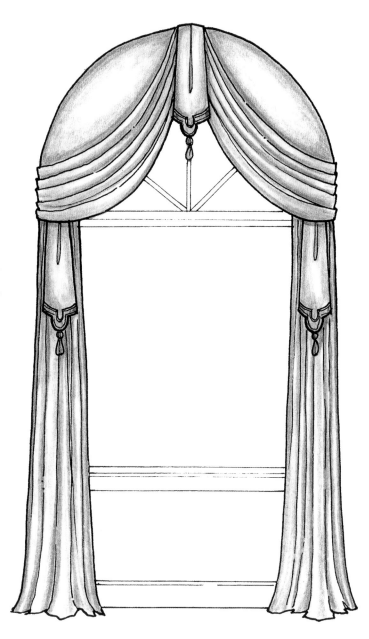

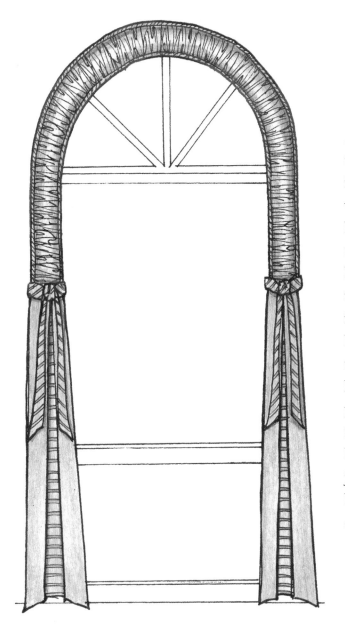

A **shirred fabric cornice** trimmed with **decorative braid** follows the graceful arch of the window. It stops just above the halfway measurement of the treatment where it is embellished with a long **bias-cut tie** in a contrasting fabric. An **inverted box-pleated jabot** hangs from the base of the cornice and ends in a **slanted hem**. The interior of the box pleat is done in the contrasting fabric to create a strong vertical line to balance the cornice. The jabot should be made in a full-bodied fabric that will hold a crisp pleat.

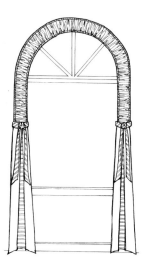

This **asymmetrical design** is achieve by draping a swag at the top of the arch over a **puddled full-length panel** pulled back using **Italian stringing**. A slim cascade placed opposite the long panel brings the design into balance.

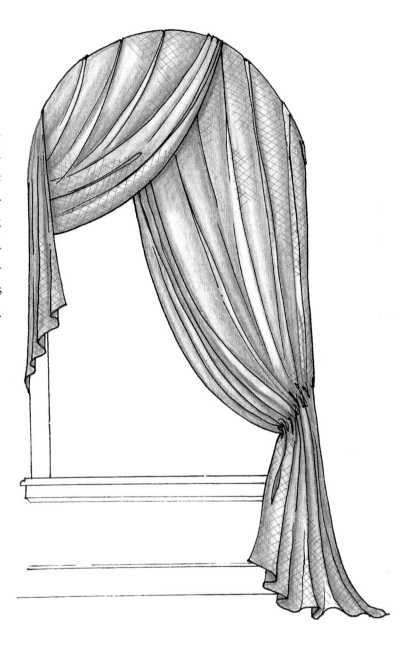

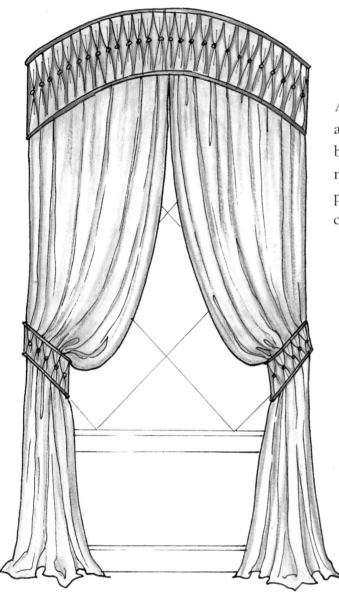

An arched **cornice** is faced with a row of **fabric bands** that have been cinched together in the middle with **glass beads**. Full panels and matching **tiebacks** complete the treatment.

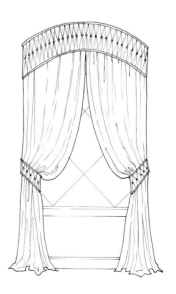

Unique **scrolled hardware crowns** are hung at an **angle** at each side of this eyebrow-arched window. **Contrast-lined scalloped panels** have been **cut at a matching angle** so they will hang straight without drooping. They are held back with matching decorative scrolls.

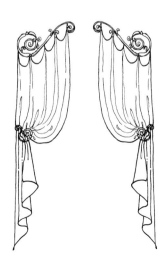

A beautiful **custom arched rod** has been made with **stationary hooks** at the back and embellished with matching leaves at the front. The **deeply scooped pleated valance** hangs in a graceful arch from the hooks on the rod. Complementary side panels are mounted on rods set at an angle behind the valance.

This delicate treatment is **swagged** at the bottom hem of the arched valance. Long, narrow side panels are pulled up into **bishop's sleeve cascades**. **Pointed crosses** are placed at key points to create movement around the window.

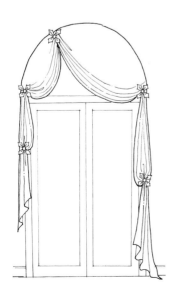

Wrought-iron medallions are placed in an **asymmetrical arrangement** around this arched window frame to hold a **loop-topped panel,** which is swagged back on one side to form a cascade. **Key tassels** adorn each medallion and hang from the cascade.

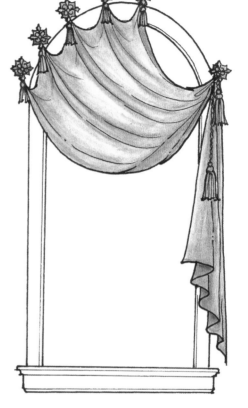

A **shirred panel** with a **ruffled heading** covers 2/3 of the top of this arched window. The last 1/3 of the arch is occupied by a smaller panel that is **swagged** over the top of the treatment and gathered into a **pouf** at the side. The side panel is tied back and decorated with a matching pouf.

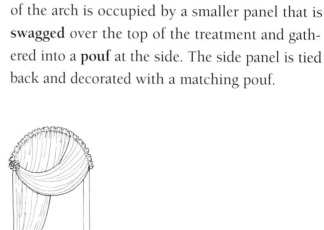

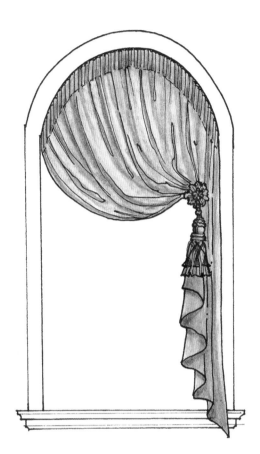

This **pencil-pleated arched panel** is mounted inside this window and held back with a medallion that is mounted on a small board or L bracket behind the treatment. A large **key tassel** is hung from the medallion.

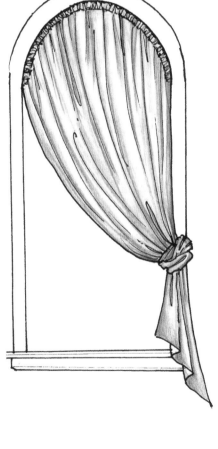

Shirring tape is used to gather the heading of this panel, which is mounted with **Velcro** to the inside of the window frame. A simple **knot tied** in the end of the panel and hooked in place adds a lovely detail to this otherwise plain design.

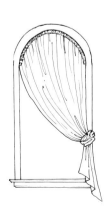

A **triple-swagged valance** with **under-mounted** cascades tops this arched window. A **sheer panel** shirred on **café rods** and mounted inside the frame provides privacy.

The most elementary treatments such as this shirred panel mounted on café rods can be turned into an elaborate master-piece with a few pieces of trim and some great hardware.

An **arched pelmet valance** is **draped** with two **contrasting scarves**, which are **picked up** at the sides of the pelmet and topped with **double cascades** and **crosses**. A matching cross adorns the high point of the arch that is outlined in **decorative braid**.

This window is topped with an arched **turban swag** cornice with crisp **double cascades**. The cornice is trimmed in two sizes of **ribbon loop fringe** to accentuate its outline. The fringe is made into **rosettes** and **tassels** that are placed at the high and low points of the swag.

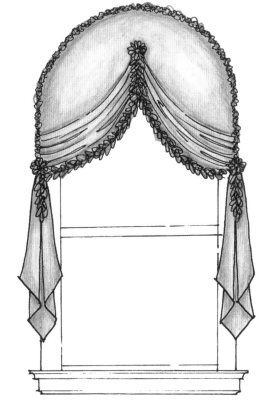

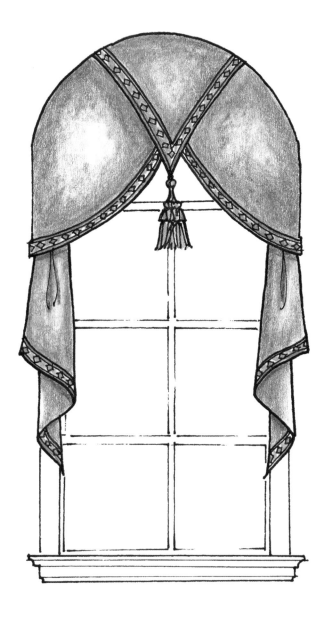

Beautiful **embroidered tape** follows the interesting lines of this **cornice** with **reversed bell cascades**. A large **key tassel** is hung from the center V section to create a **focal point**.

The magnificent **hardware** is the **focal point** of this swagged design.

Top Treatments

A top treatment can be used by itself or in combination with other soft treatments. The choice made in combining treatments can greatly affect the finished look of the treatment.

Valance only

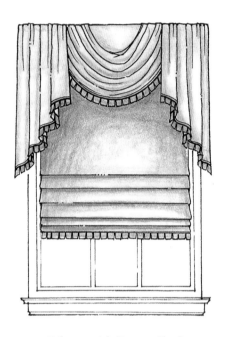

Valance with Roman Shade

Valance with Tie-Back Panels

Valance with Traversing Panels

Top Treatments

A top treatment is a valance, cornice, lambrequin, or scarf that is hung at the top of the window. It can be used as one element of a complicated treatment or by itself.

- ⚜ Top treatments frame a window or finish a full treatment.

- ⚜ They add or reinforce detail and shape.

- ⚜ They can complement or highlight architectural details.

- ⚜ They can cover unsightly hardware and mechanics.

- ⚜ They can cover pleats and headings of functional draperies or shades.

- ⚜ They can add or reinforce horizontal design elements.

- ⚜ They can manipulate the appearance of the height and width of the window.

- ⚜ They soften the appearance of hard treatments.

- ⚜ They can unify the appearance of different types of under treatments used in the same room.

- ⚜ The top treatment can be an opportunity to introduce coordinating or contrasting fabrics and colors.

- ⚜ Many top treatments are easy to make and are cost effective due to the small amount of materials used.

- ⚜ Always self-line any part of the treatment that can be seen from the front, from below, or from above.

- ⚜ Use drapery weights to control the hang of the treatment.

- ⚜ Interline where necessary to control light or color bleed-through.

- ⚜ A top treatment can easily be added to existing or store-bought panels to create a whole new look.

Flags are one of the most versatile elements used in today's drapery designs. They can be hung in several different ways:

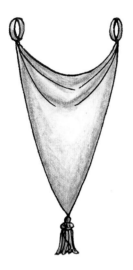

Sewn-On Drapery Rings can be hung on a decorative pole, swag holders, or knobs.

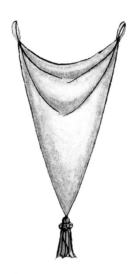

Fabric Loops can be hung over swag holders or decorative knobs.

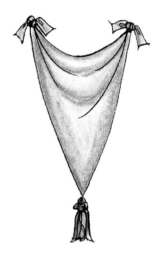

Ties can be tied directly to the decorative rod, to drapery rings, swag holders, or knobs.

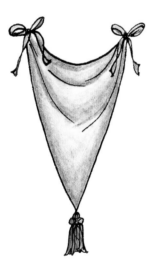

Bows can be tied directly to the decorative rod, to drapery rings, swag holders, or knobs.

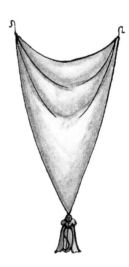

Drapery Hooks can be hooked to a traverse rod or to decorative rings.

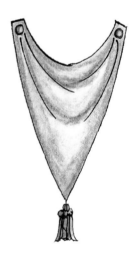

Button and Buttonhole can be used to attach the flag directly to the panel.

Flags

A flag is a pennant-shaped, vertical, decorative embellishment that is hung from two or three points at its top hem.

- Flags are very versatile. They can be used alone, on a valance or cornice, or with functional or nonfunctional panels.

- Flags are economical due to the simplicity of their construction and the small amount of fabric and trim used.

- Flags can provide a substantial visual impact for very little cost.

- Flags should always be self-lined or contrast lined.

- Use string welt to create a sharp edge to the flag.

- Do not topstitch the flag. Topstitching impedes the hang of the fabric.

- Interline or use fusible interfacing on thin or unstable fabrics when making flags to give them body and drapability.

- Flags can be made reversible by using contrast lining. This will allow a quick change to the look of the treatment. It's a great tool for creating seasonal variety in your decor.

- Flags can be taken on and off easily to change the look of the treatment or to be cleaned and pressed.

- Flags can be hung from a wide variety of hardware.

- Flags can be used to embellish store-bought panels and give them a custom appearance.

- Flags can be easily added to an existing treatment to change its look.

Double-point flag

Triple-point flag

Triple-point flag

*Triple-point flag
with folded edges*

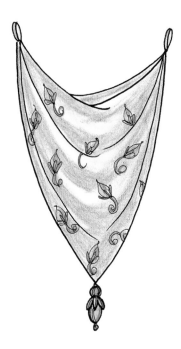

Flat single-point flag

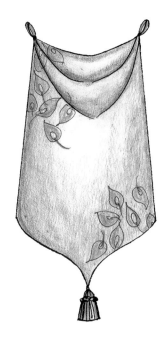

Triple Moroccan-point flag

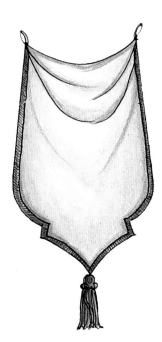

*Triple-point flag
with rounded corners*

*Triple-point flag with angled
corners and a Moroccan-point*

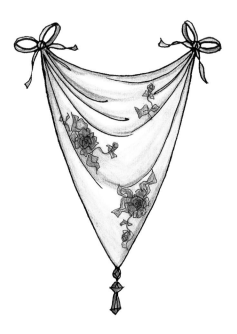

*Single-point flag
with matching ties*

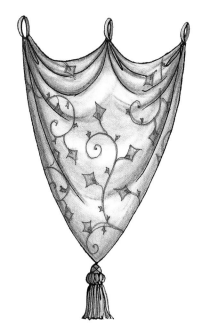

*Raised swag top,
single-point flag*

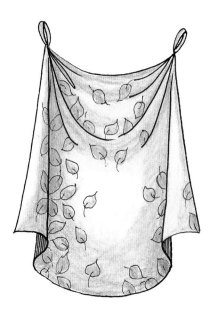

*Double-point flag
with a rounded bottom*

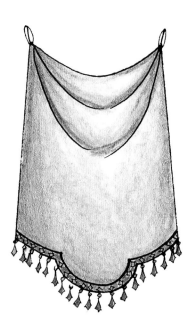

*Double-point flag with
a specialty shape bottom*

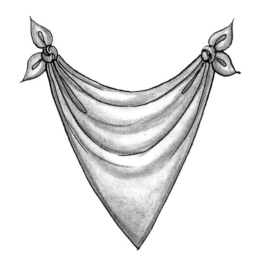

*Single-point
handkerchief flag*

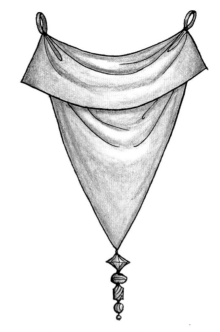

*Single-point flag with a
fold-over heading*

*Wide cascading
triple-point flag*

*Shirred reverse triple-point
flag with top ruffle*

Shirred triple-point flag

Open-swag single-point flag

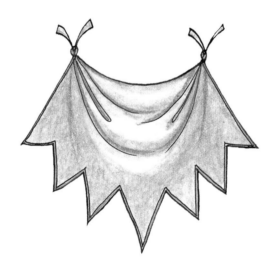

Zigzag flag

Scalloped flag

*Shirred and knotted
bishop's sleeve flag*

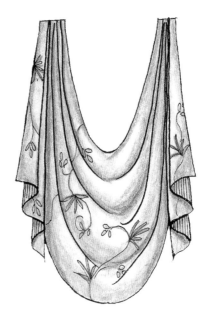

*Open-swag flag with
attached cascades*

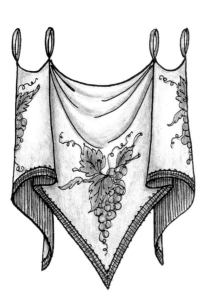

*Empire single-point flag
with single cascades*

*Empire single-point flag
with double necktie jabots*

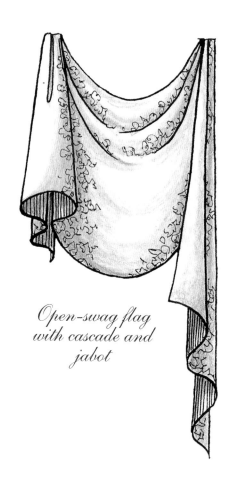

Open-swag flag
with cascade and
jabot

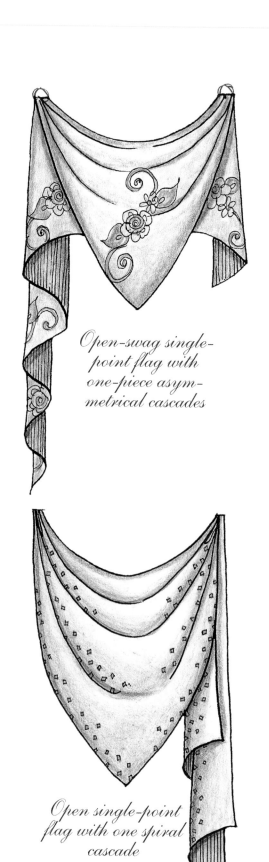

Open-swag single-
point flag with
one-piece asym-
metrical cascades

Open single-point
flag with one spiral
cascade

*Empire swag with inte-
grated reverse jabot
and cascade*

*Empire swag
with cascades*

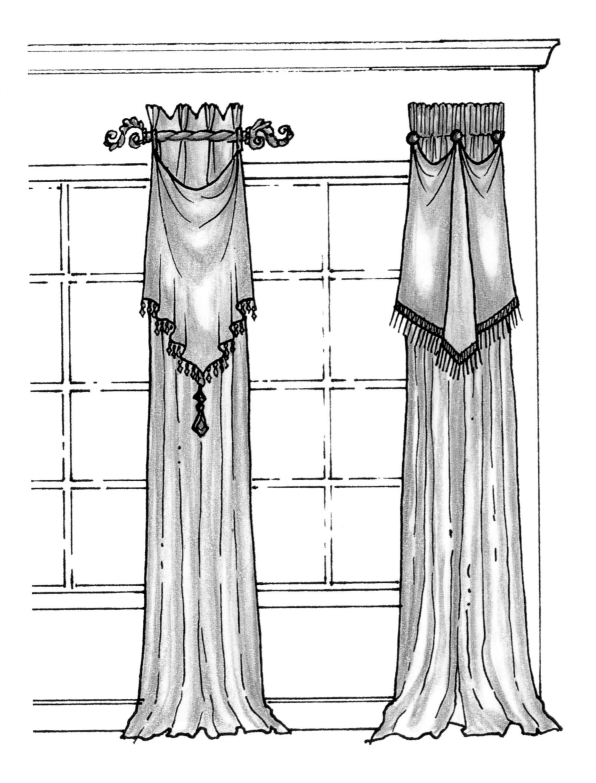

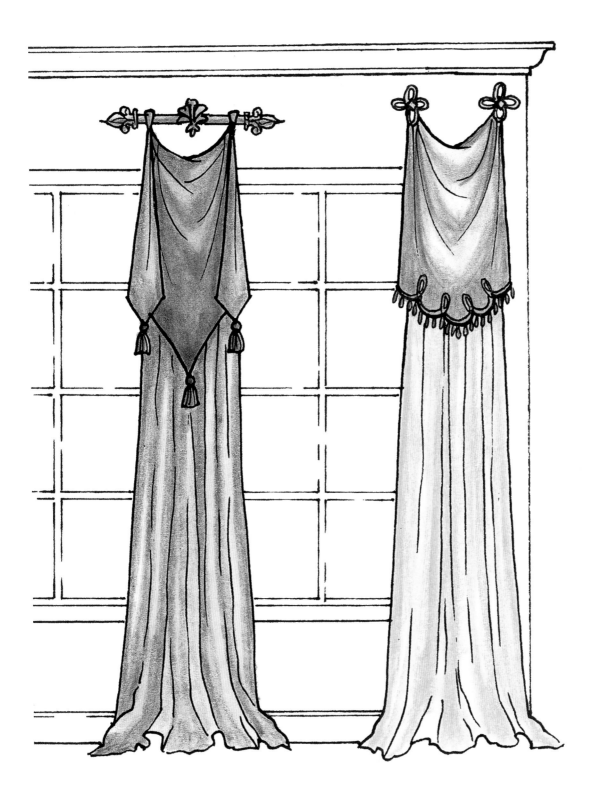

Flag Treatments

Medieval France is the inspiration for this design comprised of **banners** and **scarf swags**. The banners are stiffened with interfacing and embellished with a contrasting border and **embroidered fleur-de-lis**. They are lined in the contrasting fabric and finished with a **key tassel**. The self-lined scarves and the side panels are done in a complementary fabric. All of these elements are hung on three separate decorative poles.

Pinch-pleated side panels with a slouched heading are mounted to separate boards at each side of the window. Two **triple-point flags** with a **center swag** are hung from medallions attached to the board mount. The flags and center swag are made of sheer fabric with rolled hems. **Key tassels** add weight to the sheer flags.

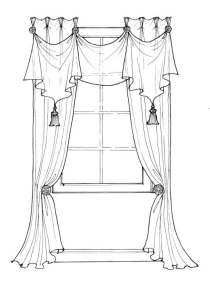

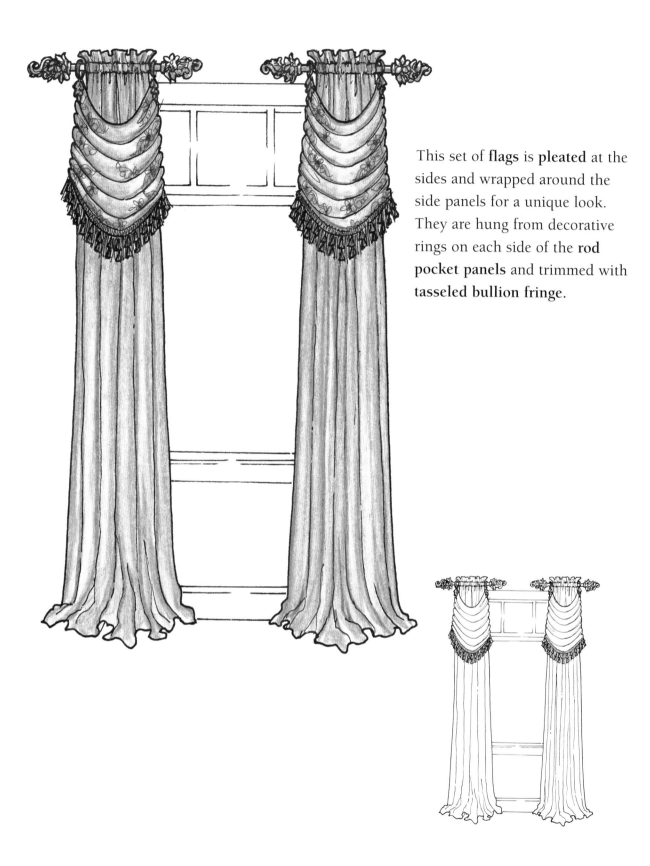

This set of **flags** is **pleated** at the sides and wrapped around the side panels for a unique look. They are hung from decorative rings on each side of the **rod pocket panels** and trimmed with **tasseled bullion fringe**.

These plain puddled panels have a **hidden rod pocket** heading with an attached, **fold-over single-point flag** done in a contrasting pattern. When the panels are threaded onto the rod, the self-lined flag is folded over the rod to the front to create the **waterfall** look seen here. **Tassel tiebacks** are looped over the panels and attached to the rod at the back. Hardware and trim are the keys to setting the mood for these classic styles. They can be starkly modern or opulently traditional.

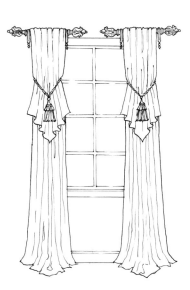

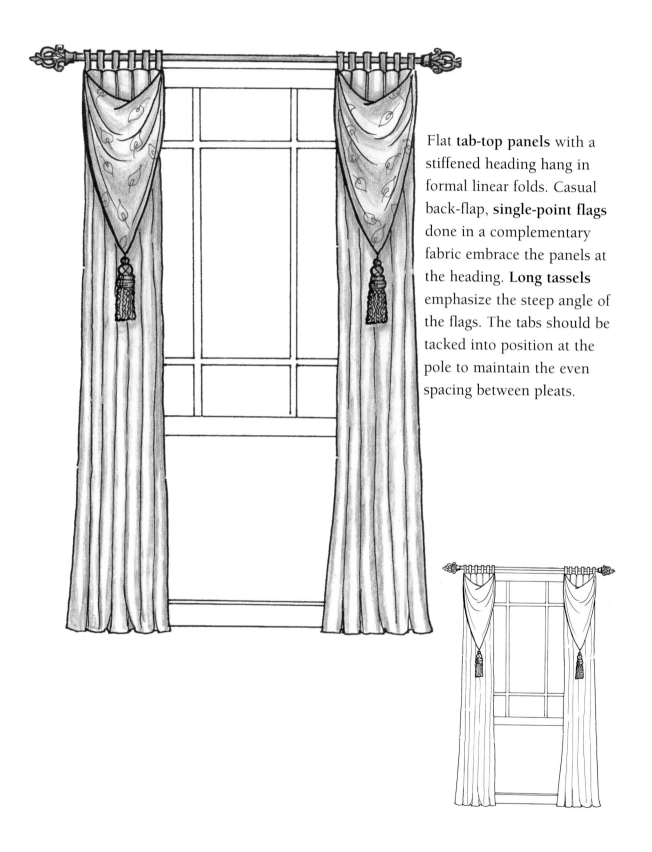

Flat **tab-top panels** with a stiffened heading hang in formal linear folds. Casual back-flap, **single-point flags** done in a complementary fabric embrace the panels at the heading. **Long tassels** emphasize the steep angle of the flags. The tabs should be tacked into position at the pole to maintain the even spacing between pleats.

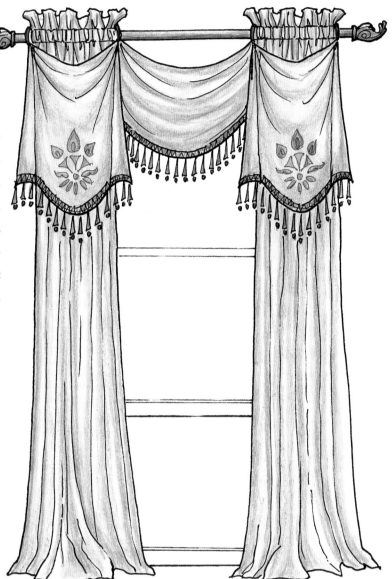

Rod pocket side panels provide the backdrop for a matching set of **triple-point flags** and a **center swag**. While the panels are threaded on the rod, the flags and center swag are hung from the rod on decorative rings placed on each side of the panels. Exotic **wooden tassel fringe** add a unique flair to this design.

This design is the utmost in old-world elegance. The **graduated series of flags** trimmed and lined in a contrasting fabric are embellished with beautiful **iron pins** and **leaf tassels**. The drapery rings have matching leaves to continue the rhythm of the design. The side panels have a hidden **"no show" top** to accentuate the continuous scallop created by the tops of the flags.

Accordion pleats head up this flowing multilayered design. The **sheer under treatment** is mounted on a board just beneath the decorative rod so that it will appear to be on the same line as the top treatments. The side panels and valance are pleated together and hung from decorative rings on the rod. Only the side panels have a return so the valance hangs flat. The valance is a simple **straight panel** that has been **tied up in the center**. The tie is knotted at the end and tacked to the panel heading.

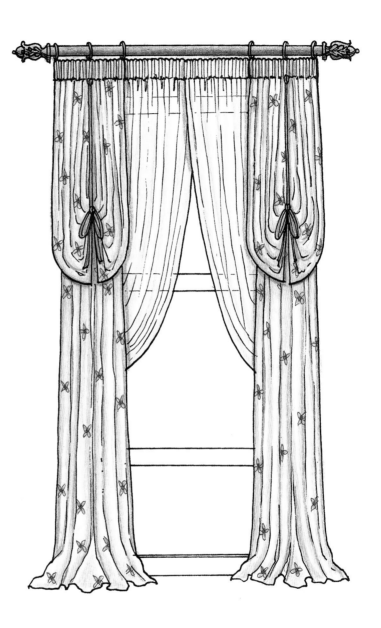

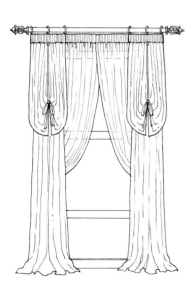

This stunning treatment is very simple in design. The panels are **knife pleated** with a very deep **inverted box pleat** at the center. The knife pleats are folded to the outside edge, away from the center on each side of the panel. The center pleat is sewn closed down the length of the panel until just above the point of the pelmet. A generous puddle in the panel allows the center pleat to open and expose the contrasting fabric. The **pelmet flags** are attached to the panel and folded over the rod. The panels are then secured directly to the rod.

The graceful lines of these **over-the-rod open empire swags** are highlighted by the application of **contrasting gimp** at the edges. The **scalloped hem** is made even more dramatic by the added curls on the face. To maintain the open swag at the heading, the pleated side panels are under mounted on a board. The crisp formal pleats of the panels provide a nice contrast to the soft drapery of the swags.

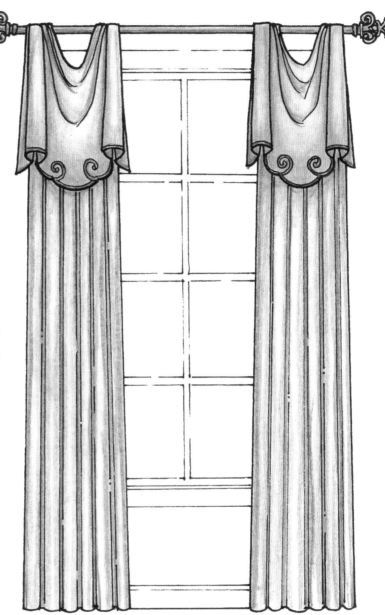

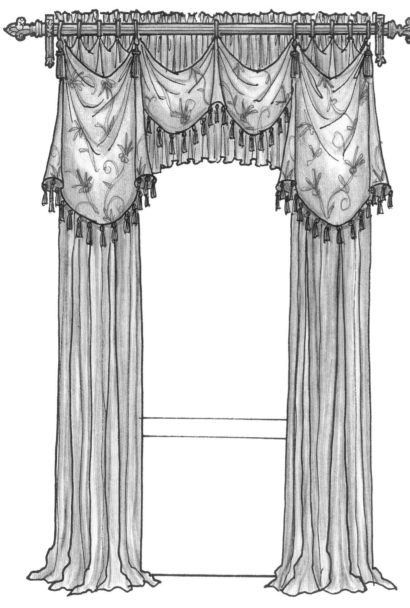

This design is perfect for those situations in which the window is mounted too low on the wall, leaving a large gap that needs to be covered. By backing the entire treatment with a set of rod pocket panels and center valance, the wall is covered. The rod can then be mounted at the ceiling to add height to the room. Here, we top the under-treatment with **contrasting side panels**, **flags**, and a **center swag** all hung on decorative rings. The rod is hung directly over the rod pocket of the under-treatment.

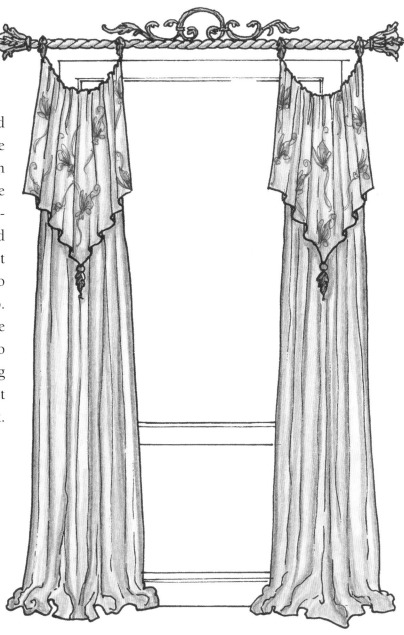

These "**no show**" **panels** and **shirred scalloped flags** are constructed as one piece with a casing sewn in along the seam joining the two sections. A flat ribbon is inserted in the casing and pulled tight to gather the two pieces into a **graceful scoop** at the top. The ends of the ribbon are used to tie the treatment to the drapery rings. A matching **leaf tassel** is used to weight the flag point.

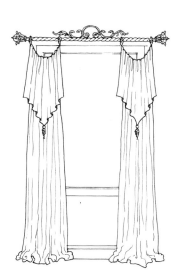

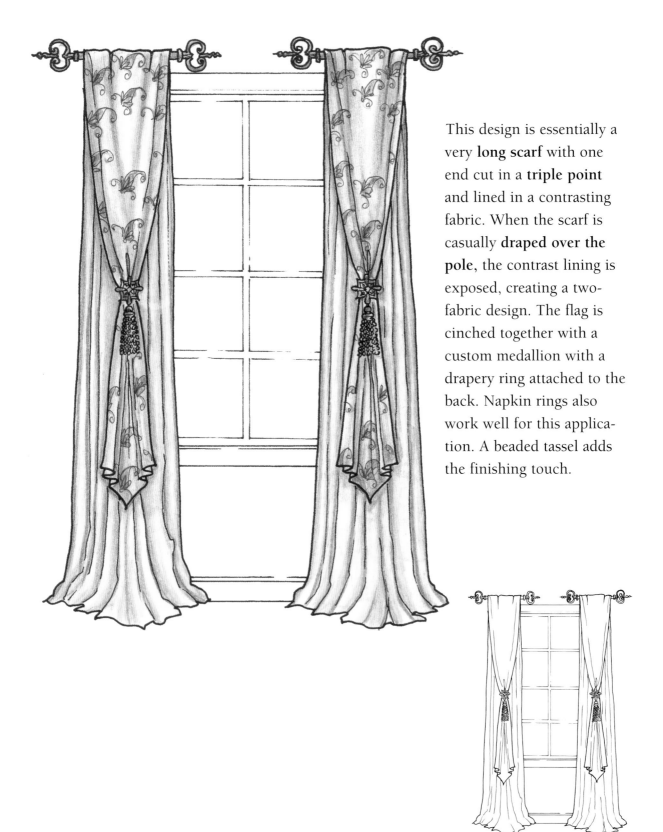

This design is essentially a very **long scarf** with one end cut in a **triple point** and lined in a contrasting fabric. When the scarf is casually **draped over the pole,** the contrast lining is exposed, creating a two-fabric design. The flag is cinched together with a custom medallion with a drapery ring attached to the back. Napkin rings also work well for this application. A beaded tassel adds the finishing touch.

Rich tassel fringe and a contrasting border transform these simple fold-over valance, hidden rod pocket panels into a rich, luxurious treatment.

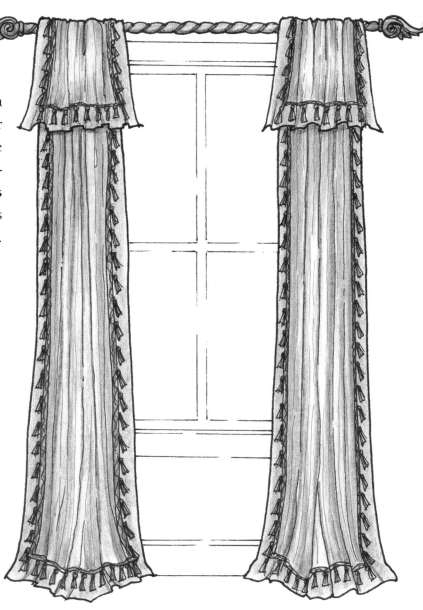

Valances

A valance is a soft, fabric-top treatment. It can be used alone or in conjunction with full-length panels, shades, or hard treatments.

- A valance can frame a window or finish a full treatment.

- A valance can add or reinforce detail and shape.

- A valance can cover unsightly hardware and mechanics.

- A valance can cover pleats and headings of functional draperies or shades.

- A valance can add or reinforce horizontal design elements.

- A valance can manipulate the appearance of the height and width of the window.

- A valance can soften the appearance of hard treatments.

- A valance can unify the appearance of different types of under treatments used in the same room.

- A custom valance can be easily added to store-bought or existing treatments to create a new look or seasonal variety.

- Always line or self-line a valance.

- Do not topstitch the valance unless it is an integral part of its design. Topstitch the face fabric only, if possible.

- Do not topstitch trim through the lining of the valance.

- Use drapery weights to control the hang of the valance.

- Increase the return of the valance if hanging additional treatments underneath.

Many of the valance designs shown in this chapter are expandable and most can be used with side panels, drapery, shades, or blinds.

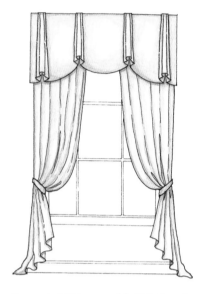

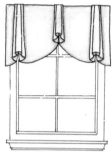

Valance   *Expanded Valance*   *Expanded Valance with Side Panels*

When expanding or using with other elements, remember these tips:

- ✤ Adjust the proportions and scale of the valance to suit the size of the window, the room, and the overall treatment.

- ✤ Specify a hard face and leg structure to your expanded valance. This will fortify the elongated shape and eliminate sagging.

- ✤ Specify your wide valances to be made in multiple sections to facilitate an easy installation, as well as to avoid tricky delivery and accessibility problems.

- ✤ Remember to increase the return on any valance to be used with panels, drapery, or blinds.

- ✤ Specify a 6" to 8" self-facing at the hem of all non-self-lined valances to avoid visibility of the white lining from below.

- ✤ Specify drapery weights where appropriate to control the fabric and make it hang well.

- ✤ When hanging a valance by itself, consider the light intensity at the window to avoid bleed-through and overexposure. Use interlining, French lining, or blackout lining where necessary.

Key Terms for Valances

Arched valance: A valance treatment that is arched along the upper or lower edge.

Austrian valance: A soft, stationary valance fabricated like the Austrian shade, with the vertical row of shirred fabric that forms a scalloped bottom edge.

Balloon valance: A soft, stationary valance fabricated like the balloon shade that is known for the poufs at the bottom edge.

Banding: Strips of fabric sewn to the edge of drapery and curtains. Banding is made with a fabric complementary to the fabric of the main portion of the window treatment.

Banner valance: A series of fabric triangles attached to a mounting board or threaded on a rod; also called a handkerchief valance.

Cascade (aka tails): Often used with swags, a fall of knife-pleated fabric that descends in a zigzag line from the drapery heading or top treatment. They should be self- or contrast lined.

Cloud valance: A stationary top treatment similar to the cloud shade that cannot be raised or lowered.

Contrast lining: A decorative fabric used as a lining or decking when parts of it may show from the front of the top treatment.

Cording (aka welt cord): A rope that is covered with fabric, also referred to as piping or welting.

Cutout return: A buttonhole or rectangular cutout at the top return of the panel or top treatment to allow the return to go back to the wall in a pole-mounted treatment.

Decorative hardware: Hardware (such as swag holders, rods, poles, tiebacks, and rings) that can add aesthetic appeal to a window fashion, as well as serve functional purposes.

Double-top heading: This heading is commonly used for both pinch pleat and rod pocket draperies, where the heading has another full layer of fabric under the visible layer on the backside.

Drapability: The ability of a certain fabric to hang in pleasing folds.

Draping: Technique of looping and securing fabric in graceful curves and folds.

Dust board: The portion of the mount board or cornice to which the legs and/or the face are attached.

Festoon: A decorative valance made of folded fabric that hangs in a graceful curve over the window.

Hem: Refers to finished sides and bottom edges of a drapery.

Layered valance: A valance that has multiple layers of fabric stacked on top of each other to create contrast and visual interest.

Holdbacks: A decorative piece of hardware used to hold back draperies or hold up swags

L Bracket (aka angle irons): A metal bracket in the shape of an L, used to install valance and cornices.

Passementerie (aka trims): The French term for a range of decorative cords, bands, and tassels used on window fashions and furnishings, to give definition or add decorative detail.

Pelmet valance: A valance that features flat, stiffened panels, sections, or shapes as the main design element.

Pillowcase seam (aka pillowslip): The technique where face fabric and lining fabric are seamed together, usually with a 1/2" seam, then turned and pressed so the seam becomes the very edge of the item.

Pleated valance: A board-mounted treatment that contains pleats as its main design element.

Pull-up valance: A valance that has high and low points in the heading. The valance is hung by the high points using hardware.

Pouf valance: A top treatment similar to the cloud, but the effect is one continuous pouf rather than separate poufs, and the pouf valance does not have a skirt.

Rod bottom valance: Any valance that has a drapery rod suspended from the hem.

Rod pocket valance: A valance that contains one or more casings sewn into the treatment through which drapery rods are inserted for the purpose of shirring the fabric and, or hanging the valance.

Rod-top valance: Any valance that has been hung from a rod using rings, ties, bows, hooks, tabs, loops, or grommets.

Roman valance: A soft, stationary valance fabricated similarly to a roman shade with stationary horizontal folds.

Rhythmic valance: Contains one or more elements that are used repeatedly to create rhythm in the design.

Stagecoach valance: Used on narrow windows, this is a panel of fabric mounted on a board and attached to the inside frame of the window. It is rolled up and tied in the center with a ribbon.

Swag: A fabric top treatment that drapes into soft semicircular folds of fabric. Swags can be used with draperies or as a top treatment only.

Swag holder: Provides support for loosely draped treatments such as a throw swag. The harp shape allows fabric to be secured in a pouf fashion.

Under-draperies: A lightweight drapery, usually a sheer, closest to the window glass. It hangs beneath a heavier over-drapery.

Valance: A horizontal decorative fabric treatment used at the top of draperies to screen hardware and cords or as a stand-alone decorative element.

Valance board (aka mount board or dust board): The flat board without a front or sides from which a valance is hung.

Valance board with legs: A flat board with boards extending down each return end. It looks like a cornice without the front. This board is used when it is necessary to anchor the sides of the valance.

Window jewelry: Small pieces of decorative hardware used as accents on fabric, usually serving no functional purpose but to add interest.

Rod Pocket Valances

A rod pocket valance contains one or more casings sewn into the treatment through which drapery rods are inserted for the purpose of shirring the fabric and, or hanging the valance.

- They are some of the simplest styles to construct but they can also be quite elaborate.

- They should have at least 2.5 times the fabric fullness, 3 times the fullness for lightweight or sheer fabrics.

- They are not suitable for heavy fabrics or fabrics with very large patterns.

- When using patterned fabric, take into consideration how your fabric will look shirred at the fullness you are using and if your pattern is suitable.

- If using interlining, exclude it from the casing area to prevent bunching.

- Allow for take up in your valance just as you would in a rod pocket panel.

- If you are using decorative trims such as tassel fringe, tape, or bullion, make sure that it is flexible. Do not use stiff trims as they will impede the draping of your valance.

This **single-ruffle** valance is made in three sections, one **center swag** and **two cascades**. The bottom borders are trimmed with beaded fringe.

The self-lined ends of the three **tubular swags** of this valance are pulled up and gathered together with drapery rings.

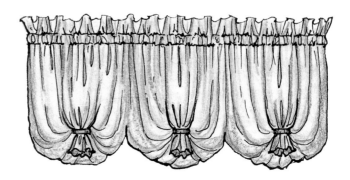

This rod pocket **London swag** has contrasting ties that are used to cinch up the panel, creating the curved tails at each side.

A single ruffle tops this **ballooned valance**. A series of casings have been sewn through the face fabric and the lining so that cording can be threaded through and tied in bows, shirring the panel into a **graduated arch**.

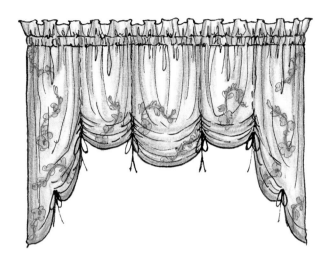

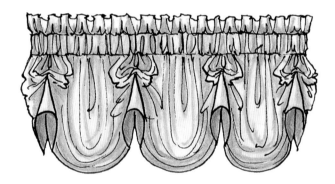

Pull-up jabots create rhythm in this **ruffled top** valance.

A flat panel with a **single-ruffle heading** is **swagged** up with contrasting **fabric ties** inserted between the rod pocket and the panel. A matching bottom ruffle is added to accentuate the swagged hem.

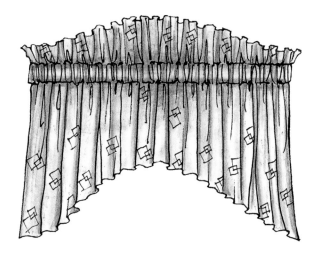

The strong lines of the **shirred arch** of the heading ruffle is repeated in the opposite **inverted V** hem of this valance.

A plain, straight valance gains visual impact by adding a gentle scallop to the bottom hem. A **bright ribbon border** applied just above the hem mirrors its curves.

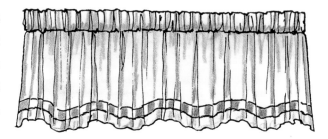

This panel is folded to create a series of **jabots** and **swags** at the bottom of the rod-pocket heading.

Two layers of self-lined fabric cut in **alternating zigzags** are joined together with a hidden rod pocket and a single-ruffle heading.

The **scalloped hem** of the top panel of this valance reveals a **contrasting under layer.** Rosettes accentuate the high point of the scallops.

Matching scallops on the **top ruffle** and **bottom hem** of the top layer of this valance are highlighted by ribbon at the edges. The arched contrasting under layer provides a backdrop for the bottom hem.
Pattern: M'Fay 9224 Petal Valance

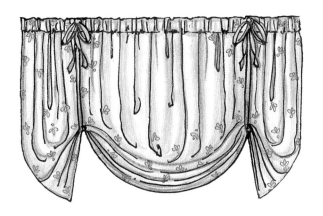

A **straight rod-pocket panel** is **pulled up** with ribbons that are tied in bows.

Cascades with a **contrast lining** and a top ruffle are attached to a **straight panel**, creating a simple yet attractive design. Fold the leading edges of the cascades back to expose more of the lining fabric.

A **plain ruffled panel** with a wide scallop hem is balanced with two **point-topped jabots** held in place by medallions and trimmed with bullion.

Three **single-point rod pocket swags** with a top ruffle are threaded together on the same rod, creating a rhythmic design. Tassels are added to weight the points and add detail.

Double-inverted-V-cut layers are centered with a contrasting double cascade and a choux.

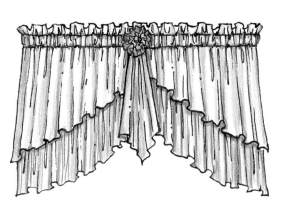

Pull-up swags with contrasting rosettes add interest to this plain panel. Use self- or contrast lining as it will show where the fabric has been raised.

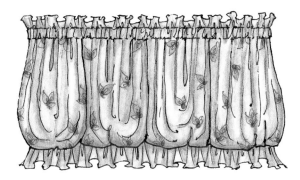

Less is more with this simple **top and bottom rod valance** with ruffles. Many times this style of valance needs some help to look full. Stuff the bottom with pillow batting or tissue paper for a crisper look.

Rod pocket swags are held up with contrasting ties that are looped over the rod and knotted at the bottom.

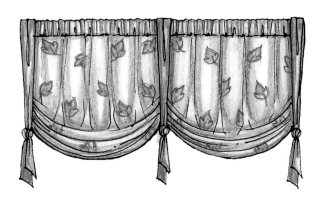

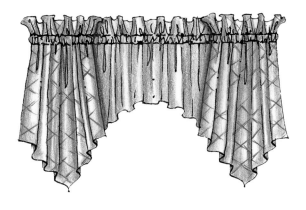

This single-ruffled rod-pocket valance has a **W-shaped hem** that is flanked by separate contrasting **double cascades** that follow the hemline.

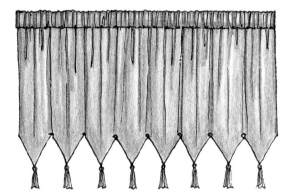

Use your imagination when choosing a **hem shape**. Even the simplest valance can be made glamorous with an interesting hemline.

Sheer or lightweight fabric should be used for this valance. It is a **double layer** shirred tightly at 3 to 3 1/2 times the fullness. The top layer is unlined and has a **lingerie hem**. It overlaps at the center in a quarter circle while the bottom layer remains straight. The center is adorned with a **double choux** and ties.

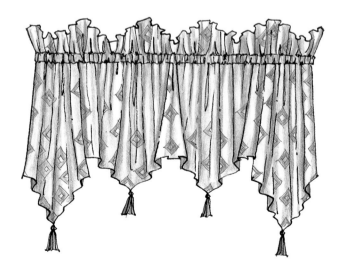

A **zigzag heading** and **graduated zigzags** at the hem perk up this simple valance.

Long and short **single-point flags** are alternated in this whimsical rod pocket valance. The flag points are weighted with **hand-painted wooden tassels**.
Pattern: Butterick B4095

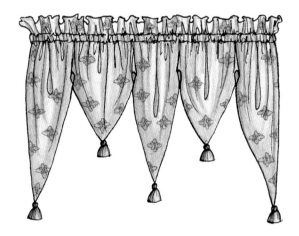

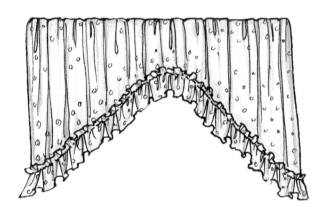

This light and airy valance has an **inverted V-shaped hem** embellished with an **edged ruffle** that has been topstitched to the face.

Rather than being threaded on a rod, this valance is **shirred at the top** and **mounted on a board**. The **contrasting ties** are embellished at the ends with big silk roses for a supremely feminine look.

Swagged Valances

Swagged valances can be composed of any combination of all or some of the following components:

Swags

Pelmets

Jabots

Tails

Cascades

Scarves

- ✤ In order for them to drape properly, swags should always be cut on the bias unless you are working with a stripe.

- ✤ Use soft pliable fabrics. Drapability of the fabric to be used is key to the success of your design.

- ✤ They are not suitable for very heavyweight fabrics or fabrics with large patterns.

- ✤ Using a striped fabric can be difficult. Always consult your workroom on which direction the stripes will be placed on each element.

- ✤ Contrast or complementary lining and string welt should be used whenever possible.

The side edges of this **casually draped** self-lined swag are rolled back to expose the **under-mounted cascades**.

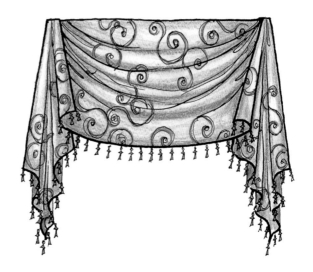

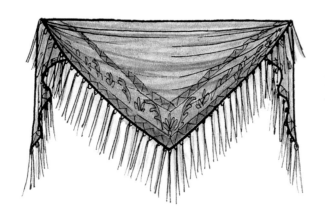

This **handkerchief swag** is made to look as if it were constructed from a scarf by adding **decorative trim and tied fringe**.

A pair of **cascading swags** is topped by a smaller, second pair of **cascades**, creating a **multilayered** look.

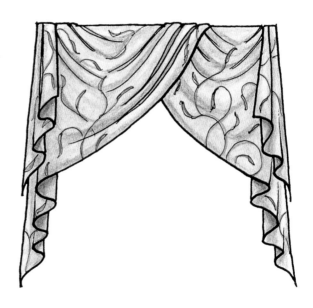

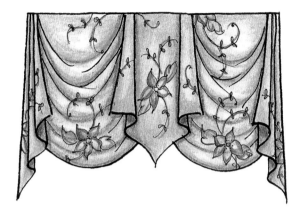

Long **Kingston swags** are centered with a **wide double cascade**. Thin cascades at the sides help to counteract the width of the center cascade and elongate the valance.

Raised double jabots with a long, thin center point and **matching cascades** frame a set of **three Kingston swags**. Decorative cord is run along the heading of the valance to cover the stitching on the cascades and jabots. It also serves as a unifying line through the treatment.

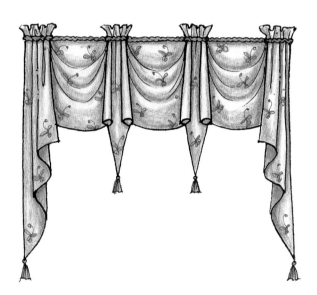

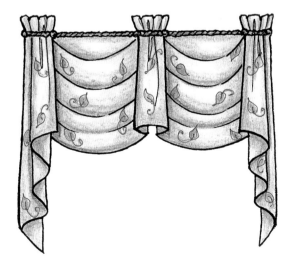

Ruffled cascades and a **matching center jabot** frame two **Kingston swags**. Decorative braid is used to unify the top line of the valance.

Two **half swags** are hung over a **center swag** to form this classic valance.

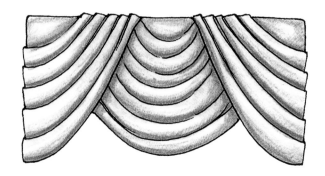

A **large swag** is set on top of a **knife-pleated under panel** to create this graceful valance.

This **Keystone swag** is aptly named as it resembles an upside-down version of the keystone in a stone arch. Pattern: Patterns Plus Keystone Swag.

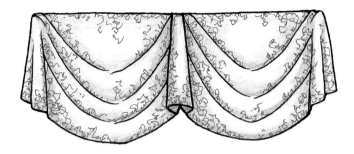

A set of **waterfall swags** are separated with a **center jabot** in this swag valance.

This swag has a **shirred heading** and **three deep swags** at the bottom. Use one by itself or a series of them in a row. Pattern: M'Fay—Gathered Fan Swag 9268.

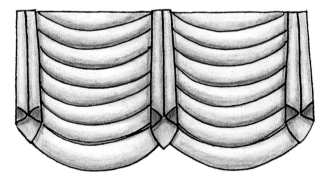

Formal **Kingston swags** are given a new look with the addition of these **double reversed jabots**.

A **pull-up swag** is framed by three **circle-cut cascades**, creating this modern design.

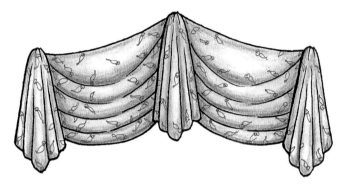

Double swags and **contrast-lined cascades** with matching outer border are embellished with **decorative rope and tassels.**

This very traditional swag valance has all the classic elements: **swags, jabots** and **cascades.** The decorative tape that is placed at the hems is repeated on both sides of the cascades so it is seen on each exposed turn.

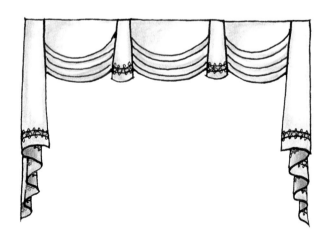

The **angled draping** of this swag is folded into a cascade at the low point. A larger cascade on the other side provides balance to the design. The angle is highlighted by the placement of the two **Maltese crosses** at each end.

Casually draped **flowing layers** of fabric reminiscent of a Roman toga create a sumptuous swag and cascade.

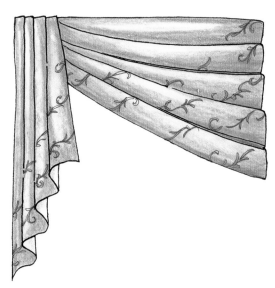

The **opposing angles** of this deeply pleated **swagged half-panel valance** and its long cascade create a harmonious balance.

This pair of deep **casual swags** with **shirred jabots** is topped with opulent tassel fringe to create a strong heading. Patterns Plus—Rod Pocket Swag 5921.

By adding an **interesting shape** to the bottom of this swag, a new **updated look** is produced Pattern: Patterns Plus—Classy Swag 5951.

The two **stacked swags** in this design are unified by the placement of an **iron scroll** at the center where they meet.

This casual flowing **scarf swag** and **jabots** are attached to a shirred back panel. The high points of the scarf are accentuated with **large velvet roses** and leaves, creating a romantic look.

A **long center panel** is shirred at the **top** and tied in a **large loose knot** at the hem of the back panel to form this casual swag and cascade. Another **set of cascades** at the sides of the valance frame the center.

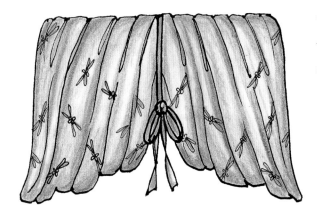

The top and bottom hems of this valance are pleated and then shirred to form large **billowing** sections. The **center** is then **pulled up** with a ribbon tie and bow to create a focal point.

Casually draped **asymmetrical swags** and cascades done in **complimentary fabrics** combine to create this rich design.

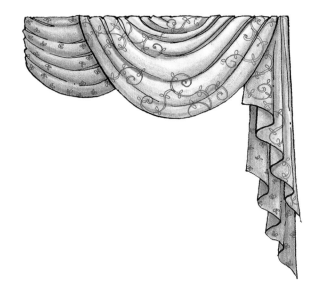

Fan top jabots are linked together with decorative rope to form a unified line in this swagged valance.

Carefully placed pleats cause this valance to fall into **graceful folds**.

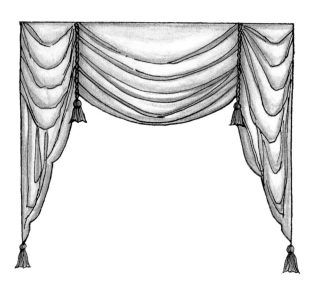

A small **box pleated heading** tops this wide swag with cascades.

Reversed cascades flank a center swag that is topped with a **contrasting band**.

A **decorative medallion** centers this pair of **front facing swags**.

A wide **rectangle swag** is hung over a **pelmet** and tied at the top corners to form jabots at the sides. **Triple-stacked tails** are mounted under the sides of the swag. Pattern: Butterick B3117

A pair of wide **shirred cascades** trimmed in **brush fringe** flank a center **raised swag**.

Open accordion swags are hung from a padded board covered in shirred fabric. **Ribbon-loop fringe** is run down the face of the swags ending with **key tassels**.

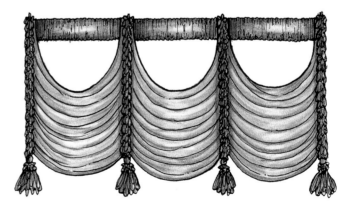

A set of **pleated panels** are mounted on this **eyebrow-arched** valance and tied back to expose a contrasting **festoon**.

A stationary **balloon shade** is hung from this arched **cornice topper**. Pattern (cornice only): M'Fay Curved Valance

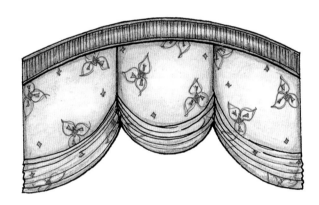

This **mock balloon shade** valance has a **camel back–shaped arch** and contrasting ties.

Rhythmic Valances

A rhythmic valance has one or more elements that are used repeatedly to create rhythm in the design. These elements can include:

Pleats

Jabots

Tails

Cascades

Scallops

Points

Arches

Pelmets

- A rhythmic valance usually has several large sections that are perfect for displaying a fabric's central motif. Choose your fabrics accordingly and plot your pattern on your worksheet so the workroom knows where you want it placed.

- Some flat designs can accommodate thicker, crisper fabric as drapability is not a big issue. Other styles with swags or gathers need a more light-weight flexible fabric.

- Interlining or interfacing should be used to prevent drooping and to add stability where needed.

This simplified version of a **Queen Anne valance** is a great design to showcase a bold pattern.
Pattern: M'Fay—Imperial Valance

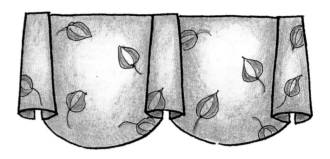

Double jabots with contrast lining create rhythm in this **triple-pointed valance.**
Pattern: Patterns Plus—Parasol valance 5937

Cross-over jabots are edged in **contrasting welt** and lined in a complementary fabric to highlight the key tassel hung from inside.

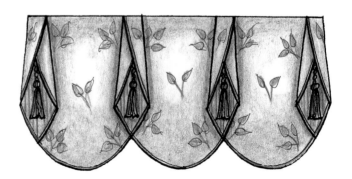

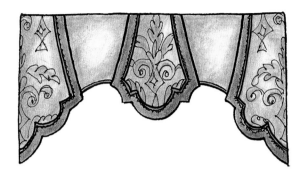

Graduated pelmets with **contrasting borders** and trims are repeated across the face of this arched valance.

A **swagged valance** is the backdrop for a set of **open-throat jabots** that are enhanced with contrast lining and a matching tie. Pattern: Patterns Plus— Swag–n-Bell 5911

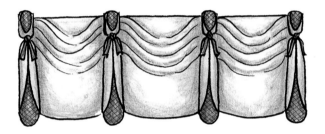

Cross-over jabots with **rosebud goblets** at the top are repeated across this **scalloped valance.** The rounded hem of the jabots creates a second set of scallops in the hem.

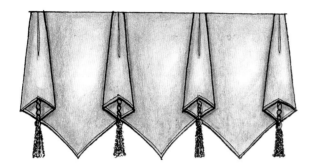

One **triple-pointed panel** is pleated to create **integrated jabots.** Contrast lining highlights the opposing angles of the hemline. Tassels are hung from the interior of the jabots.

The **flat areas** of this valance present a good opportunity to highlight a **bold pattern**.

Beaded fringe placed at the hem of the **jabots** in this valance adds emphasis to their **V shape** and creates additional length.

Two separate **layers of points** and **necktie jabots** are stacked to create this design.

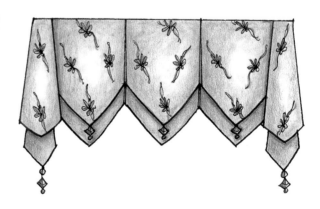

The series of **double jabots** used to frame and center this valance create a **soft undulating effect**.

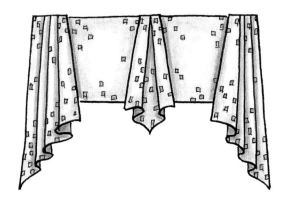

Traditional **cascades** on a **straight valance** are brought up to date by using a contemporary fabric.

The leading edge of the **shirred cascades** on this valance is rolled back to expose the **contrast lining**, which is repeated at the center.

The **cascades** and **center jabot** in this design are **knotted** at the top for a casual look. They are mounted with a pair of swags on top of a **shirred back board**.

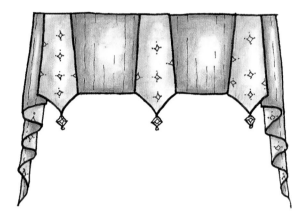

Necktie tails are used in place of jabots on this straight valance. **Cascades** with contrast lining matching the tails complete the design.

Accordion-pleated cascades and **chandelier crystals** hung like jewelry lend a dressmaker's touch to this glamorous valance.

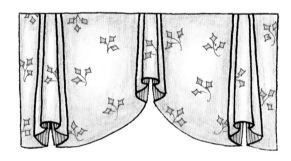

Contrast lined, **integrated stacked jabots** are created by folding the fabric.
Pattern: Patterns Plus—Legacy 5961

Switchback cascades flank uniquely shaped panels separated by **inverted box pleats.**

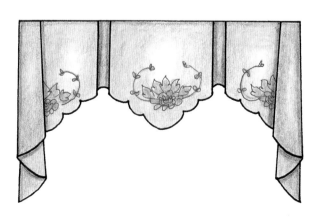

Using a **contrasting fabric on the face** of the **jabots** and **cascades** rather than for the lining makes these elements standout.

A flat valance is the backdrop for **shirred raised jabots** topped with **short, open swags**.

Graduated jabots are placed between the scallops of this valance, creating an **inverted V hemline**.

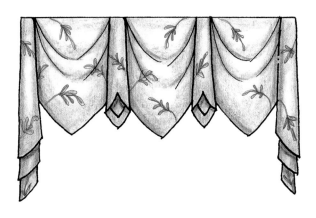

Single-point swags are separated by **stacked cascades** and **jabots**.

A **soft arched hem** on this valance is followed by the lengths of the jabots and cascades. The **decorative braid** adds emphasis to their raised headings.

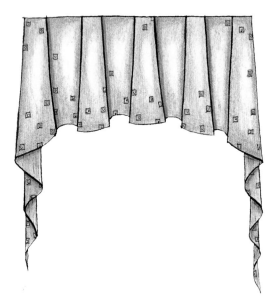

Box pleats that form a **slight arch** at the hem and long, thin cascades create a linear balance to this tailored valance.

This **M-shaped valance** is softened by adding two **raised double jabots**. The **decorative tape border** is placed to appear to run in one continuous line across the valance.

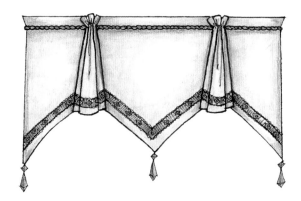

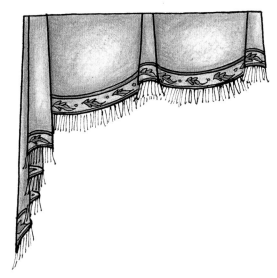

An **asymmetrical balance** is achieved by using **graduated jabots** and a **single long cascade** on this slightly scalloped valance.

A series of **graduated tails** are **stacked** together to form a cohesive surface in this interesting design. **Wooden beads** of different shapes and sizes are sewn to the tips of the tails to accentuate their individuality.

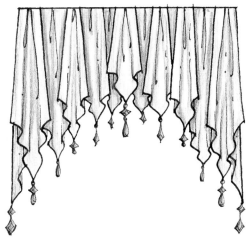

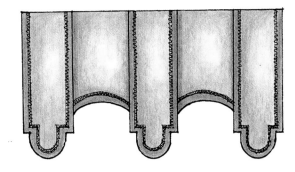

A row of **single-scallop pelmets** are evenly spaced across this **arched bottom pelmet valance**. Each section is rimmed with a contrasting border.

Rod-Top Valances

A rod-top valance can be any design style that has been hung from a rod using any of the following devices:

Rings

Tabs

Ties

Bows

Hooks

Ribbons

* Many board-mounted valances can be altered to allow them to be hung from a rod by adding tabs or ties, etc.

* Always specify the diameter of your rod to your workroom so they can make the necessary adjustments.

* Always secure the hanging devices in place on the rod to prevent drooping.

* Add 1" to the length of valances hung by taps or loops as then will shorten slightly when hung on the pole.

This valance is designed to **highlight fabric panels** with a strong pattern as if they were works of art. They are **trimmed** with **gimp** and **hung by ribbon** from decorative hooks.

The flat surface of this inverted pleat valance is appropriate for a large pattern as long as the motif is placed in the same location on each section.

A **contrasting band** of fabric serves as the backdrop for the decorative pole threaded through a **belt-loop heading** in this imaginative valance. Pattern: Pate Meadows— Mellissa Valance

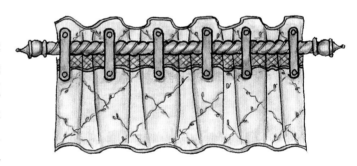

A simple **half-circle arched panel** with a **tabbed heading** makes a strong statement when it is made with rich fabrics, trims and hardware.

Flat scallops are embellished with a **shirred insert** at the center of each scallop. A contrasting **top border** and **button-down tabs** complete the valance. Pattern: Patterns Plus—Cachet-5964

Over-the-rod cascades separate **flat scalloped panels** with an **open heading**. Tassels and cording cinch the cascades together at the top of the valance. Pattern: Pate Meadows—Celebration Valance

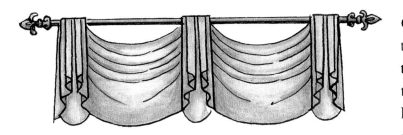

Open pole swags back up the scallop hemmed-**over the rod-double-cascades** that are folded back at the leading edge to expose the contrast lining. Pattern: Patterns Plus—Renaissance Swag 5929

Bias-cut cascades at each side frame a pair of **scalloped pelmets** that are centered with an **inverted box pleat** with a **single point** at the hem.
Pattern: M'Fay Jackson Valance 9282

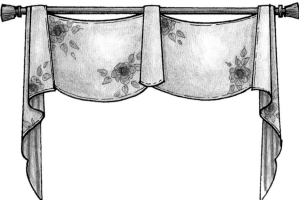

This **Imperial pole swag** is framed by an interesting **tapering cascade.**
Pattern: Butterick B4208

Queen Anne swags are modified to **wrap over the pole** in this valance.

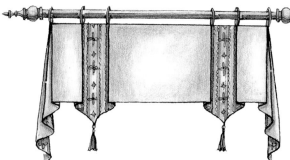

A flat panel is opened up with **exposed inverted box pleats** with **Moroccan hems.** The integrated cascades are pleated to the back, allowing the top panel to form a sharp square profile.
Pattern: M'Fay—Baroque Valance 9292

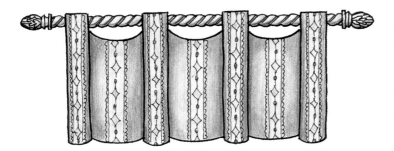

A **box-pleated tab panel** with a scalloped bottom hem and open heading is a good choice if using a striped fabric.
Pattern: Patterns Plus—Box Pleated Tabs 5942

This valance adds a creative twist to a standard **box-pleated tab heading** by using an exposed pointed end on the **button-down tab.**
Pattern: Pate Meadows—Julia Valance

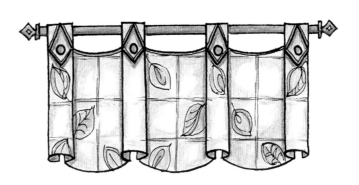

Rounded button-top tabs are used to hang this swagged valance with jabots.

The **large scallops** formed by the heading and hem of this valance are repeated in the **smaller scallops** in the hem of the jabots.
Pattern: Patterns Plus—Lexington 5968

The base layer of this valance is topped by a smaller **contrasting top layer** that appears to be held in place with **buttons**.

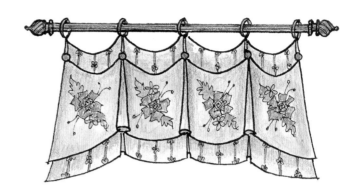

This design is a **relaxed** version of an **empire valance** with fewer pleats in the swags. The valance is attached to the drapery rings with contrasting ties. Pattern: Pate Meadows—Marley Valance

The top of this valance is **shirred down** to create a **swagged heading**.

A **stationary London shade** makes a lovely casual valance when a **tabbed heading** and decorative rod are added.

This **casual swag** is hung on a decorative rod with hidden brackets. **Ribbons** are draped over a matching medallion, giving the illusion that the valance is hung from it.

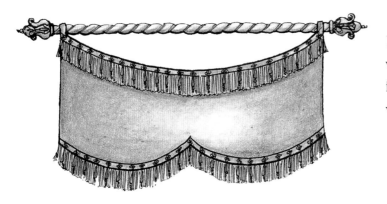

Elaborate **bullion fringe** with crystal beads is the focal point of this **pelmet valance**.

Rod-Bottom Valances

This valance is simply a **button-down tab-top panel** that has been **turned upside down** and mounted on a board.

Another **tab-top panel** with a **scalloped heading** has been rotated 180 degrees and board mounted.

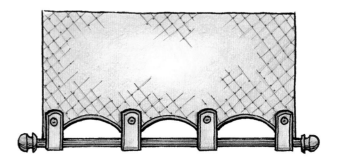

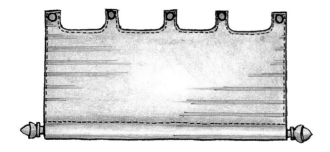

This valance combines two headings: a **tab top** secured directly to the wall and covered by buttons and a **simple casing** at the bottom to hold the rod.

This **board-mounted** valance has tabs at the ends of the **zigzag hem** through which the pole can be threaded. The **scarves** are cinched tight over the rod after it is hung and **silk flowers** are placed to hide the ties.

Many times rod-bottom treatments do not require a return. Here, a **flat panel** is **hung by medallions** flush to the wall.

Decorative ribbon is placed in stripes down the face of this valance and secured at the ends to hold the pole. The ends are then tied into **bows**.

Pull-Up Valances

A pull-up valance is one that has high and low points in the heading. The valance is hung by the high points using the following types of hardware:

Medallions

Crowns

Knobs

Wall Hooks

Ceiling Hooks

Tiebacks

Rings on Knobs or Hooks

+ Most designs are not suitable for very heavy fabrics.

+ Drapability is an important consideration with any style containing a swag or cascade.

+ Consider the lack of return space available when using wall hooks or knobs.

+ Use interlining to add stability to lightweight or limp fabric.

+ Always use self- or contrast lining.

+ Using a striped fabric can be difficult on swagged designs. Always consult your workroom on which direction the stripes will be placed on each element.

This **pull-up valance** is given a French flair by adding **delicate scalloped hems**. Pattern: M'Fay Parisian Raised Swag

Two **double cascades** frame the **wide swag** at the center of this classic valance.

Knotted headings on the **cascades** and **center jabot give** this valance a casual look.

Take inspiration from your hardware to create unique designs such as this **pull-up valance** with **double sets of jabots** at the sides.
Pattern: Pate Meadows—Pull up Valance

Multiple elements are combined beautifully in this imaginative valance.
Pattern: M'Fay—Karmen Valance 9283

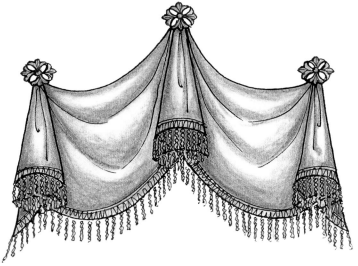

Drapability is the key when choosing fabric for this valance.
Pattern: Pate Meadows—Pull up Valance

The creative use of hard-ware can turn any design into a couture treatment such as this **tabbed valance** with **drapery rings** hung on **decorative hooks**. Pattern: Pate Meadows— Haley Valance M'Fay— Oxford Valance 9290

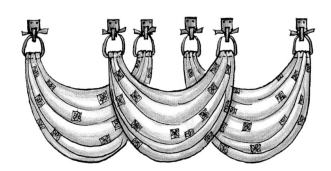

Ties are **threaded through casings** at the top of these **open swags** so they can be hung from **wall hooks**.

Plain **swag holders** can be **embellished** with silk flowers for a custom touch.

A **Queen Anne valance** is updated by the addition of a **swagged heading**.

A series of swags are dressed up with **gusset jabots** and a **turned cuff heading**.
Pattern: Pate Meadows— Gusset Valance

Button-down flags on a flat backdrop are highlighted by a **turned cuff heading** with **rosettes**.
Pattern: Pate Meadows— Rosette Valance

A **continuous contrasting border** emphasizes the graceful lines of this treatment.

A flat pelmet with a **zigzag hem** is embellished with **shirred rope with tab tops** and **tassels** at the end.

This **pelmet** has a **boldly shaped hem** and tabs set with grommets to enable it to be hung with wall hooks.

Drapery finials are attached to the ceiling and the valance is hung from them with **simple tabs** creating a dramatic design.

Loops at the heading allow this swagged valance to be **hung from medallions.**

Ceiling hooks can be used in conjunction with **wall brackets** or **medallions** as in this **pull-up valance.** This is a great solution if you have crown molding but need additional height to your design.

Let your hardware inspire you as with these **ceiling hooks.** They can be a great choice if you have a wallpaper border or trim you don't want to cover up.

The **dramatic peak** of this **raised set of swags** and **cascades** will add height to any space.

A combination of **swag holders** and a **decorative rod** is used for this **multi-tiered swagged valance**.

Pleated Valances

A pleated valance is a board-mounted treatment that contains pleats as its main design element.

- ⚜ Choose fabrics that are crisp and able to hold a fold.

- ⚜ Choose fabrics that can be ironed at high heat to press folds in place.

- ⚜ Not suitable for very heavyweight fabrics or 100% polyester fabrics.

- ⚜ If interlining is needed, do not use "bump" or heavyweight flannel unless you do not want a crisp look. Use a cotton poly interlining that will hold the fold of the pleats.

Inverted box pleats done in a contrasting fabric are **tied together** at the hem.

A **knife pleated ruffle** trims the bottom hem of a **single flat panel valance**. Decorative tape is applied at the edge and between the scallops.

Bell pleats are cut to create a point at the hem that is banded with contrasting fabric and welt and **embellished** with a **button**.

A **series of angled pleats** and a **carefully designed hem** combine to produce this beautiful valance.

This valance is made interesting by the design of the **zigzag hem on the cascades**.

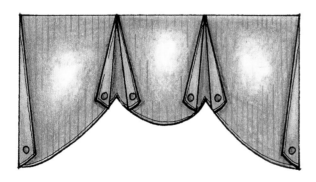

The placement of a **tuxedo pleat** at the sides of this valance and the scalloped hemline help to soften this masculine treatment.

Knife pleats fold outward on each side of the center box pleat. The **inverted V hem** is banded with decorative tape. Pattern: Decorate Now— Windsor Valance

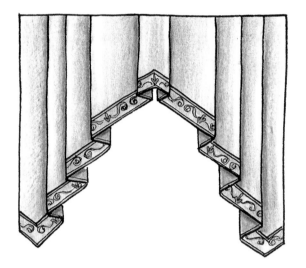

Large box pleats are given a designer touch by placing **grommets** at the top of each pleat through which a **tie** can be threaded.

Inverted box pleats are tacked in place with a **double set of buttons** on each side of the pleat.

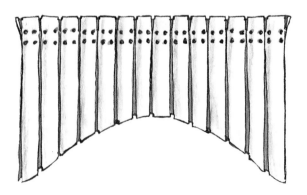

Simple construction combined with **graceful lines** and good proportion creates this classic valance.

An innovative **combination of elements** and **balanced repetition** are the keys to success for this treatment. Pattern: Pate Meadows— Madelyn Valance

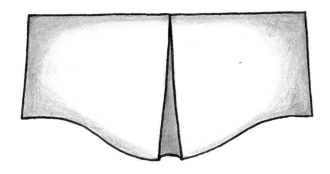

Simplicity is the key here. **One deep inverted box pleat** and a **reverse scallop** at the hem create a classic design.

Several **different pleat styles** are juxtaposed to create this **angular valance**.

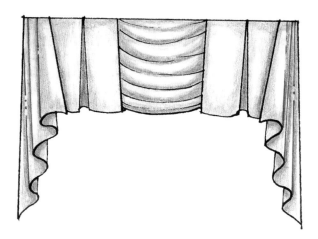

A **scalloped cornice topper** supports this **simple box-pleated valance**.

The center panel of this valance has **knife pleats** running in opposite directions from the center and **pelmets** with a **sinuous scalloped hem** at the sides.

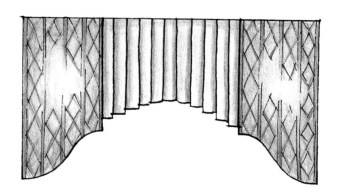

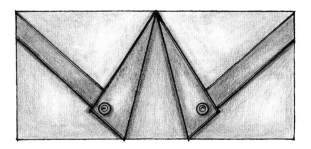

A **V-shaped top panel** with a contrasting border is cut in a **tuxedo pleat** and **tacked back with buttons**, exposing the under layer.

The **classic tuxedo valance** is pleated in the center and buttoned back to expose the under layer of contrasting fabric.

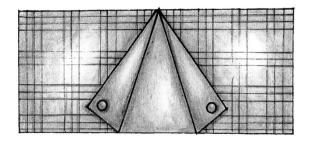

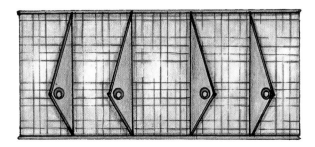

In this design only one half **of the tuxedo pleat** is used. The pleats are then folded away from the center and secured with a button.

This **mock roman shade** valance is embellished with **contrasting buttoned bands**. Pattern: Decorate Now— Mock Roman Shade

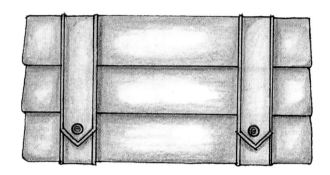

A **mock roman shade** with **gussets** is given added interest by placing buttons at the gussets and creating **notches** to allow tassels to hang at the hem.

Using a **custom shape** at the **bottom hem** of any mock roman shade can give a new flair to a plain design.

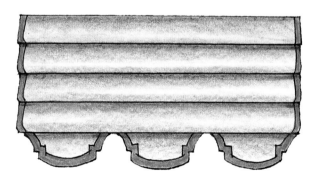

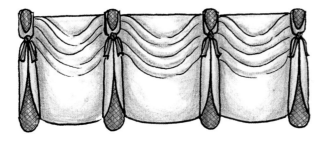

Swagged sections of this valance are flanked by **open-throat goblets** that are also left open at the front, exposing the contrasting lining.
Pattern: Patterns Plus—Swag–n-Bell 5911

A straight goblet-pleated valance is embellished with a **scarf** that appears to be **threaded through the pleats** and tied in bows at each side.

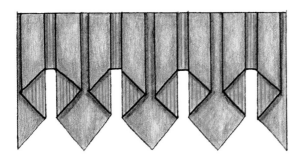

Crisp folds and **contrast lining** make this an interesting design.

Use your imagination to take a basic design and make it your own. Here, **nail heads** have been added to the **cornice topper** for a new look. Pattern: M'Fay Curved Valance

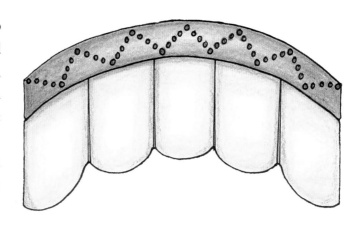

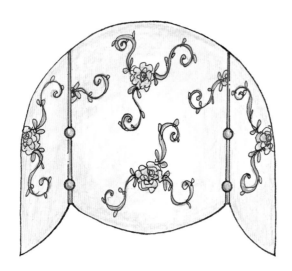

A **full half-circle arch** with **inverted box pleats** and a scalloped hem can make any square window appear to be a tall, graceful arch.

An upholstered arched **cornice topper** edged in contrasting welt provides a base for a separate **scalloped valance with inverted box pleats**. Pattern: M'Fay Curved Valance

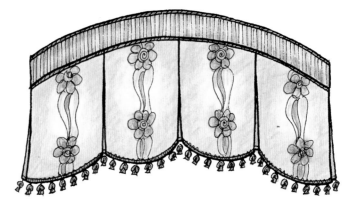

Layered Valances

Layered valances are designs that have multiple layers of fabric stacked on top of each other to create contrast and visual interest. They usually consist of one or two under layers and the top layer.

- Contrasting fabrics are the key to the success of these designs. Use fabrics that provide that contrast in color, pattern, and texture.

- In some designs heavy fabrics can be used for the under layer but should be avoided for the top layer. But for the most part, these designs are not suitable for heavy fabrics.

- Large patterns are not suitable for the under layer.

- When choosing the colors of your layers, remember that dark colors come forward and light colors recede.

- It may be necessary to use a heavyweight interlining or stabilizer in the under layer to prevent drooping and ensure that it maintains its shape.

This valance uses **classic proportion** rules and a **contrasting insert** in the jabots to achieve balance.
Pattern: M'Fay—
Tucker valance 9278

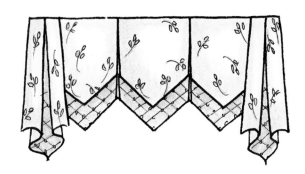

Another version of the valance above has been **elongated** to almost double its original length. The jabots and under layer have been lengthened accordingly.
Pattern: M'Fay—
Tucker valance 9278

This classic arrangement consists of **open swags** with a center jabot and cascades mounted on a **shirred background.**

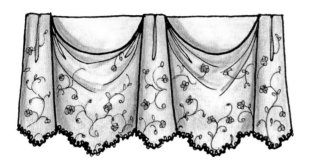

Open swags expose a **contrasting under layer** on this scalloped edge valance.

This **lace-up valance** has a contrasting under layer that creates a separate set of scallops at the hem.

The under layer of this valance is a backdrop for its **scooped heading**. **Contrasting welt and ties** add continuity to the separate elements of the design. Pattern: Pate Meadows: Claudine Valance (modified)

A **classic turban valance** is enhanced with a **knife-pleated bottom ruffle**. The contrasting tie helps to center the treatment and add emphasis to the high point of the swag. Pattern: Decorate Now—Petticoat Valance

A simple **inverted box-pleated top layer** with a **Moroccan hem** is given a rich appearance with the addition of **balloon swags underneath**. Tassels reinforce the vertical line of the top layer through the hem.

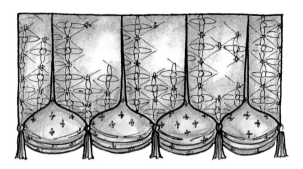

The top layer of this valance has a **scooped pleated heading** with a **swagged cuff** between each pleat. The slightly rounded hem of each section repeats the line of the swags.

This classic valance is made interesting by breaking the top layer into **separate sections**. The pieces at the sides are mounted on top of the center panel. They are cut longer to create a **graduated hem**.

Separate **reversed cascades** and **jabots** are mounted on top of a **swagged under panel** to create this valance. A **contrasting under layer** provides a striking base to emphasize the shape of the swags.

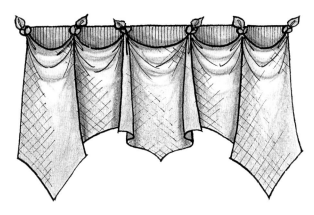

The three **handkerchief flags** are hung on top of a separate **swagged under panel** to create a sense of **depth**. The under layer provides a base for those elements.

Pattern placement is key on this valance. A strong central motif can be highlighted quite well on this design.

This **lace-up design** has a **contrasting band** at the top that matches the pelmets mounted underneath the top layer. Pattern: Pate Meadows— Lace Up Valance

A plain **inverted box-pleated valance** has been given a series of **festoons at the bottom** to crate a striking contrast in styles.

Balloon Valances

A balloon valance is a stationary design in which the bottom hem is pulled up with pleats, shirring tape, or rings and cording to create a series of balloon swags.

- ❧ Most designs are not suitable for very heavy fabrics or those with large patterns. Lightweight, pliable fabrics will produce a beautiful treatment.

- ❧ Drapability is an important consideration for most designs.

- ❧ Use interlining to add stability to lightweight or limp fabrics.

- ❧ Some balloon valances may need some assistance to retain their shape. Use inserts of bubble warp covered in lining fabric to add volume and body.

The hem of this flat **pelmet** is draped with a **scarf swag** and embellished with graduated rope and tassels.

Two **necktie jabots** frame this series of **balloons** with **inverted box pleats.**

Accordion swags with a **graduated hem** are separated by decorative cord and tassels.

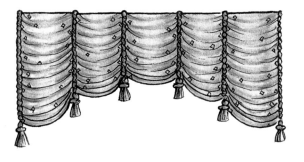

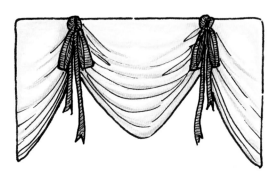

This **casual mock London shade** is pulled up with shirring tape that is hidden by the **long ribbon bows.**

Rings and **cord** are used to create the **deep swags** of this **mock London shade.**

Long contrasting ties hold up the center swag of this **mock balloon shade.**

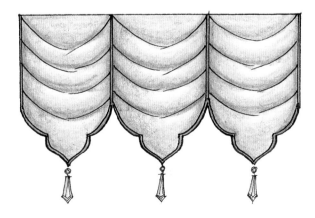

Contrasting welt is used to **separate the three sections** of this valance and to create a border at the outside edge.

The pleats in this **balloon valance** are placed far apart for a casual look. **Glass beads** are used to add emphasis to the points.

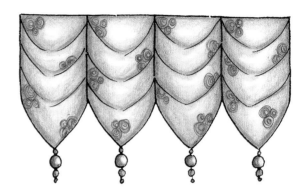

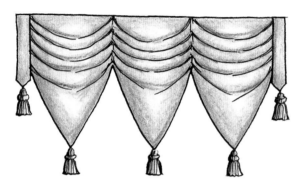

Necktie jabots are placed at either side of this valance in order to frame the interior swags.

Balloon swags are hung under a **diamond-shaped valance** mounted on an **iron cornice**.

A **faux London shade** is topped with **deep scalloped flags** edged in a **box-pleated ruffle**.

This **mock balloon valance** has a **scalloped hem** and heading with a contrasting edge and banding.

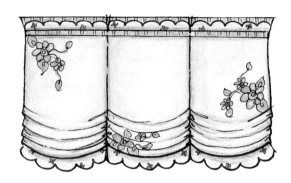

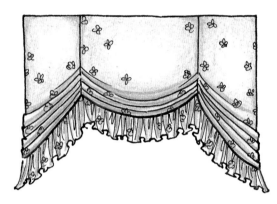

The **deep accordion-pleated ruffle** at the hem of this **mock London** shade adds a light feminine touch.

This design highlights a **bishop's sleeve jabot** that has been **knotted** at the end as a center element.

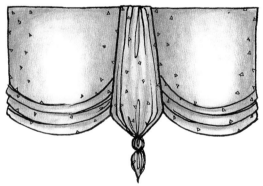

A **single casual swag** is flanked by **two knotted bishops sleeve jabots**.

Pelmet Valances

A pelmet valance is a design that features flat, stiffened, panels, sections, or shapes as the main design element.

Pelmets can be used in combination with:

Jabots

Cascades

Tails

Swags

Flags

- Pelmets should be stiffened and interlined to avoid sagging and rippling.

- Some designs are suitable for large patterns.

- Select a motif and plot pattern placement carefully.

- Heavy fabric can be used on flat elements of the design.

- Use welting and borders to accentuate the shape of the pelmet.

Contrasting borders separate this **pelmet** into three sections while small wooden drapery finials are used as tassels.

Decorative cord and **tassels** separate this pelmet into sections corresponding to its **zigzag border**.

The **distinctive shape** of the **insets** in this **pelmet** dictate the shape of the under layer and border.

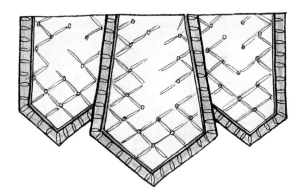

A **W-shaped under panel** is topped by a **wide necktie-shaped pelmet**, creating an interesting hemline.

Two layers with **opposing zigzag hems** combine to create a **diamond-shaped** border.

A series of **full** and **half triangles** are **stacked** on top of each other to create this angular design.

Bordered and **non-bordered banners** combine to make this gothic-inspired design.

Top-mounted and under-mounted scallops and **half scallops** make up this simple treatment. Fabric bells with beads finish the side points.

An **arched under panel** provides a backdrop for **three bordered banners**.

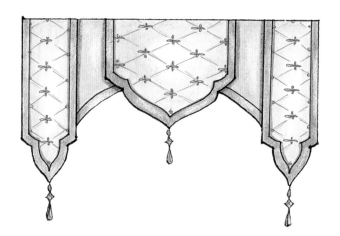

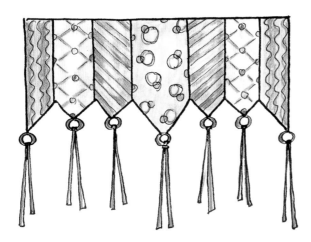

This **necktie valance** is finished with **rings** and **ties** for a playful look.

Single-point flags are stacked to create a **multi-layered treatment**.

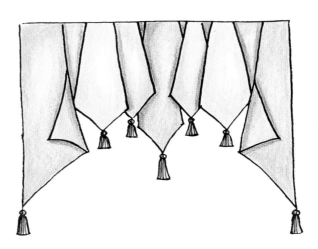

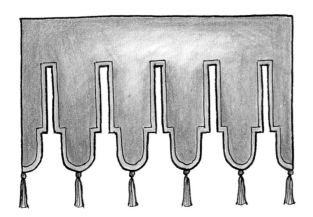

A **single pelmet** is cut with an **elaborate hemline** and bordered with contrasting gimp to give the appearance of multiple sections.

A **rounded pelmet** appears to swag across the face of this valance even though it is flat.

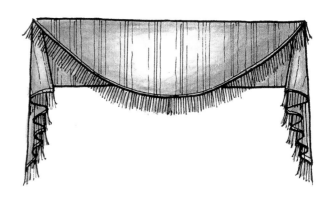

Contrasting gimp and **rosettes** are used to create a pattern designed to call attention to the scalloped hem of the pelmet.

Two **identically shaped pelmets** are **stacked** on top of each other, exposing the bottom layer. The shape of the jabots repeats the shape of the pelmet point. Pattern: M'Fay— Moroccan Valance

This **arched pelmet** has a **gusset** at each side that is held closed by **ribbon ties.**

An **arched pelmet** serves as a backdrop for **matching cascades.** Pattern: M'Fay Bordeaux valance

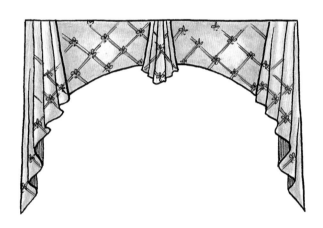

This **pelmet with attached cascades** appears to be made as one continuous piece.

Deep **inverted box pleats** tied closed with **luxurious silk bows** make a rich statement in this simple design.

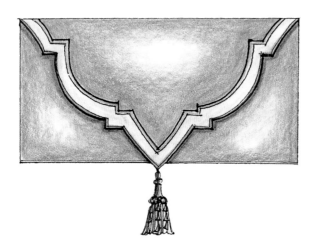

A straight cornice is embellished with a **large flap cut in an elaborate shape** and bordered in a contrasting fabric and trim.

Banners of **graduated lengths and widths** are simply draped over a decorative rod. Multiple layers of trim finish the design.

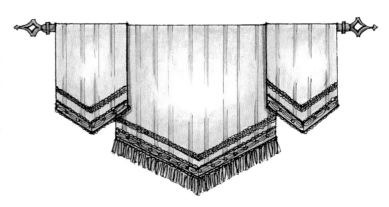

The **steep peaks** of this pelmet are embellished with **crystals and tassels.**

Single-point pelmets are stacked on top of each other to create this **multilayered arched treatment.**

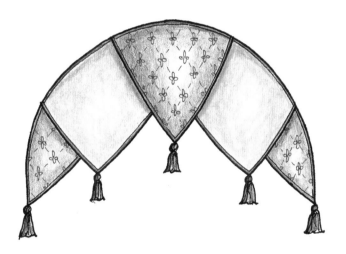

A center pelmet with an elaborate **Moroccan point** is set underneath a pair of pointed pelmets at each side.

The **crisscrossed center** of this **pelmet** is balanced with the simple jabots at each side.

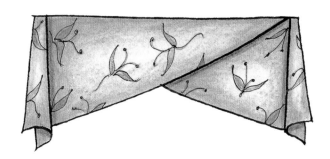

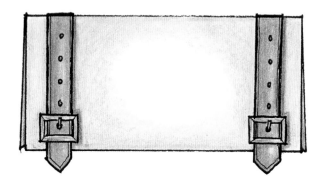

Leather belts with brass buckles are used to **embellish** this flat pelmet.

The many **carefully placed lines and angles** in this complicated design create a beautiful treatment.

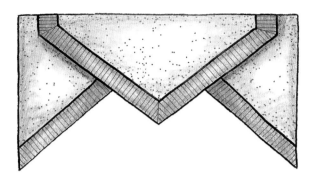

The **juxtaposed angles** of the **triangular shapes** in this treatment create a central balance to the design.

Two **graduated triangular pelmets** fold over the **wide cascades** at the sides of this valance. Pattern: Decorate Now— Casta Valance

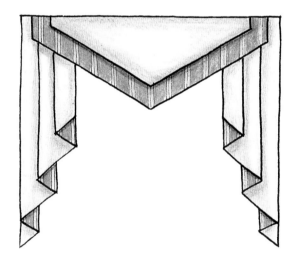

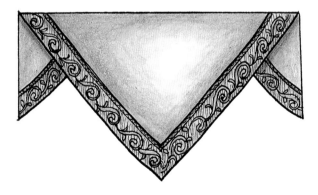

Wide embroidered trim and gimp are used to create a strong **border** on this pelmet.

Deep scallops in varying sizes are **stacked** and trimmed with tied tassel fringe.

Pointed banners are trimmed with **contrasting welt** and mounted on this flat valance. Pattern: Decorate Now—Kensington Valance

The **pleats at the corners** of this design help soften its hard edges.

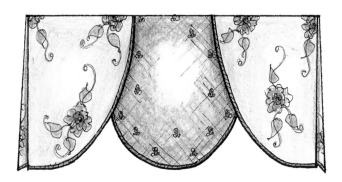

The **center pelmet** of this valance presents a great opportunity to **highlight a large motif.**

An **inverted box-pleated valance** is topped with **three single-point banners.**

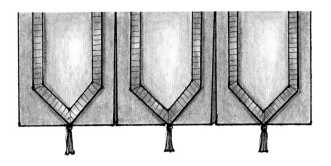

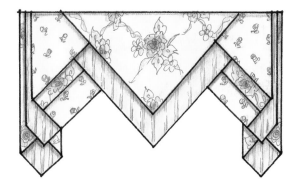

Precisely folded layers of fabric form an intricate **geometric design.**

The **bold shape of the bottom hem** of this valance is repeated in the top layer and on the matching cascades.
Pattern: M'Fay Milan Valance 9291

A **pointed pelmet** with a tassel serves as the center for these **unique one-piece cascades** that meet in the middle of the valance.
Pattern: M'Fay Milan Valance 9291

Extra-wide one-piece cascades flank a **center pelmet with jabots**, creating a flowing treatment that appears to be made from one continuous width of fabric.
Pattern: M'Fay Sofia Valance 9294

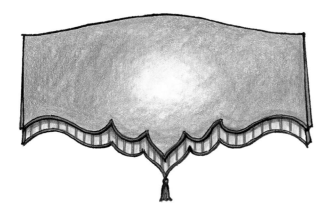

The **eyebrow arch** of this pelmet bows out in a graceful curve in the center. The **under panel** peeks out at the bottom, showing a contrasting stripe.
Pattern: M'Fay Window # 310 9293

This **angled pelmet** is balanced by the **opposing angle** of the cascade at the other side.

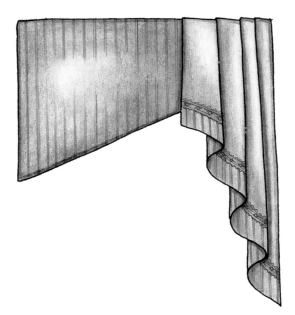

A set of **triple arches** tops this **box pleated valance** while a scalloped bottom is highlighted by tassel fringe.
Pattern: Patterns Plus—Boxter 5972

The **zigzag hem** on the **center pelmet** of this valance is repeated on the **shirred side panels**.

Shirred side panels are draped over this **arched pelmet**. Pattern: M'Fay—Melody Valance

An **iron drapery crown** is mounted **upside down** over the pelmet to create this rich design.

The center pelmet of this valance is almost fully covered by the **shirred cascades** and **center jabot**. Pattern: M'Fay Jessi Valance 9277

Three **open swags** are hung over a straight pelmet that is framed by two **cascades with a rounded, reversed, leading edge**. Pattern: Butterick B3117

An **arched pelmet** with an **inverted box-pleat** center at the center is hemmed with **tied fringe with beads**.

Valance Treatments

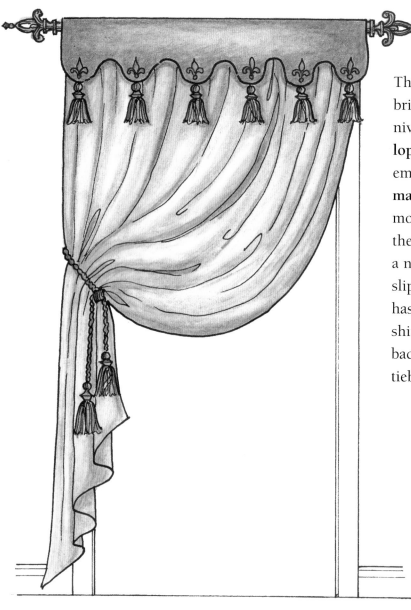

This **short pelmet valance** brings to mind a Medieval carnival tent. The continuous **scalloped edge** is trimmed with embroidered **fleurs-de-lis** and **matching key tassels**. It is mounted on a board just above the rod. The valance return has a notch cut out for the rod to slip through. The under panel has a rod-pocket heading and is shirred onto the rod and pulled back with matching tassel tiebacks.

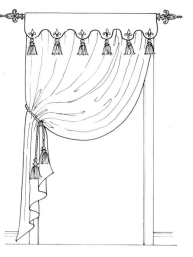

Shirred side panels that have been trimmed with a **contrasting border** and welt at the leading edge have been wrapped over the top of this scalloped pelmet valance. Both have been trimmed at the bottom hem with contrasting **tassel fringe** to give the appearance of a unified bottom line. The stationary pleated under panels are trimmed in a **matching border** that continues the **vertical line** created by the valance border.

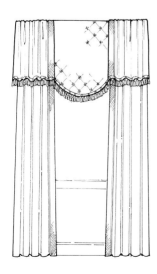

Shirred waterfall cascades frame the center pelmet of this **M-shaped valance.** Decorative braid is appliquéd to the face of the treatment in an elaborate design that complements the pattern in the panel fabric. It is also used along with beaded fringe to border the bottom hem.

Straps made of decorative embroidered ribbon hold up the sides of this mock London shade valance. Beaded tassel fringe edges the hem, providing another vertical element. The ribbon is repeated as banding at the hem of the panels to bring the bottom of the treatment into balance with the top.

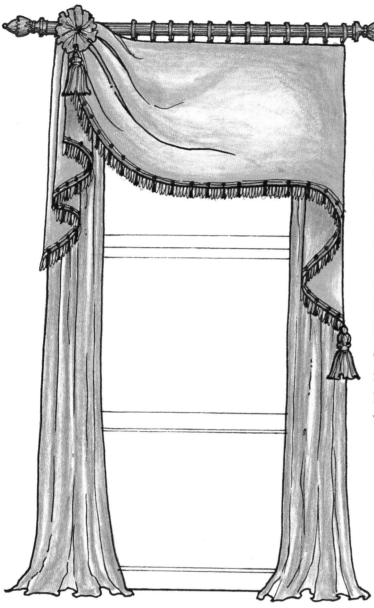

This flat pelmet with its dramatic **one-sided swag** is pulled up to meet a **stacked cascade** and **choux**. The **integrated cascade** on the other side of the panel creates a harmonious balance. The **contrast lining** and **decorative trim** with matching tassels accentuate the flowing lines of the valance. Shown here hung with rings on a decorative rod, it can also be board mounted.

Pattern: M'Fay - Moreland Valance

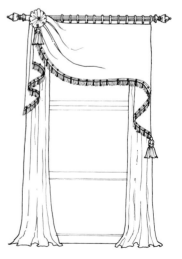

Borders of contrasting decorative tape accentuate the softly **rounded corners** of the top and bottom layers of this **pelmet valance**. The contrasting fabric used for the bottom layer of the valance is repeated in the **border at the leading edge** of the panels. Rosettes with button centers finish the valance.
Pattern: Decorate Now—Magnolia House Valance

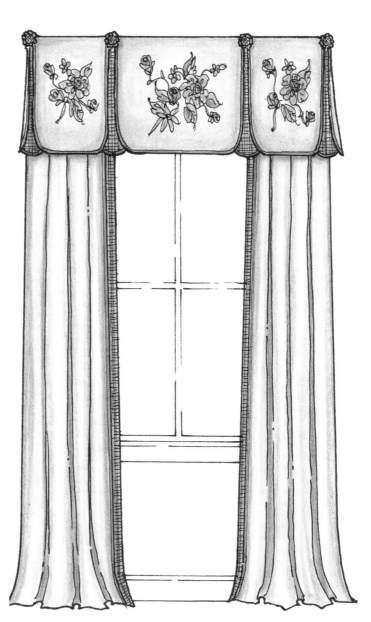

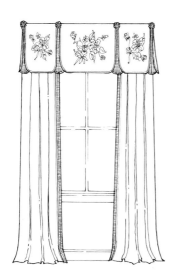

Two quarter circles converge at the center of this **pelmet** with another section mounted underneath, showing a **scalloped hem**. The scallop is repeated in the **reversed scallop** of the border used on the top layer, the hem of the panels and the hem of the **under-mounted roman shade**. The multilayered look of the treatment is reinforced by adding a **false under layer** to the drapery panels. The top layer is shortened to show off the scalloped hem. The panels are mounted on a traverse rod under the valance. Be sure to allow a deep return on the valance to accommodate the under treatments.

This design has a whimsical look created by the series of **graduated points** in the valance. The **swagged heading** adds softness to the sharp lines. **Contrast lining** is exposed at the fold over of the side points. **Wooden beads** painted to match the fabric add emphasis to the tips. The side panels are mounted with a rod-pocket heading on sash rods beneath the valance, which is board mounted.

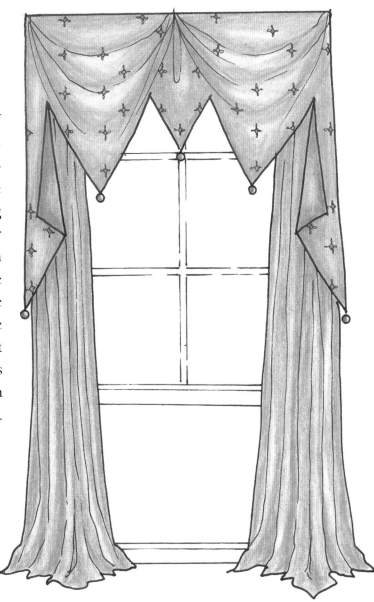

This intricately detailed **pelmet valance** uses multiple elements to create a **harmonious balance**. Decorative braid tops the treatment while **flat tape** or **gimp** is used to border the bottom hem and create the **fleurs-de-lis** highlights at each point. **Chair-tie tassels** are hung from the points to emphasis the openness of the design. **Stationary drapery panels** are pulled back in a graceful swag and tucked behind matching fleurs-de-lis holdbacks set high and at an upward angle to lead the eye towards the beautiful valance.

The sinuous lines of this rich treatment are repeated in the **swagged scallops** of the valance and the long **bishops sleeve cascades**. A strong focal point is established by continuing the swags across the face of the valance to the top. A **braided rosette** is placed at the high point of each swag and at the bishop's sleeve. The under drape is mounted on sash rods at the wall while the cascades are mounted directly to the board mount of the valance so they can hang freely.

A **short pelmet** with a distinctive shape and **edged with a contrasting fabric tops** this beautiful pair of cascading swags. The contrast fabric used for the lining of the swags is repeated in the **stationary side panels**. They are cinched tightly just out of sight to create a very **slim profile** to the panel, which allows the puddle to flair widely for a dramatic look. To maintain the slim width of the panel, the heading is shirred and mounted on a small board. This design is also quite lovely without the pelmet.

A strong center point domi-
nates this flowing swagged
valance. **Long waterfall cascades** frame the center swags
and add to the fluid look of
this design. **Contrast lining**
peaks through, and a single
tassel emphasizes the long
lines of the treatment. The
valance is board mounted
while the side panels are
hung with a rod-pocket
heading and sash rods.

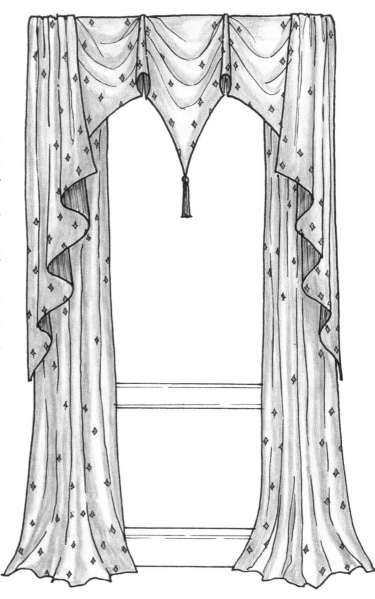

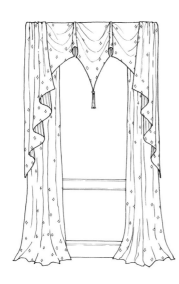

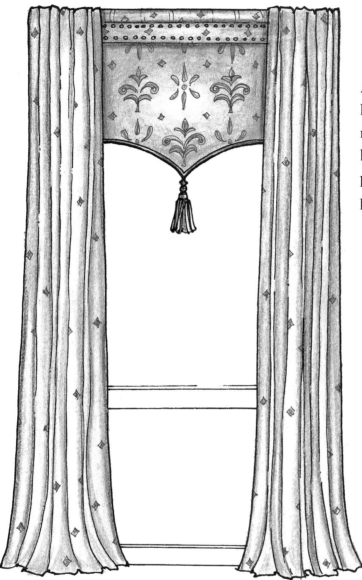

A **center pelmet** with a **banded heading** is embellished with **nail heads** and weighted by a **large key tassel**. **Waterfall side panels** flow over the top of the pelmet to frame the window.

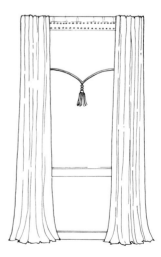

Contrasting scalloped trim highlights every element of this design to add a playful side to this decidedly traditional treatment. The swags and cascades that make up the valance are centered by a **cross-over jabot.** A contrasting fabric is used on the cascades and the inner lining of the jabot. It is repeated in the **string welting** that separates the scallop trim and the panel. **Matching tiebacks** complete the design.

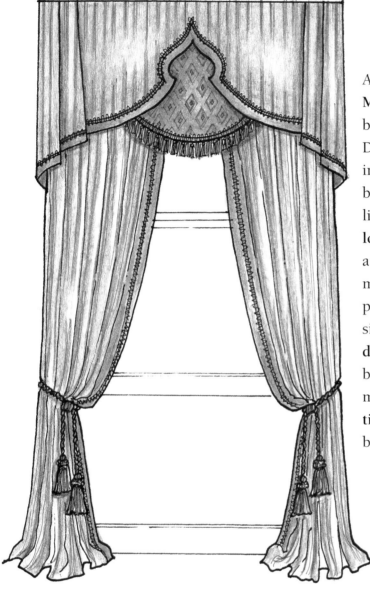

A **center pelmet** with a **Moroccan** cutout is flanked by **layered cascades.** Decorative braid follows the interesting line of the bottom border and cascades to highlight those elements. A **scalloped center pelmet** done in a contrasting fabric is mounted below the center point, adding further emphasis to the valance. **Traversing draperies** are mounted beneath and trimmed with matching braid. **Tassel tiebacks** are used to pull back the panels.

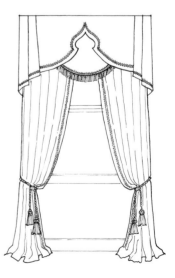

These **pointed pelmets** with under-mounted swags impart a strong **geometric appearance** to this valance, which is reinforced by the strong lines created by the formal pleated under drape. The points are edged in a contrasting border.

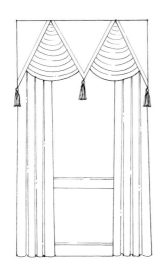

This unique valance is constructed using **flexible board**. It is separated into **rounded sections** that are cut into a detailed scalloped and arched hem. A contrasting **wide swag** and side panels are hung beneath it and in front of a **flat roller shade** made of the valance fabric, which provides **light** control and **privacy** while providing a backdrop to highlight the swag.

This design expertly mixes several distinct design elements without overdoing it. The **flat scalloped cornice** is flanked by **jabots** and **cascades** and wrapped in a **scarf swag** that creates a strong focal point to the treatment. The **scarf** is repeated at the **leading edge** of the panels draping gracefully behind the holdbacks, which match the **center medallion** on the cornice. Using this many conflicting styles can be risky, but when it is done well, a beautiful result can be achieved.

The **small diamond appliqués** and the **vertical banding** and **welting** on this **pelmet valance** are balanced by the **horizontal banding** at the hem. These two elements are anchored by the larger diamonds at the intersection of the bands. The side panels are **box pleated** to ensure an out-facing fold at the center of the panel to allow the **diamond appliqués** to lay relatively flat at the front of the panel.

The **dramatic shape** of this **pelmet valance** is bordered with a contrasting fabric and trimmed with coordinating **tassels**. It is mounted on a board with a drapery track attached to the underside to hang the drapery panel. The **custom tieback** repeats the design elements in the valance, creating a well-balanced treatment.

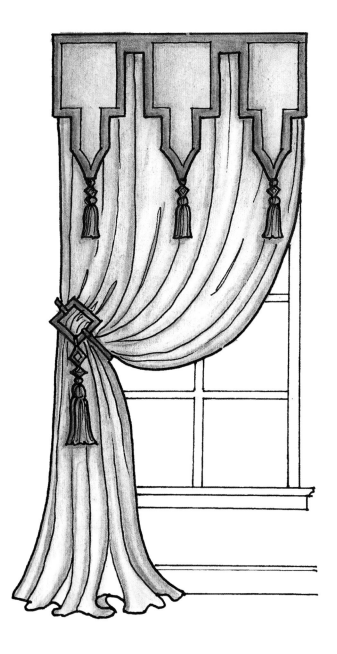

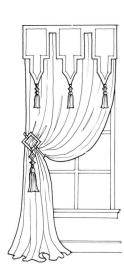

Valance Outlines

For a complete inventory of all valance outline art, please refer to *The Design Directory of Window Treatments* companion CD-Rom.

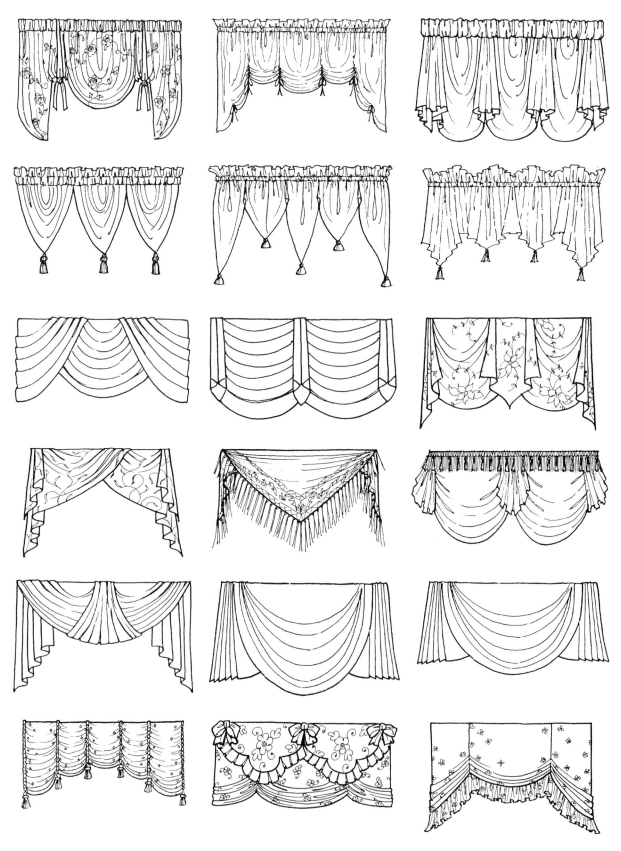

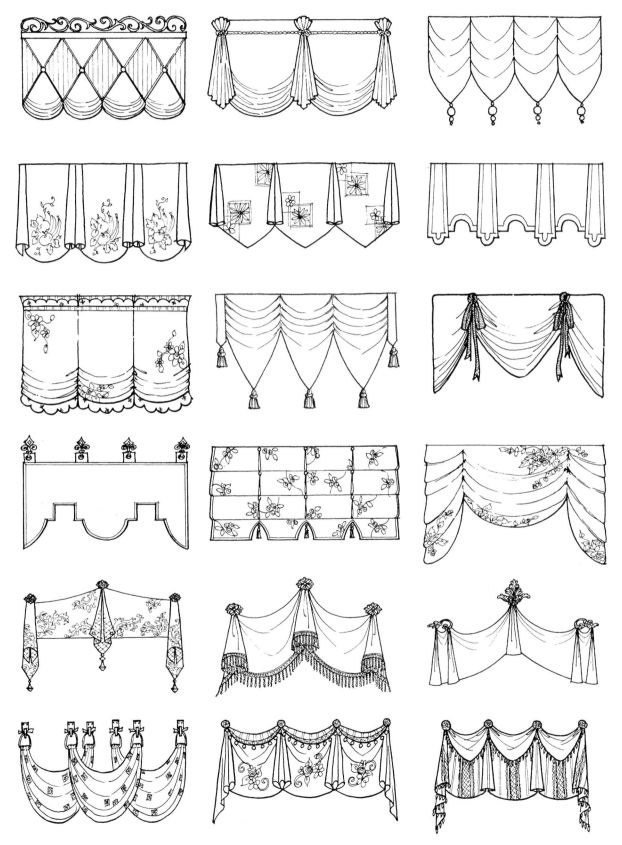

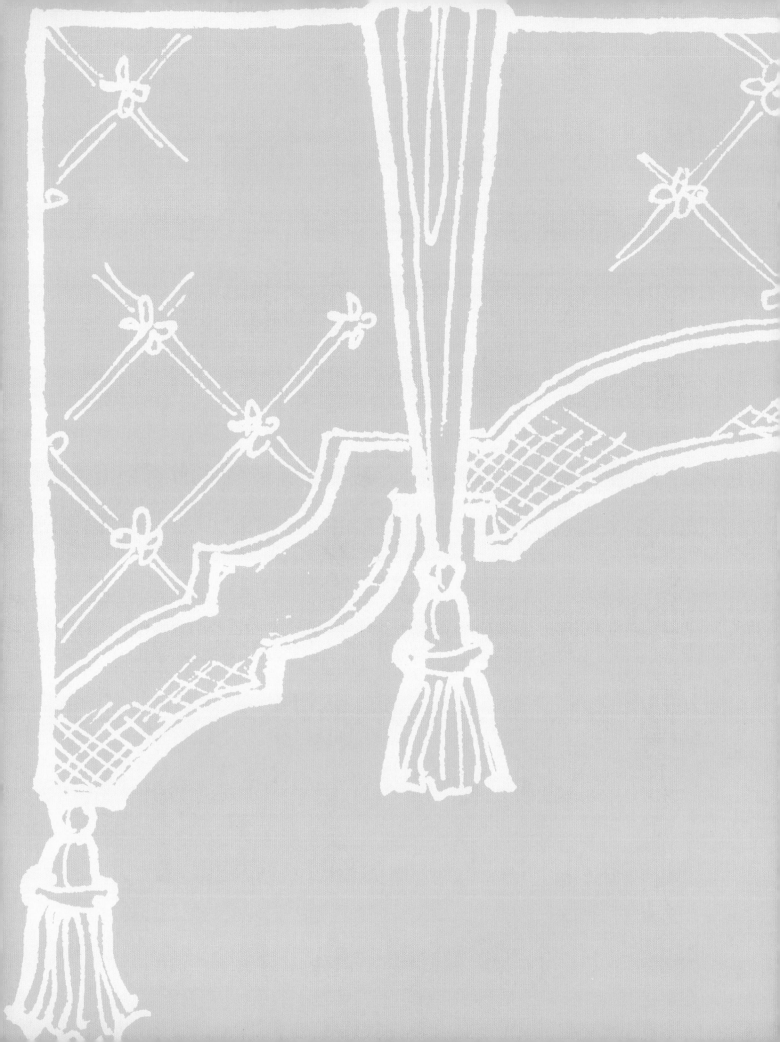

Cornices

〜∞〜

Hard Cornices

A cornice is a hard-framed top treatment that can be used by itself or in combination with other elements.

- A cornice can create architectural form and detail in a plain space.

- A cornice can provide a structural framework for supporting additional treatments where hanging space on the wall is limited.

- A cornice can provide an opportunity for the use of many materials other than fabric in the treatment design.

- Remember to increase the return of the cornice when hanging additional treatments underneath.

- Self-line the dust cap if the cornice can be seen from above.

- Self-line the cornice if the interior can be seen from below.

- Consider the finished weight of the cornice when planning its location and method of installation.

- Design long cornices to be made in several sections for ease of installation and on-site accessibility.

- The hard inner frame of a cornice is usually constructed exactly to the measurements given. Cornices can "grow" after they are heavily padded and upholstered. If your cornice must fit in a tight space, adjust it by reducing the frame measurements 1/2" to 1".

Hard cornices offer many opportunities for creative design.
Think out of the box when selecting materials to be used.
You will be rewarded with a truly unique and attractive treatment.

Padded and upholstered

Combination of upholstery and
a wallpaper border

Faux finished with wood fretwork

Tin ceiling tiles or ceramic tiles

Hand painted

Bead board with wood filigree

Embossed wallpaper

Stained wood with wrought-iron details

Upholstered cornice with contrast
welting and border

Upholstered cornice with
decorative braid and tassels

Hand-painted cornice topped with a
festoon border held up with tassels

Wallpapered cornice with
fabric swags and key tassels

Upholstered cornice with
contrasting insert

Upholstered cornice
with draped braid

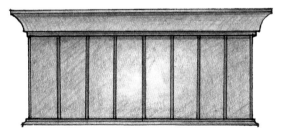

Wood-paneled cornice

Upholstered cornice with decorative
wrought-iron framework

Upholstered Cornices

An upholstered cornice is a hard-top treatment that has been padded and upholstered with fabric. Its design can include other soft elements that enhance its appearance. Use it alone or with side panels, draperies, or shades.

ANATOMY OF A CORNICE

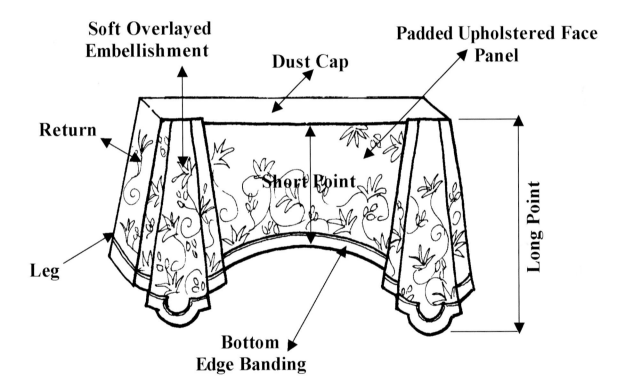

Soft Overlayed Embellishment

Dust Cap

Padded Upholstered Face Panel

Return

Short Point

Long Point

Leg

Bottom Edge Banding

Basic Cornice Shapes

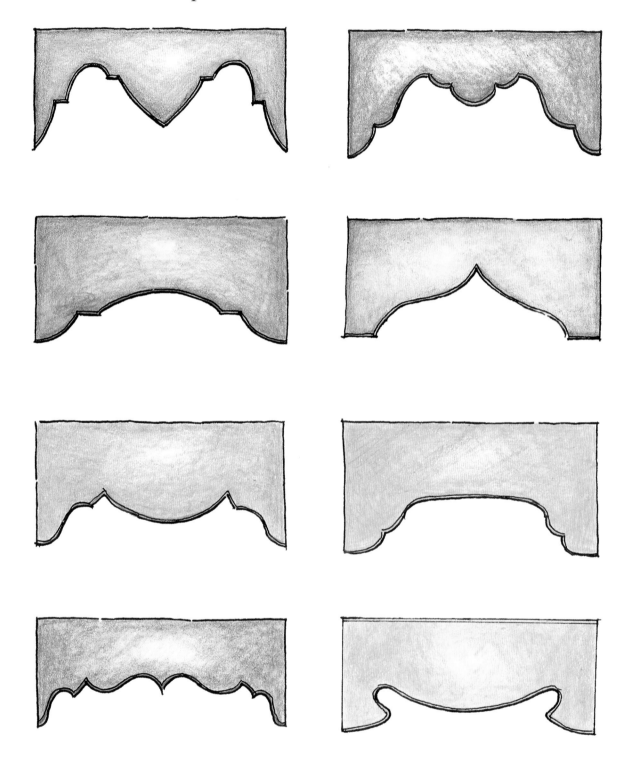

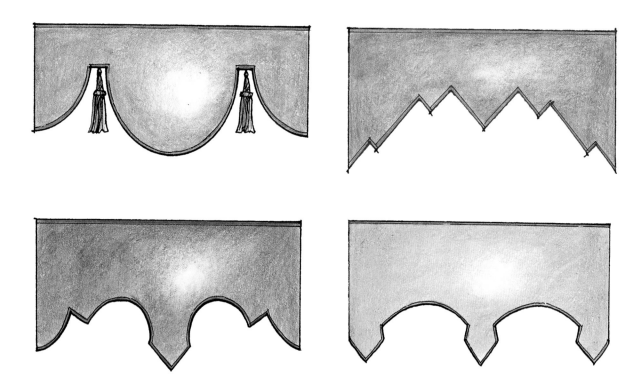

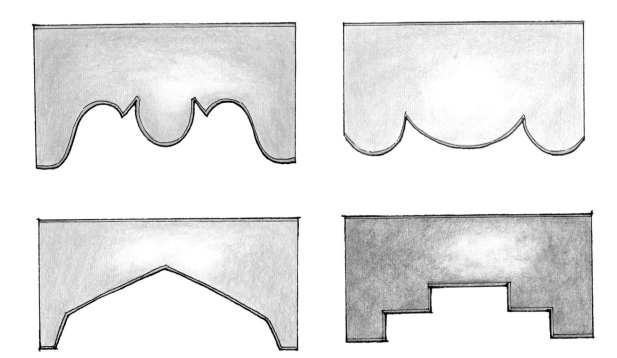

Arched Cornices

An arched cornice is a hard or soft cornice that has an arched shape to the top of the cornice board. It can add architectural structure and shape to a plain window or reinforce arched lines already present in the room.

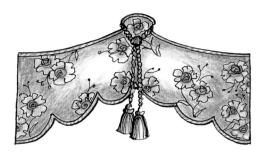

Using **bold welt** can help to minimize a large pattern. The long tassels wrapped around the **top knot** balance the center of this cornice.

Mount **decorative hardware** in unexpected ways to create **focal points** and detail to your designs.

The **center medallion** on this cornice **creates a balance** between the straight top and the scalloped bottom.

Drapery hardware does not have to come from traditional sources. Here, **antique gate hinges** are used to embellish this plain cornice.

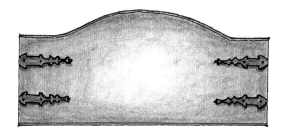

Iron drapery crowns are a great way to embellish any treatment. This one is inset in a **matching cutout** at the bottom of the cornice.

The distinctive **arched lines** of this cornice are repeated several times to create a pleasing rhythm.

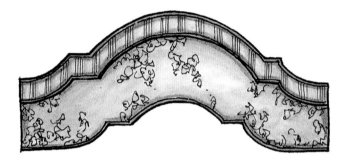

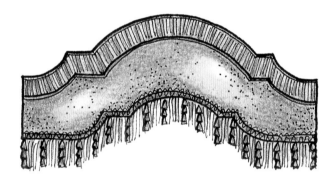

Vertical balance is added to this arched cornice by using a striped border and **tasseled bullion fringe** at the hem.

This cornice shows an effective use of a **key-hole opening** to create a focal point.

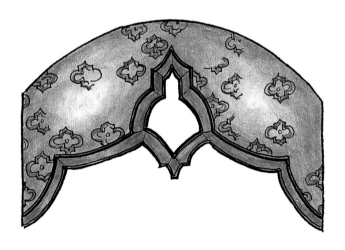

This simple cornice is placed on top of two **decorative wall brackets**, creating a stunning old-world look.

The playful use of **multiple fabrics and trims** can result in a wonderfully eclectic design.

A **classic turban swag** is draped over a contrasting cornice, framing its interesting shape and contrasting fabric.

The center medallion of this **eyebrow-arched cornice** is backed with a rosette that matches the **scarf swag** that frames the opening. Matching holdbacks secure the swag in place.

Framed Cornices

A framed cornice is a hard or soft cornice that is flanked on either side by a soft element such as a jabot, tail, or cascade. These elements "frame" the interior section of the cornice and add a linear balance.

Raised jabots are mounted flush with the top of this cornice rather than above it for a different look.

Double jabots have been given an interesting shape at the front, which is emphasized by a contrasting border and welt.

The **contrast lining** inside these jabots is exposed to create a bold contrast in this design. The **tassels** are hung from cord mounted inside the jabots.

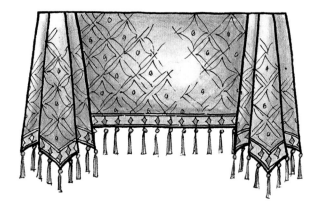

The **diamond pattern** in the fabric used on this cornice is **repeated in the shape** of the jabots, as well as in the fringe used to trim the hem.

Decorative medallions are used to embellish the **double-pointed jabots** on this cornice.

Accordion-pleated fabric is used to form unique jabots on this **asymmetrical cornice.**

Necktie tails made in an array of complementary colors are **stacked** on top of each other at each side of this cornice.

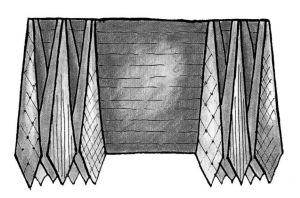

Flat-pointed side panels frame the **peaked center** of this cornice to produce a slim profile.

The **contrasting border** of this cornice is repeated on the **double-folded jabots** to establish continuity at the hem.

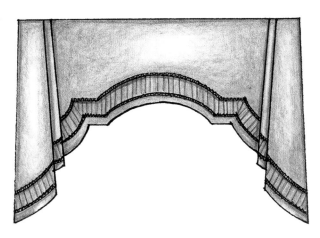

Swagged Cornices

A swagged cornice is a hard or soft cornice that includes a single or multiple swags as its key design element.

Scalloped swagged flags embellished with rosettes are draped over this valance, exposing the high point and creating a **peek-a-boo cutout**.

This simple cornice is transformed by the addition of a **swagged handkerchief flag** with a zigzag hem.

A pair of contrasting **open half swags** drapes the shoulders of this delicate cornice.

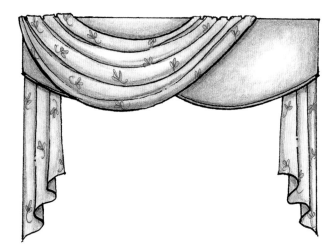

A **casual scarf swag** is draped over one side of this **double-scalloped cornice** with under-mounted cascades.

The long profile of this cornice is accentuated by **decorative cord and tassels** that run vertically to border **accordion swags** on each side of the center panel.

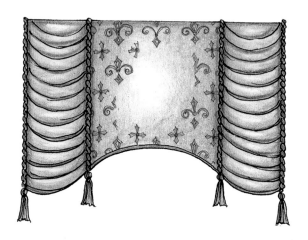

A **peaked cornice** serves as the base for a pair of short, **inverted box-pleated panels** that have been knotted to create cascades. This treatment is an option that can be used to add height to a low-hung window.

The **double arches** of this cornice are opposed by the scallops of the **double swags** hung on its face.

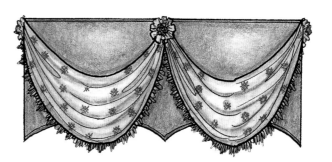

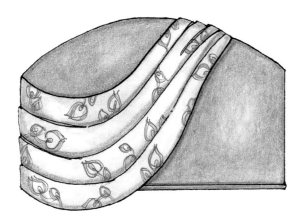

A **simple arched cornice** is softened by the casual draping of a **deep asymmetrical swag**.

Sheer lengths of fabric are draped in **casual switchback swags** over this straight cornice to achieve a **graduated waterfall**.

Scarves constructed of unlined crinkled fabric are draped over this straight cornice in **graceful swags and tails**.

The apex of this pair of **turban swags** is embellished with a flourish made of cord that matches the tassels hanging over the **contrasting under panel**.

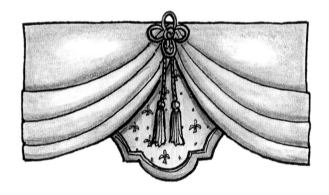

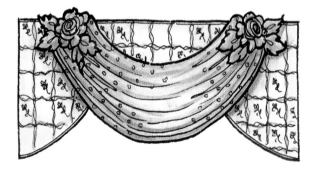

This **inverted V-shaped cornice** is draped with a **wide shirred scarf** that is swagged from shoulder to shoulder and embellished with large velvet roses and leaves.

A **turban swag** at the bottom of this cornice is centered with an oversized **double bow** with tails.

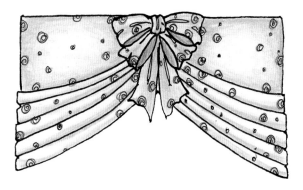

This cornice is draped with a flowing **cascade** and a **scarf** that is gathered together to create an off-centered **pouf**.

Medallions attached to the face of this cornice support a series of **swags** and **single-point flags**, with the flags at the sides wrapping around the cornice return.

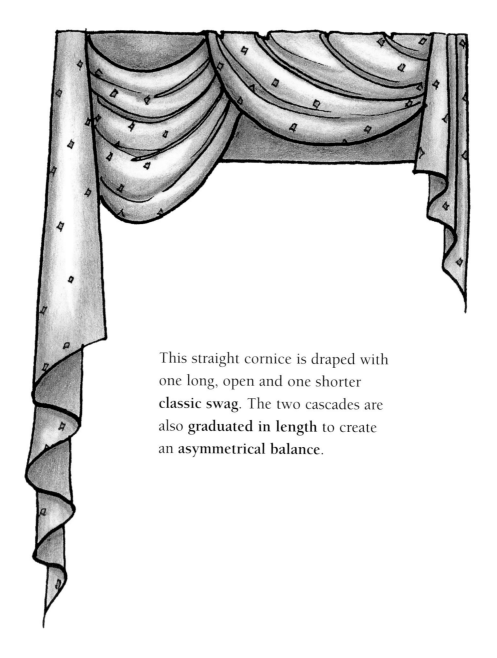

This straight cornice is draped with one long, open and one shorter **classic swag**. The two cascades are also **graduated in length** to create an **asymmetrical balance**.

Over-the-shoulder swags hang on top of wide cascades on each side of this cornice. The **long point** of one of the cascades is **extended** so it can be tied in a knot.

Bordered Cornices

A bordered cornice is a hard or soft cornice that incorporates a linear border as its key design element.

A **tent flap** overlapping the front of this cornice is held in place by a series of buttons. **Decorative top stitching** reinforces the angular lines of the flap.

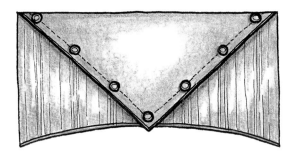

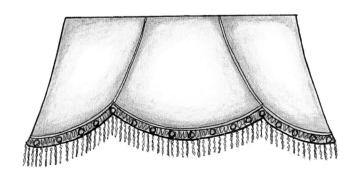

Curved welt and a **scalloped hem** add a new twist to this pagoda-style valance.

A series of shaped **banners** in contrasting fabric top this straight cornice, overlapping the hem to form a **pointed border**.

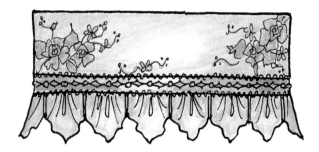

Wide-**galloon** tape and a zigzag ruffle trim out the bottom hem of this short cornice.

Pay close attention to the **geometric shapes** and **direction** created when using multiple fabrics on your treatments and adjust them accordingly.

The **single-point pennants** forming the top layer of the **double-fabric border** of this cornice serve as a backdrop for tassels hung from **jacquard ribbon banding.**

Sheer crinkled fabric is wrapped from the back of the cornice to the front, where it is **gathered together** to form a **choux** at the center.

A favorite for children's rooms, this straight cornice is tightly **crisscrossed with ribbons**, allowing mementoes and treasured keepsakes to be placed inside.

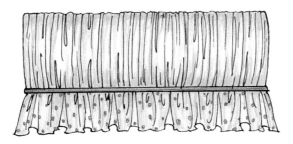

Sheer fabric is **shirred** over this straight cornice, which has been lined in white chintz. **Contrasting welt** and a **sheer ruffle** with a lingerie hem complete this effervescent design.

A simple design can be transformed by the addition of a **bold border** in tape or braid as with this cornice.

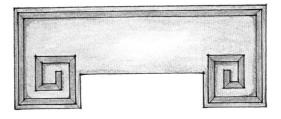

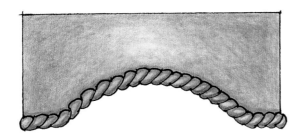

Jumbo padded rope in a contrasting fabric borders the hem of this arched valance.

Resembling a **shirt cuff**, this cornice uses simple details to make a big impact.

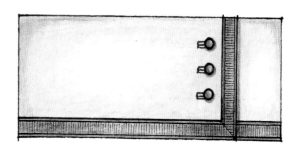

A **shirred border** and **decorative cording** create a frame for the bold pattern of the fabric of the center panel.

The **peaked top** of this cornice will add architectural interest to any plain window.

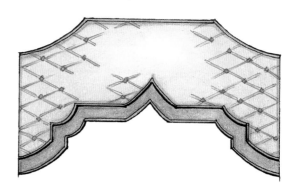

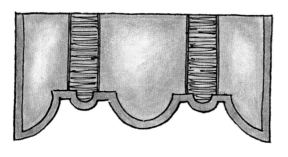

Tightly **shirred bands** of complementary fabric bordered with welt create **vertical stripes** that run perpendicular to the scalloped hem of this cornice.

Shirred Cornices

A shirred cornice is a hard or soft cornice that incorporates single or multiple bands of shirred fabric as its key design element.

A **shirred panel** of fabric resembling a **keystone** wraps around the center of this cornice to create a focal point.

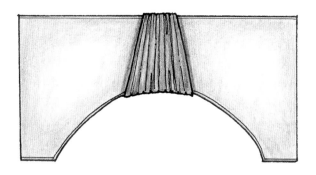

The smooth finish of the legs of this cornice is a striking contrast to the **shirred center.**

Shirred bands of contrasting fabric fit around the straight sections of this cornice.

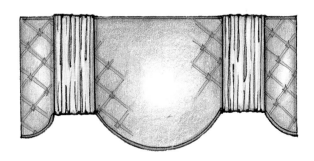

Embellished Cornices

Embellished cornices are hard or soft cornices that are embellished on their surface with trims, moldings, crystals, or other decorative elements.

Crown molding at the top and base of this arched cornice will add substantial architectural detailing to any window.

A series of **flags** are hung from **decorative knobs** on the face of this painted cornice.

You can emphasize the hemline of any cornice by adding a **contrasting border** or **tassels at key points**.

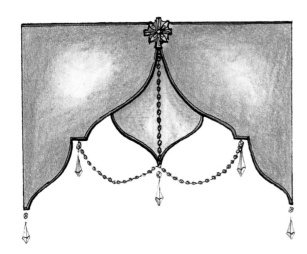

Chandelier crystals are a great way to add **glamour** and **brilliance** to any design.

Double strands of decorative **rope** and **tassels** are hung from **iron medallions** attached directly to the face of this cornice.

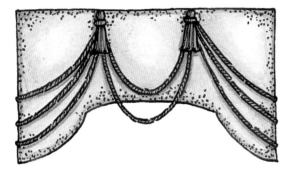

Swags are made from multiple **layers of cord** draped over the face of this valance and anchored at the top with tassels.

Contrasting bands of fabric and hanging **tassels form vertical stripes**, which are aligned with the high points in the hem of this cornice.

Notches are cut in the hem of this cornice to accommodate the **shirred ties with tassels** that are wrapped around the board.

The **tassels** on this cornice are **hung from embroidered ribbon**, which is centered at the high points of the hem.

This straight cornice is topped with a **smaller over-lapping panel**, which is held down with **contrasting ties**.

A **contrasting fabric border** and welt are used to create three **separate sections** on this cornice, which are embellished with amber chandelier crystals.

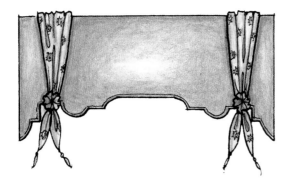

Tapered scarves are given two end tails to create the appearance of the scarf being **wrapped around the board** and tied together below the hem.

The welted border of this arched valance is **embellished with decorative nail heads**.

A **bishop's sleeve jabot** is hung behind the center of this cornice, creating a **focal point**.

Extra-large welting cord is covered with a shirred fabric casing to create these **bold rope swags** and cords with tassels.

Swags and bows made of contrasting ribbon top this simple, romantic design.

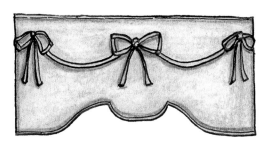

Alternative hardware can be the inspiration for new designs. Here, **wrought-iron shelf brackets** are used to embellish the interior corners of this cornice.

Tufted Cornices

Tufted cornices are soft cornices that are usually heavily padded and then tufted by applying buttons, nail heads, or other fasteners through the front of the cornice and securing them at the back, creating a specific pattern on the face of the cornice.

A large wrought-iron filigree and matching nail head borders impart a rustic look to this design.

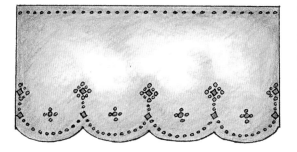

Nail heads in different shapes and sizes can be used to create elaborate patterns.

The welt and nail heads at the hem of this valance make it appear to overlap at the center.

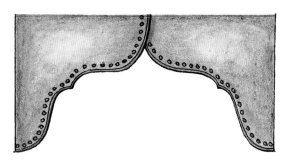

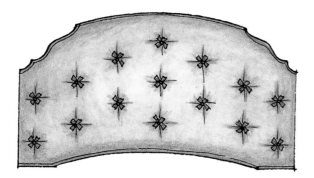

The face of this arched cornice is covered with **deep tufting**, which is highlighted by **small grosgrain ribbon crosses**.

Extra-deep square tufting with buttons forms a strong **geometric rhythm** in this contemporary design.

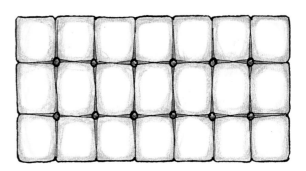

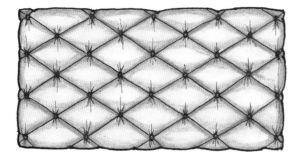

The **shallow diamond pillow tufting** of this cornice wraps around the edges, creating a very soft, **overstuffed** look.

Square nail heads are placed at the junctures of this **diamond-tufted cornice** with cascades.

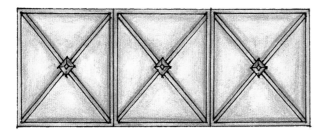

A **custom hand-painted iron frame** encases this upholstered cornice. **Diamond-shaped medallions** at the center of each section add balance to the larger square motifs.

Squares of **contrasting colors** create a **checkerboard pattern** that is enhanced by cording that separates each square. Buttons on the light squares add impact.

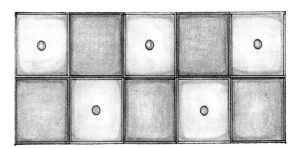

Cornice Toppers

A cornice topper is a small linear cornice box that serves to hide functional hardware for full-length panels or as a hard base from which a valance or shade can be hung.

A cornice topper with an attached balloon shade.

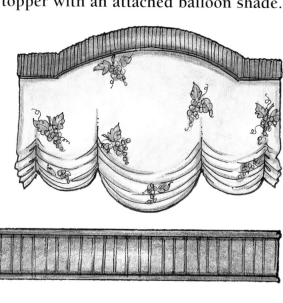

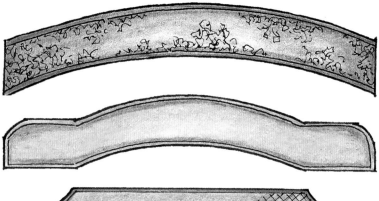

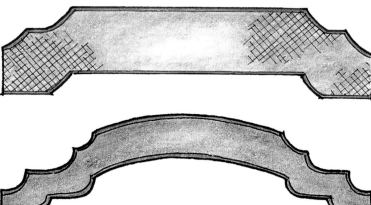

Cornice Treatments

This **pagoda cornice** is upholstered in a grass-cloth fabric and is done in a traditional Japanese style usually reserved for architecture. The curled corners are set off by **key tassels** that match the welted border of the cornice. The subtle sheen of the **shantung silk side panels** provides a contrast to the natural texture of the grass cloth.

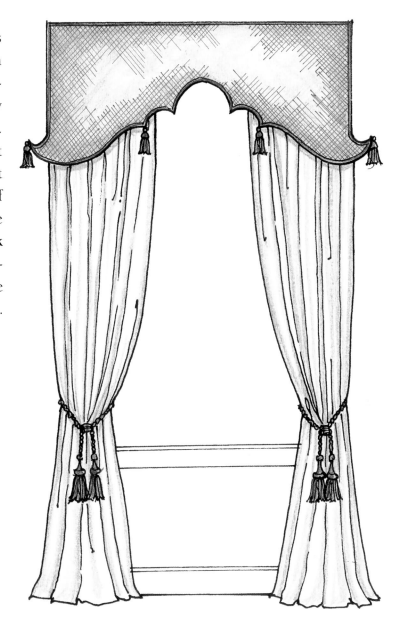

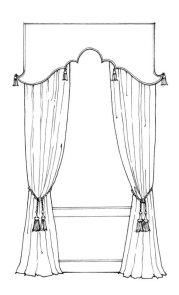

Creative designs can change the visual shape of any window and add character and architectural detailing to the space. This cornice treatment does all of that. The arched bottom of the cornice is detailed with **contrast banding** and **trim**. Decorative medallions are anchored directly to the face of the cornice and the **swagged top panels** are hung from them. Matching medallions are used to hold back the swagged top side panels.

Extra-deep overlapped **turban swags** fall into a bold pattern on this simple cornice, creating a rich sophisticated treatment. The under drapes are mounted behind the cornice on a traverse rod. The cornice base can be upholstered in a contrasting color or the swag folds can be done in **alternating fabrics** or **graduated tints** of the same color for a different look.

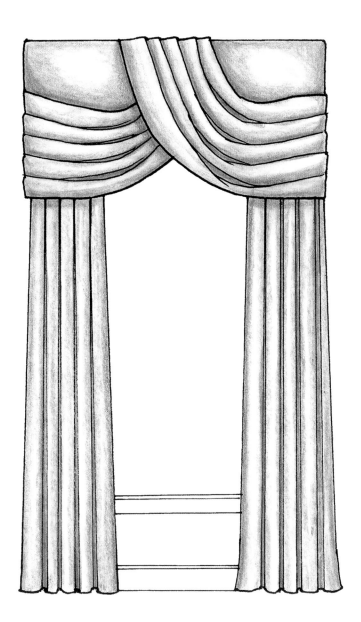

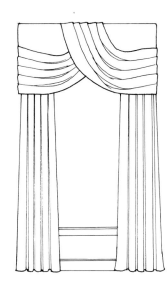

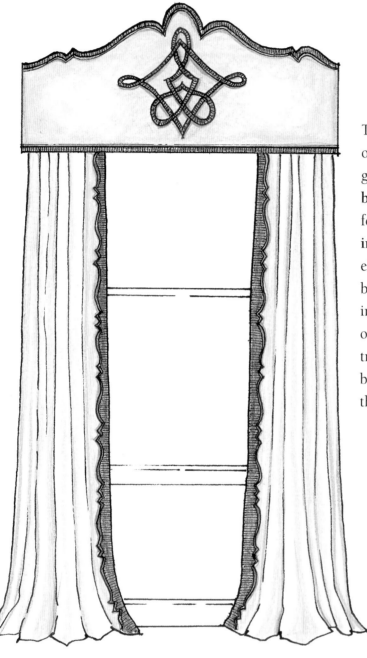

The **formal shape** at the top of this cornice is repeated to great effect in the contrast **banding** and **braid** that form the border on the **leading edge** of the under panels. The cornice itself is also banded to accentuate the intricate edgework. An elaborate **cartouche** made of the trim fabric and edged with braid marks the center of the cornice.

The inspiration for the shape of the bottom of this cornice came from the outline of the ornate **antique gate hinges** used as decorative ornaments. The edge of the cornice is welted and trimmed with **nail heads** that complement the hinges. Under panels are made in a complementary solid with a stripe that picks up both colors as a border. The stripe is repeated in the back-mounted **roman shade**. To finish the design, metal **holdbacks** and a metal-topped custom **fabric tassel** in the same finish as the hinges are added.

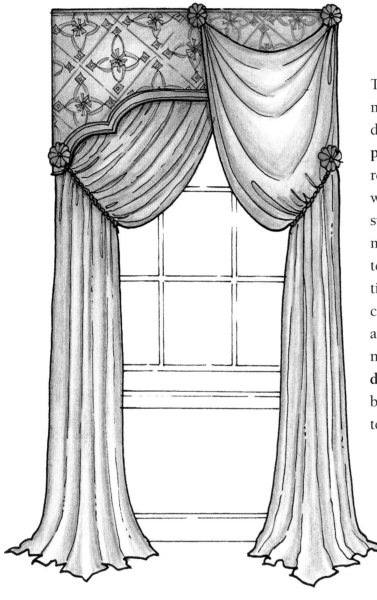

The cornice in this treatment supports the two very different panels. The **under panel** is shirred on a sash rod and mounted to the wall while the **over panel** has a swagged heading hung from medallions attached directly to the cornice face. Both are tied back with decorative cord attached to **medallions** at the long points of the cornice. The **contrasting border** and welting used at the bottom of the cornice helps to balance the treatment.

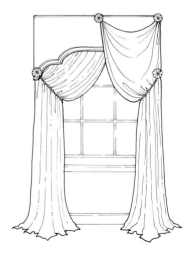

This flat, **hard valance** is faux painted to resemble leather and decorated with a pattern made of **decorative nail heads**. Accordion-**pleated double cascades** hang from the top of the cornice and are hemmed with long **beaded fringe**.

The side panels can be shirred and mounted with Velcro to the back of the cornice for easy removal for cleaning. The cornice can also be padded and uphol-stered for a softer look.

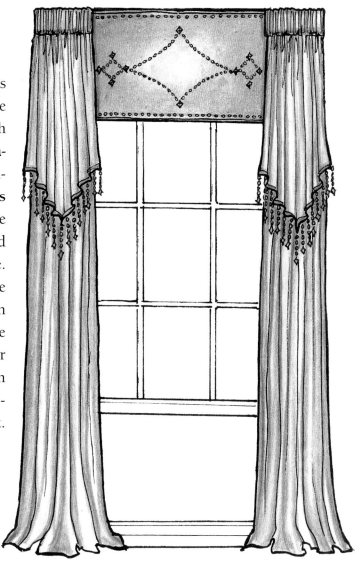

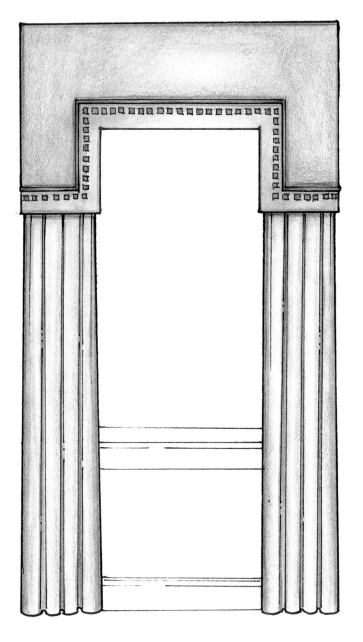

Decorative **nail heads** are generally thought of as an element in **traditional** or rustic designs. Here they are used to embellish a contrasting border at the edge of this very **modern** cornice.

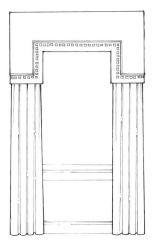

Square **keyhole openings** in the center of the larger square panels of this cornice are a unique feature of this geometric design. The squares of the cornice are delineated by applying a **flat border** of contrast fabric outlined by **string welt** in the same color. The cutouts allow an interesting **light pattern** to form on the opposing wall in the room.

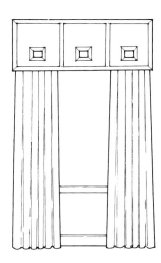

Subtle curves and angles bring out the **Oriental influence** in this design. The flared hem of the **pagoda cornice** is trimmed with a **brush fringe** embellished with long wooden beads, as are the matching tiebacks. A contrasting fabric is used for the **welting** that outlines the cornice.

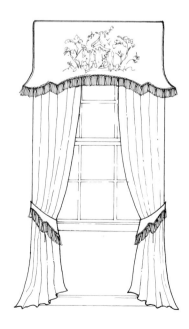

Swagged Cornice Outlines

For a complete inventory of all valance outline art, please refer to *The Design Directory of Window Treatments* companion CD-Rom.

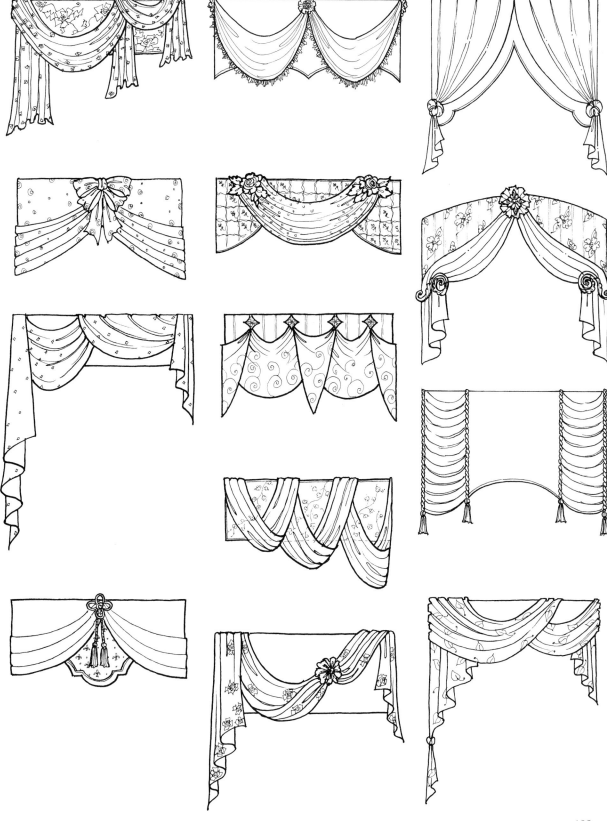

Arched Cornice Outlines

For a complete inventory of all valance outline art, please refer to *The Design Directory of Window Treatments* companion CD-Rom.

Hard Cornice Outlines

For a complete inventory of all valance outline art, please refer to *The Design Directory of Window Treatments* companion CD-Rom.

Framed Cornice Outlines

For a complete inventory of all valance outline art, please refer to *The Design Directory of Window Treatments* companion CD-Rom.

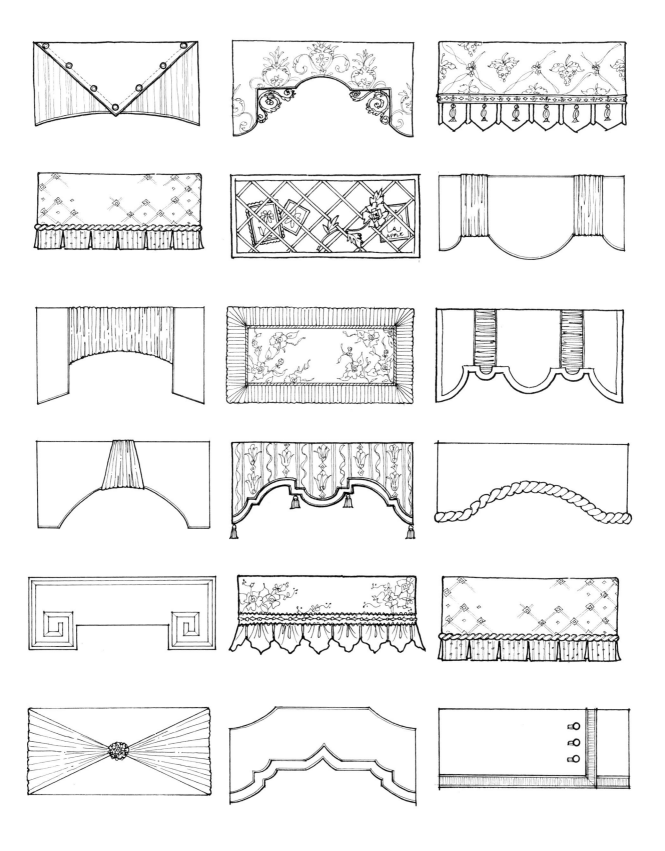

Embellished Cornice Outlines

For a complete inventory of all valance outline art, please refer to *The Design Directory of Window Treatments* companion CD-Rom.

Tufted Cornice Outlines

For a complete inventory of all valance outline art, please refer to *The Design Directory of Window Treatments* companion CD-Rom.

Lambrequins

✦

Lambrequins

A lambrequin is a cornice with long sides, or legs, that extend down to frame the window.

- A lambrequin can be painted, wallpapered, stained, or upholstered just as a cornice can.

- Its purpose is to create a strong frame around the window or to visually alter the shape of the window.

- It can add architectural detailing to a plain space.

- It can be used with under treatments such as draperies, sheers, blinds, or shades. Increase the return and clearance accordingly.

- A lambrequin can be used to unify a series of close-set windows into one treatment.

- Lambrequins should be self-lined as the lining can be seen from the inside edge of the treatment.

- A lambrequin can have a symmetrical appearance using two legs of equal length and shapes or an asymmetrical appearance with one or two legs of varying lengths or shapes.

- A cantonniere is a lambrequin whose legs extend all the way to the floor.

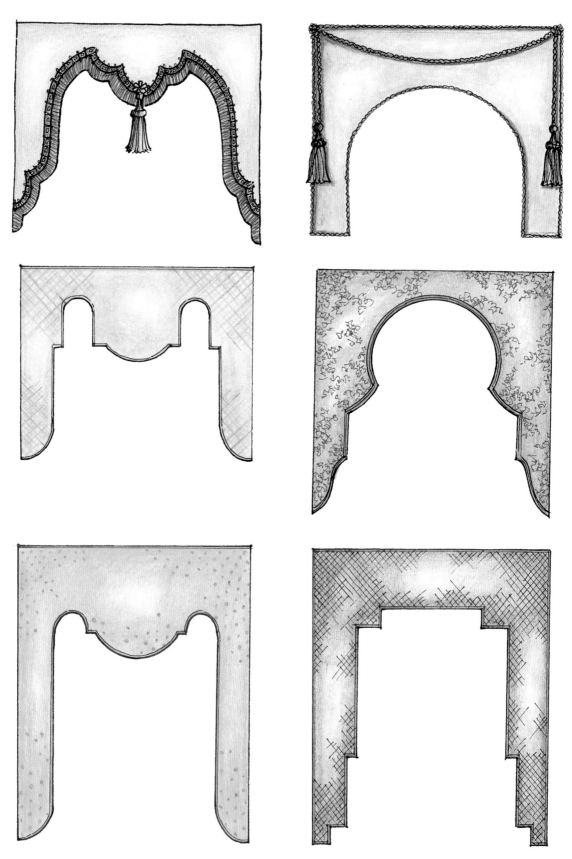

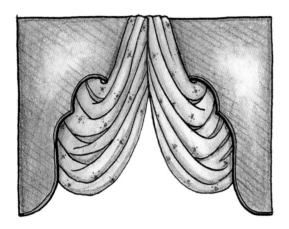

A **pair of swags** are mounted behind this short lambrequin and wrapped up over the top, creating a **keystone at the center**.

Pull-up swags and **matching cascades** are mounted behind this lambrequin, which is centered by a **large medallion** at its high point.

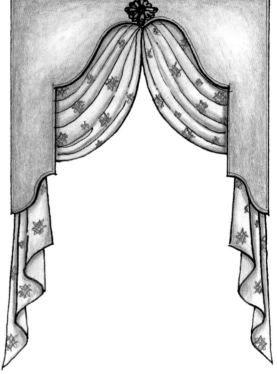

Large **tassels** are placed at this lambrequin's high and low points. A pair of panels is mounted beneath and **tied back at the bottom tassels**.

The **deep swag** of the under panel is juxtaposed against the **steep arch** of this lambrequin.

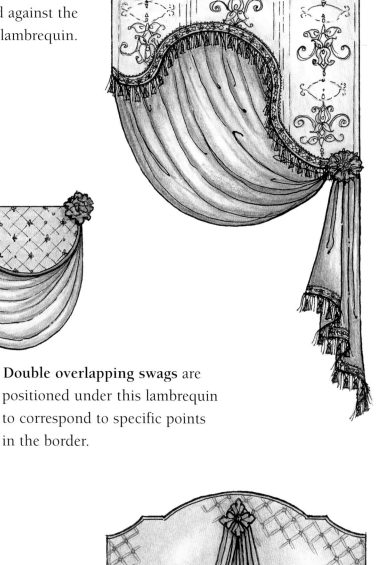

Double overlapping swags are positioned under this lambrequin to correspond to specific points in the border.

A **thin scarf swag** is pulled up from underneath this lambrequin and draped over the **decorative medallion** at the center.

Lambrequin Treatments

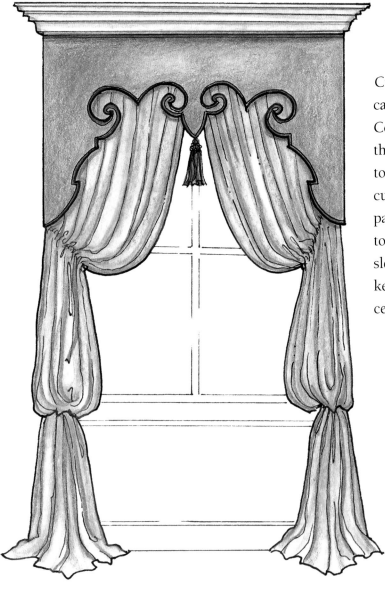

Crown molding tops this intricately bordered lambrequin. Contrasting welt winds around the edge of the cutout border to accentuate its dramatic curves. The wall-mounted side panels are Italian strung at the top and fall into a bishops sleeve at the bottom. A large key tassel creates a strong central focal point.

This one-sided lambrequin is draped from the top to the bottom with a long scarf swag. A single tied-back panel is hung underneath, completing this asymmetrical design.

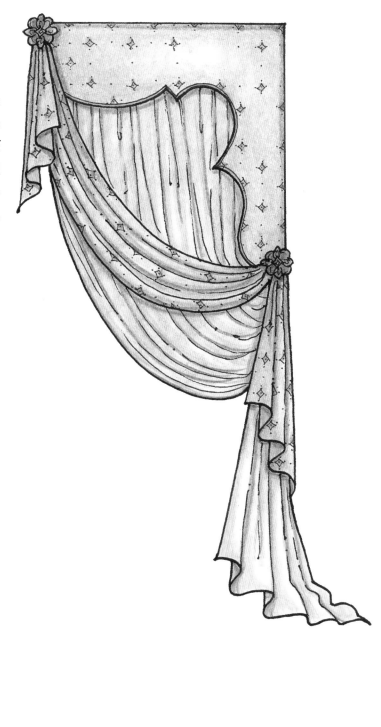

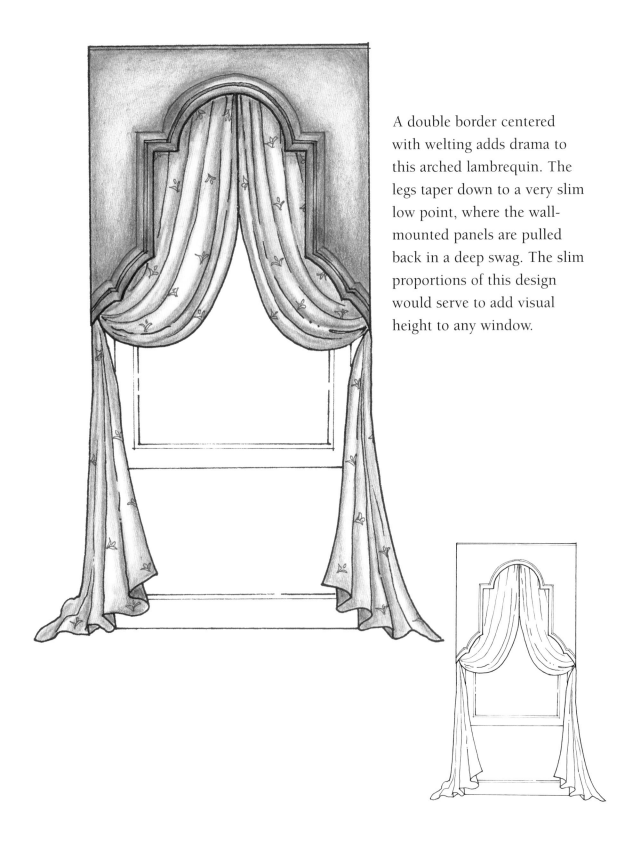

A double border centered with welting adds drama to this arched lambrequin. The legs taper down to a very slim low point, where the wall-mounted panels are pulled back in a deep swag. The slim proportions of this design would serve to add visual height to any window.

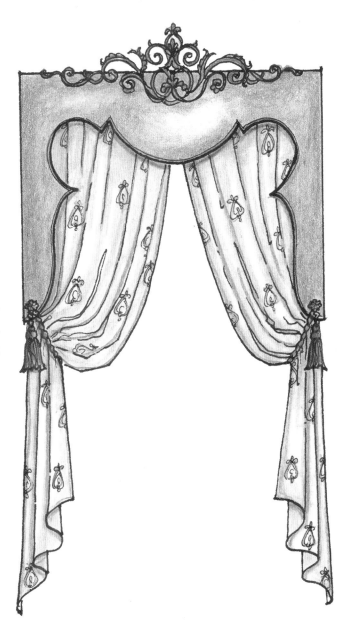

An ornate iron drapery crown tops this straight lambrequin, creating a peak. The scalloped lines of the crown are repeated in the inside outline of the lambrequin. Under panels are tied back with cord and tassels looped over small medallions or knobs at each side.

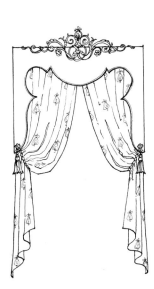

Three medallions are mounted
in an asymmetrical
pattern on this shirred
lambrequin with a contrasting
border. A slim scarf swag
is draped casually over
the medallions.

Swags

⁓

Swags

A swag is a semicircular cut of fabric that is draped in soft pleats. It is commonly used with cascades, horns, and tails to create graceful, undulating top treatments.

- Pleated swags have a tailored, formal look.

- Shirred swags are more casual and informal.

- Swags should always be cut on the bias unless working with a strong vertical pattern or stripe.

- Swags should always be self-lined or contrast lined.

- Never topstitch swags. Topstitching impedes the drape of the swag.

- Never stitch decorative trim through the lining at the swag hem.

- Placing decorative trim at the hemline of the swag can cause the trim to fold under and become hidden after it is pleated and hung. If possible, plot your trim placement after the swag has been draped to show the trim at its best.

- Interline or use interfacing on lightweight fabrics to add body and drapability.

- Test for pattern and color bleed-through in contrast-lined swags. Correct it with blackout or French lining.

- Use string weight to measure length and drop for your swags.

- Consider the effect that pleating and swaging will have on the pattern of your fabrics and adjust the pattern placement accordingly.

- Use drapery weights or string weights to control and manipulate the hang of your swags.

Anatomy of a Swag

Swag treatments are popular due to their versatility. The many individual components available can be combined to create an infinite number of beautiful, formal, and casual styles.

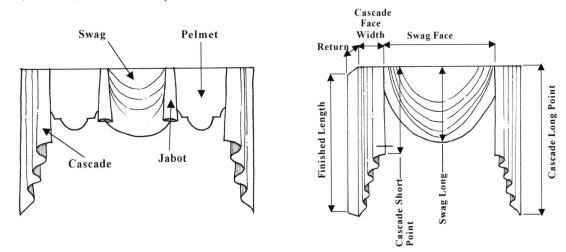

SWAG: A horizontal element in which the fabric is pleated or gathered into soft folds that are longer in the center than at the sides.

PELMET: A horizontal or vertical element consisting of a flat, stiffened panel of fabric usually cut in a decorative shape.

CASCADE: A vertical element in which the fabric is folded or gathered at the top. The fabric creates a zigzag effect between the long and short points of the tapered hem. Cascades are generally used at the sides of a swag or pelmet (sometimes called tails).

JABOT: A vertical element in which the fabric is flat or conical in shape. It is usually placed between swags or pelmets (sometimes called horns or trumpets).

TAIL: A flat vertical element usually cut in a decorative shape at the end and hung between swags or pelmets.

SCARF SWAG: Made of a continuous length of fabric that is then draped over a pole or swag holders to create the desired look.

Classic Swag Arrangements

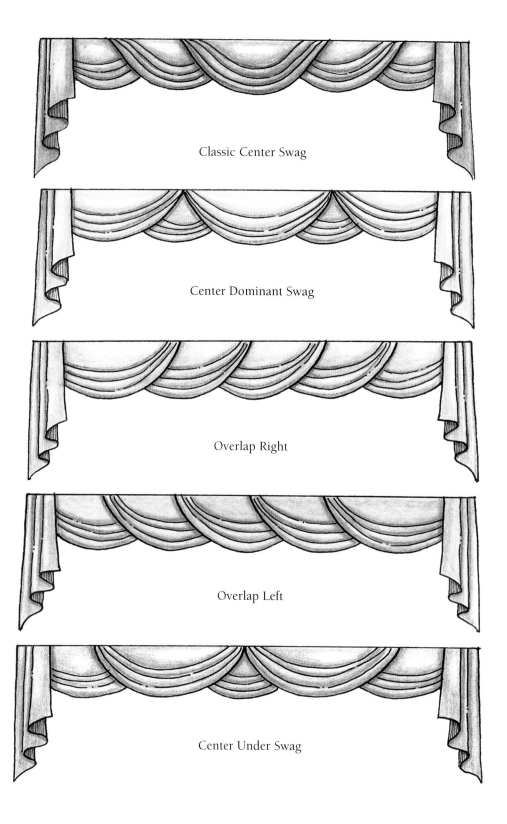

Classic Center Swag

Center Dominant Swag

Overlap Right

Overlap Left

Center Under Swag

Swag Charts

Use this chart as a guide to help calculate the number of swags needed according to the width of the window.

Board Face Width	# of Swags per Window
36" to 48"	1 swag
49" to 70"	2 swags
71" to 100"	3 swags
101" to 125"	4 swags
126" to 150"	5 swags
151" to 175"	6 swags
176" to 200"	7 swags
201" to 225"	8 swags
226" to 250"	9 swags
251" to 275"	10 swags
276" to 300"	11 swags

Use this chart as a guide to help calculate the average depth of your swags according to the width of the swag face.

Swag Face Width	Avg. Depth of Each Swag
20"	10"–12"
25"	12"–16"
30"	14"–18"
35"	14"–"18"
40"	14"–20"
45"	6"–22"
50"	16"–22"
Over 60"	18"–23"

Common Swags

Imperial Swag

Pattern: M'Fay 9109

Queen Anne Swag

Pattern: M'Fay 9107

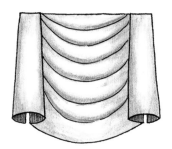

Kingston Swag

Pattern: Patterns Plus 5922

Empire Swag

Pattern: M'Fay 9284

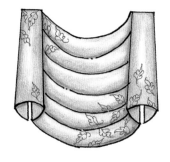

Open Kingston Swag

Pattern: M'Fay 9203

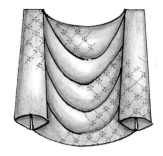

Open Empire Swag

Pattern: M'Fay9244

Empress Swag

Pattern: Patterns Plus 5918

Squire Swag

Pattern: M'Fay 9213

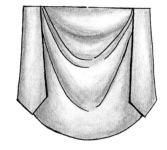

Estelle Swag

Pattern: M'Fay 9261

Murphy Swag

Pattern: M'Fay 9102

Ascot Swag

Pattern: Pattern Plus 5941

Napoleon Swag

Pattern: M'Fay 9254

Scalloped Swag

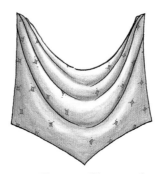

Open Triple-Point Swag

Balloon Swag

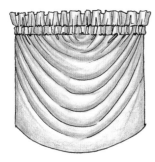

Rod-Pocket Empire Swag

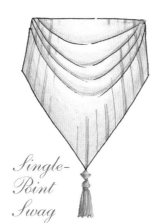

Single-Point Swag

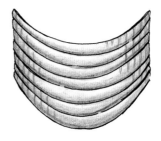

Open Boxed Swag

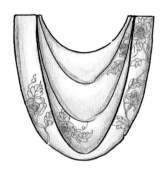

Face Front
Stacked Swag

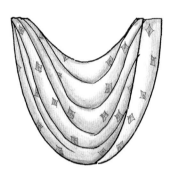

Face Front and Back
Stacked Swag

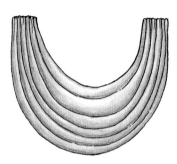

Scooped Swag

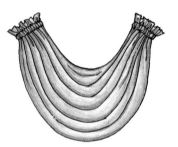

Open Shirred Swag

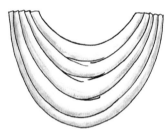

Open Classic Swag

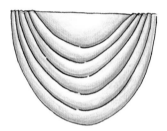

Classic Swag

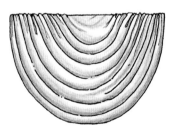

Shirred Swag

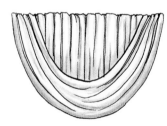

Fan Swag

Pattern: M'Fay 9002

Classic One-Sided
Swag

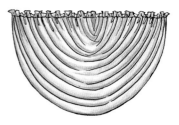

*Gathered Swag
with Ruffle*

Pattern: Patterns Plus 5921

Boutonniere Swag

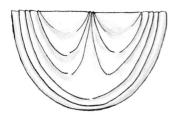

*Stacked Back-
Facing Raised Swag*

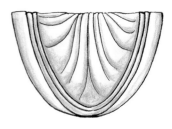

*Stacked Front-
Facing Raised Swag*

Open Raised Swag

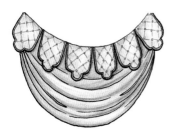

*Open Swag with a
Shaped Cuff Top*

Cowl Swag

*Side Gathered Swag
with Ruffles*

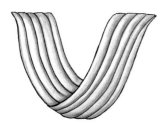

Switchback Swag

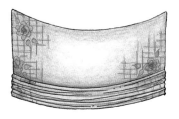

*Open Shirred
Boxed Swag*

Boxed Swag

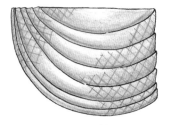

*Pleated Half
Swag*

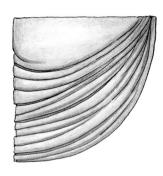

*Shirred Half
Swag*

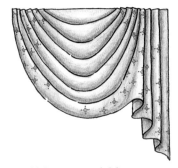

*Waterfall Half
Swag*

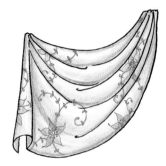

*Pull-Up Half
Swag*

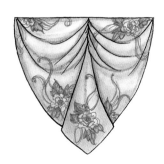

*Single Raised Swag
with Center Point*

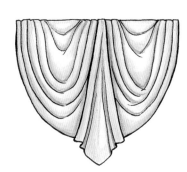

*Double Raised Swag
with Center Point*

Gathered Tudor Swag
Pattern: M'Fay 9287

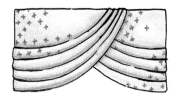

Turban Swag

Pattern: M'Fay 9225

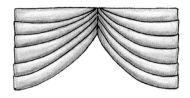

Taj Mahal Swag

Cross-Over Swag

Pattern: M'Fay 9201

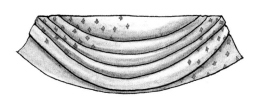

Flat-Bottom Swag

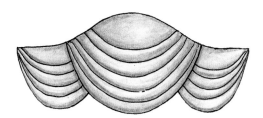

Turtle Swag

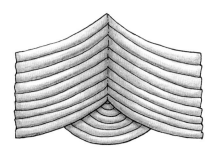

Raised Taj Mahal Swag

Switchback Swag with Cascade

Cascades, Jabots, and Tails

There are three types of vertical design elements commonly used in window treatment designs.

CASCADE

A flat, angled panel of fabric is folded or gathered at the top. The angle creates a zigzag effect between the long and short points of the tapered hem. Cascades are generally used at the sides of a swag or pelmet.

JABOT

A flat panel of fabric that is conical in shape or folded onto itself to create a sleeve. It is usually placed between swags or pelmets (sometimes called horns or trumpets).

TAIL

A flat panel of fabric usually cut in a decorative shape at the end and hung between swags or pelmets.

- Cascades, tails, and jabots should always be self-lined or lined with contrasting or complementary fabric.

- When using lightweight fabrics for these elements, you may want to interline to add body and drapability.

- Check for color bleed-through when using contrasting linings or bold patterns and eliminate it by using blackout or French interlining.

- Do not topstitch or apply trim by stitching through the face fabric to the lining as this will interfere with the draping of the element.

- Keep in mind that the backside of these elements is just as important to the look of your design as the front, and plan accordingly.

- Large patterns are not appropriate for these pieces. Plot the pattern placement carefully on each element to show it at its best.

- Because of the angle of the cascades, the return can make it appear shorter after it is hung. Add 3" to 4" to the overall length to adjust for this shortcoming.

- As a rule, the length of the cascades is usually at least 2 times the drop of the swag.

Cascades

Stacked
Cascade

Tapered
Stacked
Cascade

Waterfall
Cascade

Inverted
Waterfall
Cascade

Double
Cascade

Inverted
Double
Cascade

Reversed
Top Cascade

Single
Waterfall
Cascade

Spiral
Cascade

Switchback
Cascade

Bias-
Cut
Cascade

Scalloped
Cascade

Shirred
Spiral
Cascade

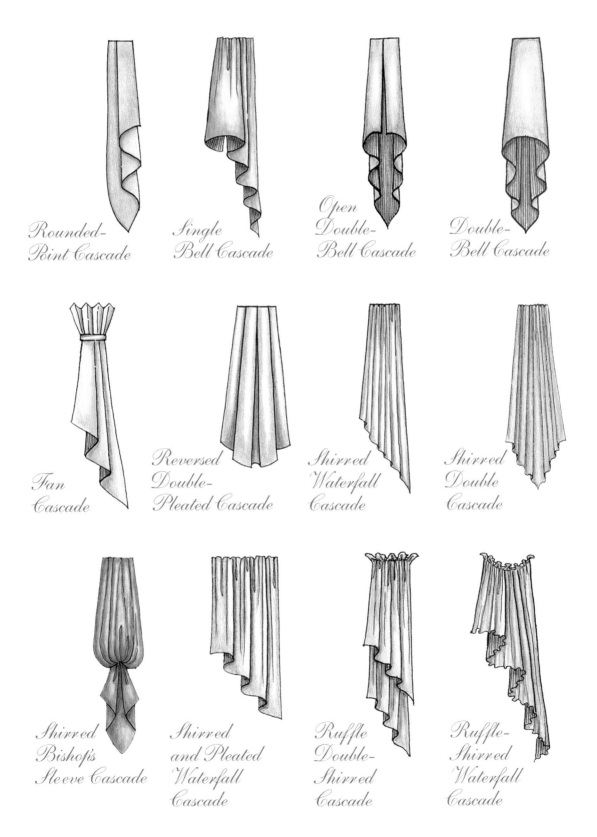

Rounded-
Point Cascade

Single
Bell Cascade

Open
Double-
Bell Cascade

Double-
Bell Cascade

Fan
Cascade

Reversed
Double-
Pleated Cascade

Shirred
Waterfall
Cascade

Shirred
Double
Cascade

Shirred
Bishop's
Sleeve Cascade

Shirred
and Pleated
Waterfall
Cascade

Ruffle
Double-
Shirred
Cascade

Ruffle-
Shirred
Waterfall
Cascade

Jabots

Horn Jabot

Single-Point Horn Jabot

Inverted Single-Point Horn Jabot

Fan Top Horn Jabot

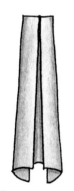

Inverted Box Pleat Horn

Triple-Bell Jabot

Cupped Necktie Jabot

Pleated Necktie Jabot

Horn with Tails

Clover Leaf Jabot

Center Pleat Necktie

Fan Top Pleated Jabot

Fan Top Bell Jabot

Necktie Jabot
with a Double
Cascade

Cross-Over
Jabots

Scalloped
Cross-Over
Jabots

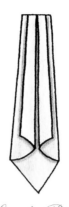

Single-Point
Top-Folded
Jabot

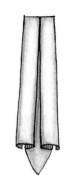

Double Horn
Jabot with
Center Point

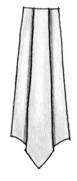

Single Round Point
Under Folded Jabot

Single Scallop Jabot
with Side Rolls

Single Scallop
Tuxedo Jabot

Handkerchief
Jabot

Single Scallop Jabots with
Scalloped Fold-Overs

Double
Stacked Jabot

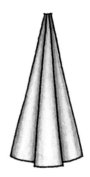

Triple Gusset
Jabot

Multiple Gusset
Jabot

Tails

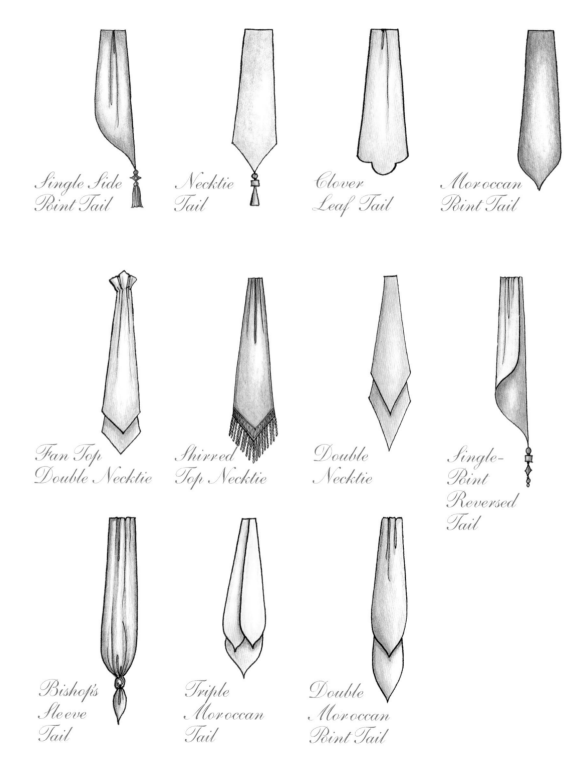

Single Side
Point Tail

Necktie
Tail

Clover
Leaf Tail

Moroccan
Point Tail

Fan Top
Double Necktie

Shirred
Top Necktie

Double
Necktie

Single-
Point
Reversed
Tail

Bishop's
Sleeve
Tail

Triple
Moroccan
Tail

Double
Moroccan
Point Tail

Over-the-Rod Casades

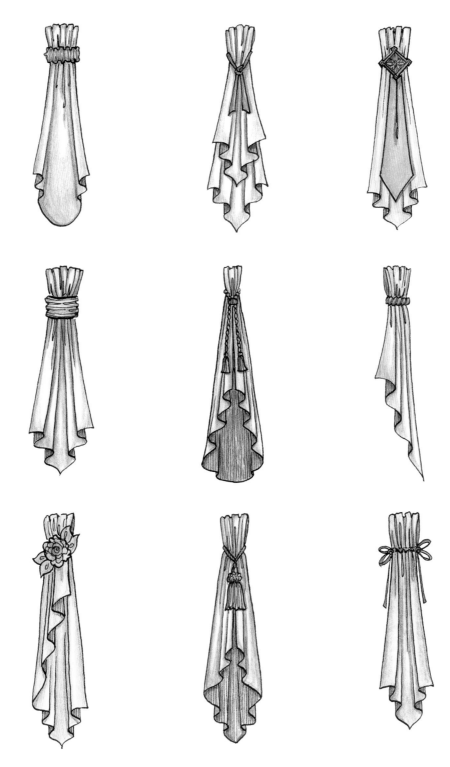

Scarf Swags

A scarf swag is a length or lengths of fabric that have been pleated or are bunched together and draped over a drapery pole or other hardware.

These treatments may include:

SWAGS

JABOTS

TAILS

CASCADES

SCARVES

- Scarf swags are usually not cut on the bias like formal swags. They are constructed of a single length of fabric.

- Use soft pliable fabrics. Drapability of the fabric to be used is key to the success of your design.

- They are not suitable for very heavyweight fabric or fabrics with large patterns.

- Using a striped fabric can be difficult on some designs. Always consult your workroom on which direction the stripes will be placed on each element.

- Contrast or complementary lining should always be used.

- Interlining will help the swag drape and hang properly.

- Drapery weights should be used to control the hang of long tails or cascades.

A one-piece **Moroccan swag** is folded, draped over the front of the rod, and secured at the back rather than winding it onto the rod.

Three distinctly shaped flat **open pelmets** are balanced with matching jabots and cascades, which fold gracefully over the rod.

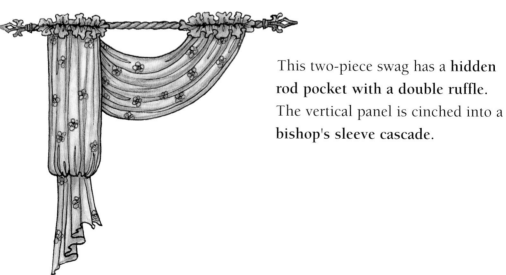

This two-piece swag has a **hidden rod pocket with a double ruffle.** The vertical panel is cinched into a **bishop's sleeve cascade.**

An **open swag** has a scalloped cuff heading in a contrasting fabric. The **asymmetrical double cascades** are weighted with **chandelier crystals** and lined in the same fabric as the scallop.

This **one-piece scarf** is draped over three medallions, creating a **triple swag and cascades.** Beaded fringe is added at the bottom hems only.

An **asymmetrical balance** is achieved in this design by using a long cascade draped to the front and a scarf wrapped over the pole, forming a short cascade at the back. The **miss-matched tassels** complete the treatment.

Multiple layers combine effectively in this creative design. Two formal **open swags** cover a separate mounting board that supports the other elements in the treatment. Attached to the panel are a **center swag** and two **double cascades**.

A decorative pole supports the two center swags of this valance while the swags at the side are allowed to drop at an angle supported by medallions at each side. The **switchback cascades** are **scalloped** to match the border of the swags.

This classic **handkerchief swag** is made up of three separate sections but looks as if it is one continuous piece. **String welt** and **decorative braid** are used to maintain the design's sharp, crisp edges. The **key tassel** creates a focal point and weighs down the point.

This single **Wilshire swag** is topped with a ribbon rosette and a long rope with a tassel to cover the center shirring. Pattern: M'Fay

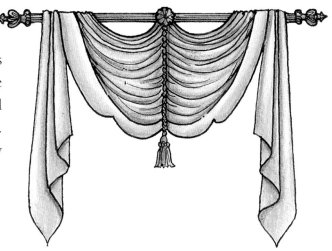

The **pick-up swag** in the middle of this design is anchored by the elaborate center medallion. Two **open swags** flank the center with two **reversed cascades** at the sides. Each piece is lined in a contrasting fabric.

Over-the-rod cascades flank a single scarf swag wound over a decorative rod. The cascades are cinched at the top with coordinating tassels.

Over-the-rod cascades cover the end points of this single center swag. **Ruched sleeves** are threaded over the cascade to cinch it in and to cover the seam at the top.

This single length of fabric is attached to **tabs** and hung from the pole. The center of the panel is pulled up in a swag by a **loop** of fabric.

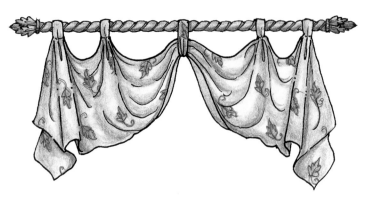

This classic **one-piece scarf swag** is draped over the top pole and secured to the medallions at the sides by matching ties that cinch the panel in order to create cascades at the tail ends.

Hidden rod pockets allow this set of double ruffle shirred swags and **bishop's sleeve cascades** to be hung with the appearance of having no hardware.

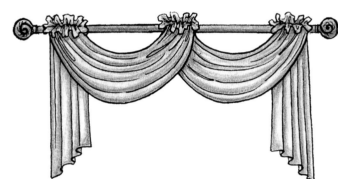

Hidden rod pockets with double ruffles head these swags and cascades.

An elaborate **medallion** on this decorative pole is placed to emphasize the **center pick** up of this scarf swag. The side pick ups are looped over the pole with an attached tab and secured to the lining of the scarf.

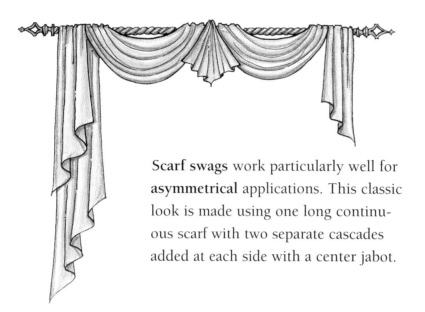

Scarf swags work particularly well for asymmetrical applications. This classic look is made using one long continuous scarf with two separate cascades added at each side with a center jabot.

Two separate swags, one casual and one formal, are draped over each other on a pole. Two sets of double cascades are hung underneath the swags.

In this classic valance, a pair of stacked cascades frames an under-mounted pick-up swag and two top-mounted open half swags.

Beautiful iron hardware is the focal point of this graceful two-piece **scarf swag**. Contrasting cord embellished with leaves matching the hardware balance the strong horizontal lines of the rods.

This valance is comprised of one full **renaissance flag** and two halves hung by **tabs** from an iron rod and weighted with **glass beads**.

A simple **one-piece scarf** can be given a very formal look by adding the right hardware or trim. This beautiful **crown** raises the swag above the matching decorative rod. The coordinating tassels add a **vertical balance** to the center of the swag.

A pair of graduated pole swags with **attached cascades** is given a **single ruffle heading** that creates a more casual country look.

Scarves or bandanas are cut in half and used to create this valance.

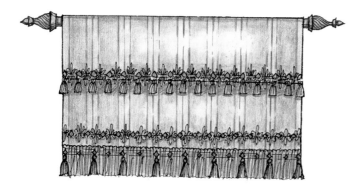

A self-lined **rectangular panel** is simply folded over a decorative rod and trimmed with multiple **coordinating trims**, forming elaborate double borders.

Swag Outlines

For a complete inventory of all valance outline art, please refer to *The Design Directory of Window Treatments* companion CD Rom.

Swag Treatments

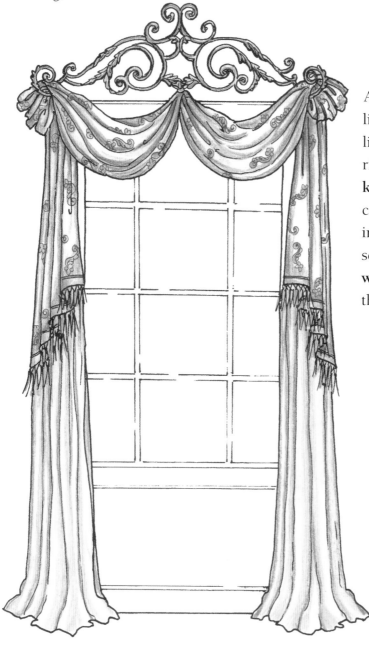

A **one-piece scarf** is interlined to add body and
lined with contrasting fabric. It is trimmed with long
knotted fringe and draped
casually over this beautiful
iron crown. To keep
scarves in place, use **florist
wire** to secure the fabric to
the crown.

Two **half swags** and a center **open swag** drape beautifully over this exquisite iron rod. The swags are self-lined and trimmed with a decorative **galon (braid)** to accentuate their graceful curves. Traversing panels are mounted under the top treatment.

Multiple layers create a rich backdrop for this intricate **iron crown** and **pair of flourishes**. A wide swag with **center pickup** is bordered on each side by **double cascades**. The larger and longer matching versions of the second layer are done in a semi-sheer contrasting fabric. Side panels made with the fabric of the top layer finish the treatment.

This **Austrian shade valance** is trimmed with contrasting decorative cord that separates the sections of the valance and forms **looped rosettes** at the top. A small **zigzag border** finishes the hem.

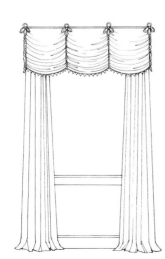

An extra-deep **pole swag** with a matching **waterfall cascade** and full-length side panel are wrapped over the front of a decorative rod. A **contrasting scarf** is then wrapped over the pole swag, creating a dramatic focal point to this treatment.

This beautiful swagged treatment appears to have been made from one continuous length of fabric beginning in a **double cascade** that wraps over the pole into an open **swag**, finally ending in a **full-length panel**. It is actually made in three sections for ease of construction and installation.
Pattern: Vogue V7984

This design is a second interpretation of the heavy formal treatment shown on the opposite page. It is given a **lighter more delicate appearance** by using a **lightweight interlining** and adding long, **beaded trim and tassels.**

Decorative tape is used as a border to accentuate the graceful lines of this classic cornice. The **swagged center panels** are topped with **double bell jabots** and **double cascades** that have been wrapped around the edge of the valance. A large medallion places emphasis on the high point of the valance and creates a dramatic focal point.

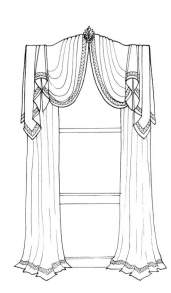

Multiple **swagged layers and cascades** in this **eyebrow-arched** valance are unified by the addition of crisp **scalloped borders** that are set apart by contrasting welt.

Medallion **swag holders** support this semi-sheer swagged valance with **single horn cascades**. The under panel is made with a **no-show heading** to maintain the open look of the swag. **Ribbon** is used as **banding** on the cascades and the bottom hem of the panel.

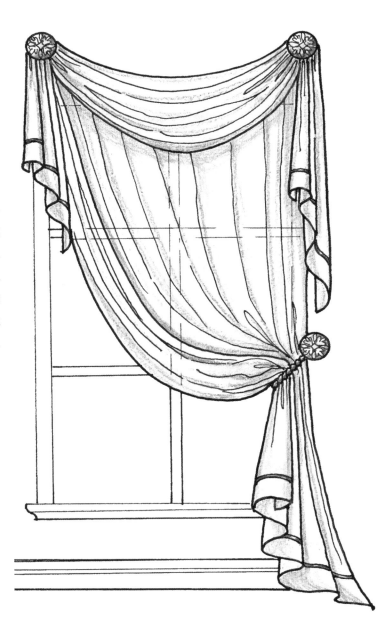

A single **scarf swag** is wrapped around a decorative pole, creating a double swag and two long cascades. A **banner swag** is draped across the front of the treatment and secured to the pole with large contrasting **rosettes**.

This extra-wide **open boxed swag** is made by sewing **casings** in the sides through which a tie is threaded. When the tie is pulled, the fabric is **shirred** up into a swag. The ends of the ties are knotted and hang free as part of the treatment. The swag is hung over pleated side panels by mounting a **hidden leg** underneath the side panels to which the swag can be attached.

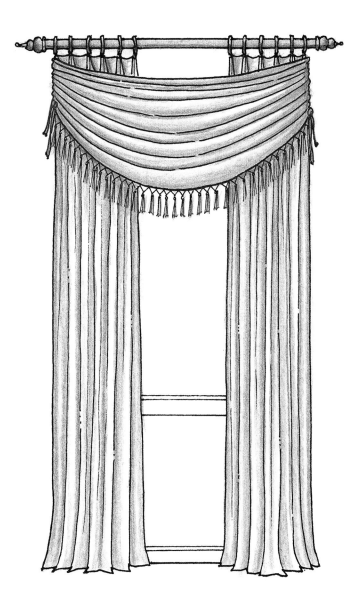

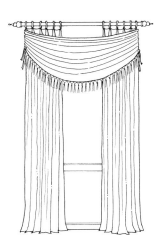

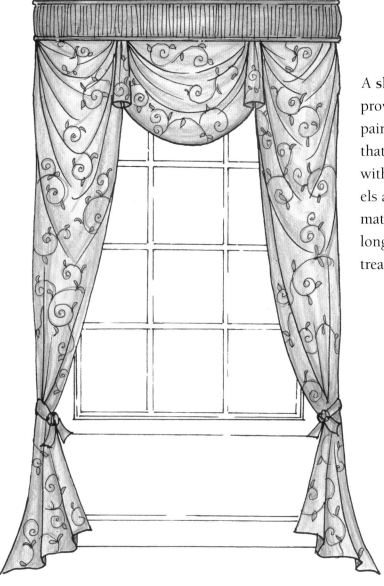

A **shirred cornice topper** provides a platform for a pair of **swagged side panels** that flank a **center swag** with **horn jabots**. The panels are pulled back low with matching ties to create a long, thin profile to this treatment.

Many times, the elaborate hardware currently available can become the star of your treatment as with this iron pole with brass finials and center medallion. A **pole swag** with cascades showing large scallops at the inside hem is **pulled up** by two ribbon ties to form its own scallops.

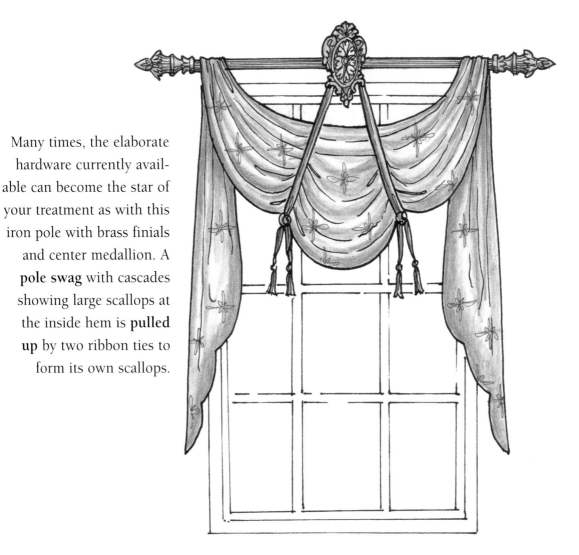

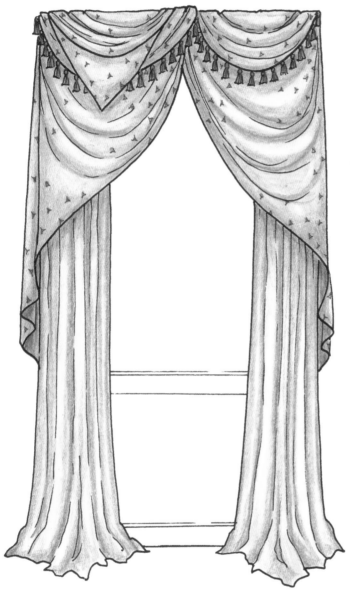

Tapered waterfall swags create the first layer of this complicated valance. Another pair of swags trimmed in **tassel fringe** and a **flag** on one side top the valance.

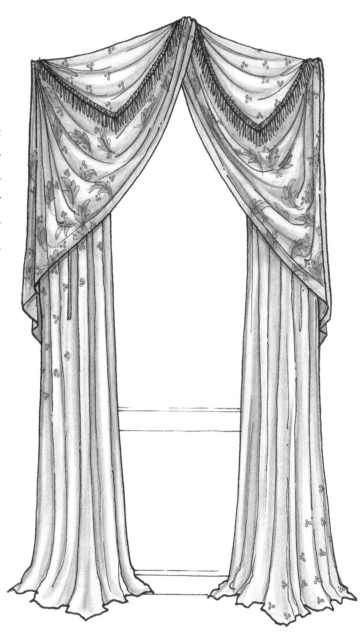

This treatment is made with a pair of **overlapped waterfall swags** pulled up at the center and topped with two **swagged flags** trimmed in brush fringe.

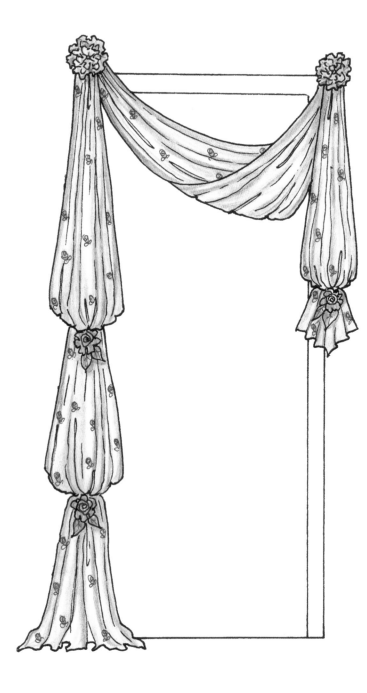

A full-length **double bishop's sleeve side panel** is topped with a **switch-back swag** and matching **bishop's sleeve cascade**. Large **poufs** cover **swag holders** at the top of the treatment while **rosettes** embellish each pull up of the sides.

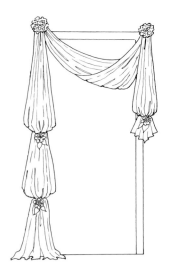

A pair of luxuriously **swagged floor-length scarves** are draped over a stunning iron rod and centered with a **double cascade. Double tassels** on long ropes are hung at each side of the pole, as well as at the tip of the cascade.

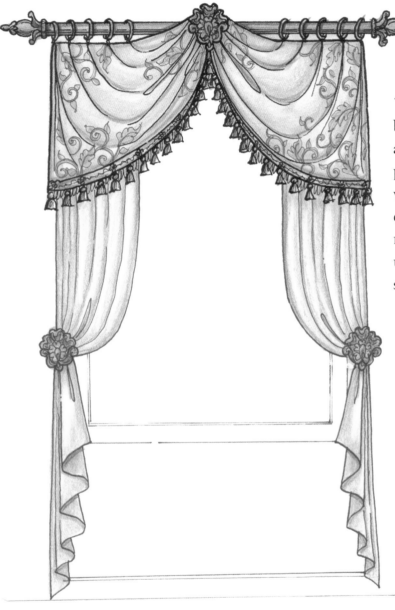

This treatment is hung by **drapery rings** attached at the **pleat points** of this raised swag while the center is draped over a large medallion. The traversing under panels are hung separately.

A **single scarf swag** is self-lined and draped over a decorative rod while another **contrasting swag trimmed with bullion fringe** is hung over the scarf swag. A matching pain of double-layer **cascades** is hung from the back of the rod underneath the scarf swag. Stationary side panels are mounted separately on the wall.

French Doors and Awnings

❧

French Doors

French doors that are hung to open inward into a room present a challenge in designing a window treatment to provide privacy and light control that does not interfere with the doors' function.

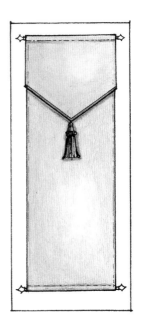

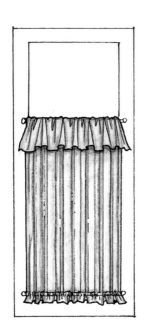

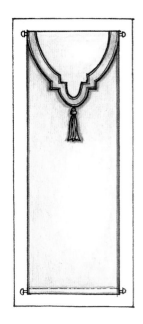

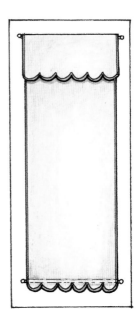

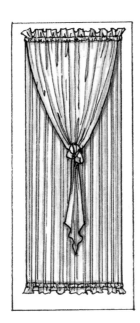

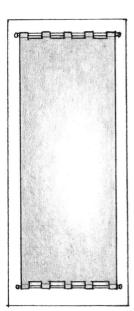

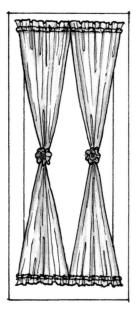

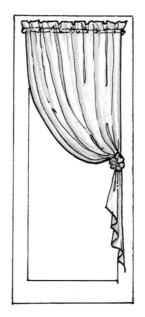

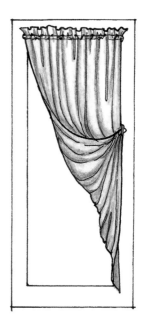

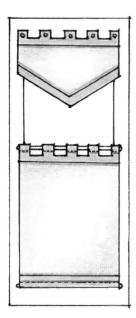

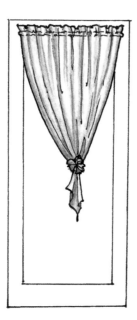

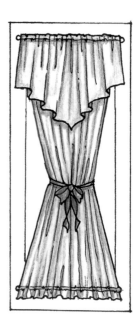

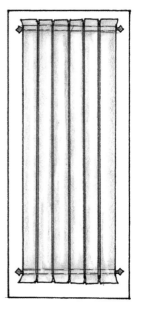
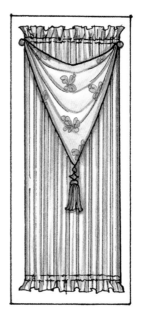
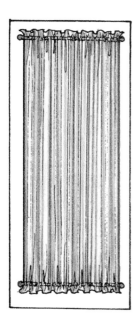
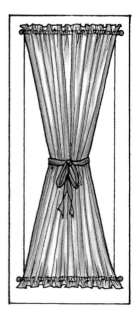
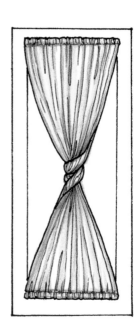
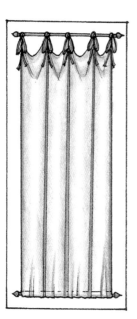

Awnings

Interior awnings are simple valances that are angled away from the wall at the bottom of the treatment.

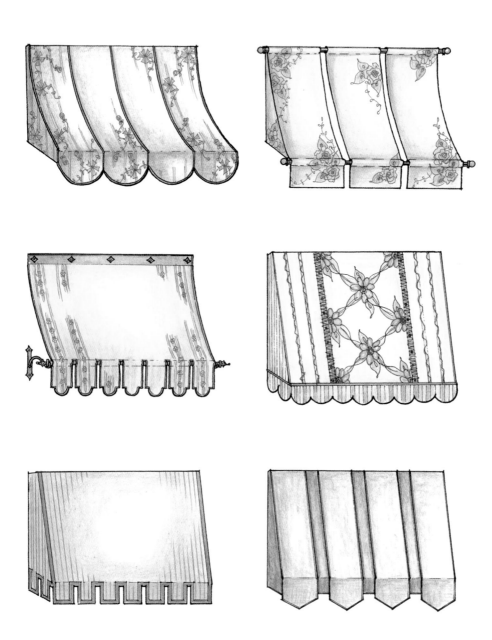

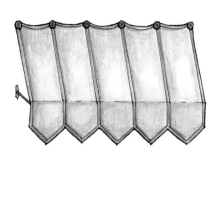

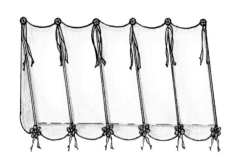

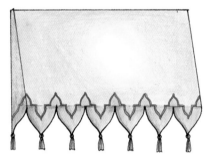

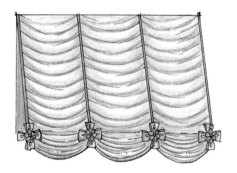

Fabric Shades

Fabric Shades

Fabric shades are versatile window coverings that can be used by themselves or in combination with any number of other over treatments. The vast number of variations possible makes them appropriate for almost any design style.

There are four types of shades commonly used today:

AUSTRIAN: This shade is drawn up by vertical shirring running the entire length of the shade into tight gathers.

BALLOON: This shade has a scalloped hem that draws up from the bottom in loose gathers.

ROMAN: This shade is drawn up from the bottom in folds.

ROLLER: This shade is rolled up from the top to the bottom.

- Fabric shades should always be lined and interlined when necessary.

- They can provide light and privacy control for any window including small, odd-sized, and hard-to-reach windows.

- They can be easily motorized.

- They can be hung on skylights and transoms.

- When specifying blackout shades, pinholes in the lining must be filled to prevent light from bleeding through.

- When mounting shades as under treatments, calculate the return of the over treatment to accommodate the full stack-up depth of the shade.

- If specifying shades in a space where children are present, consider the safety concerns related to shade cords. Always specify continuous loop or other safe mechanisms when available.

Balloon Shades

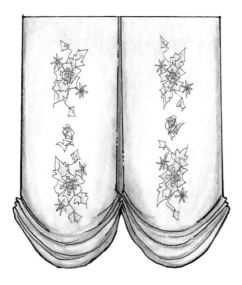

Center-Pleated Balloon Shade

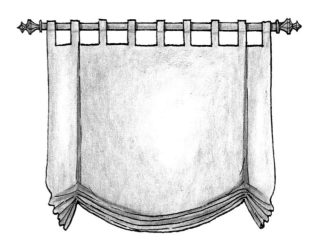

Tab-Top Pleated London Shade

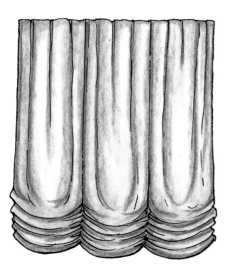

Cloud Shade

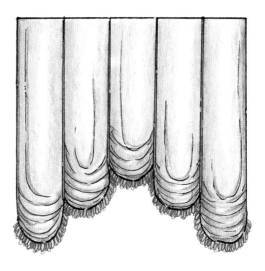

Opera Shade

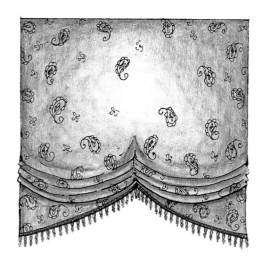

Balloon Shade with a London
Bottom

London Shade

Simple Balloon Shade

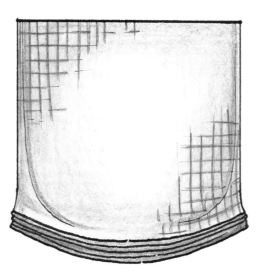

Slouched Roman Shade

Gathered Column London Shade

Cloud Shade

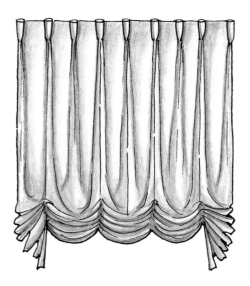

Top-Pleated Cloud Shade

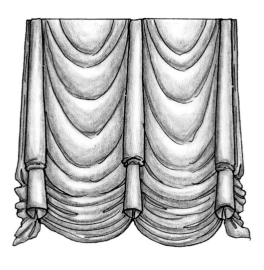

Empire Shade

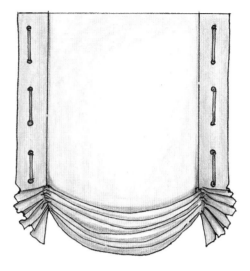

Linen Fold Shade

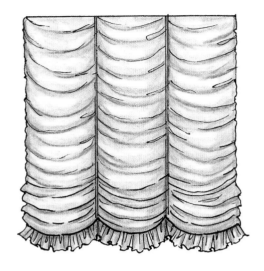

Austrian Shade

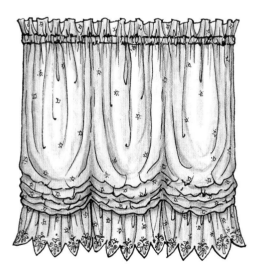

Rod-Pocket Cloud Shade
with a Ruffled Hem

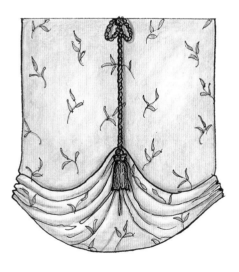

Raised Balloon Shade

London Shade

Pleated London Shade

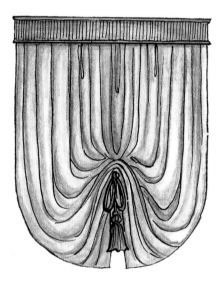

Center-Drawn Cloud Shade

Roman Shades

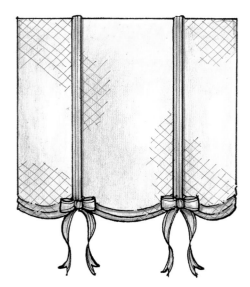

Stagecoach Roman

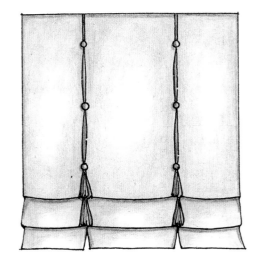

Open-Pleated Roman Shade
with Buttons

Stagecoach Shade

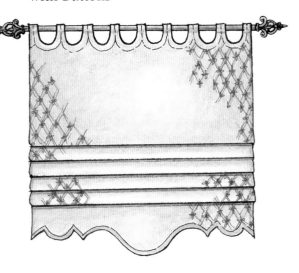

Tab-Top Roman Shade with
Scalloped Hem Detail

Shirred Roman Shade

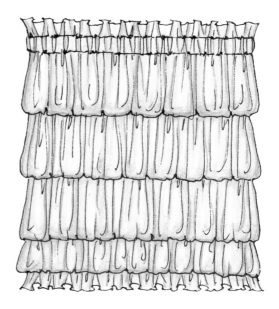

Rod-Pocket Roman Shade

Gathered Roman Shade

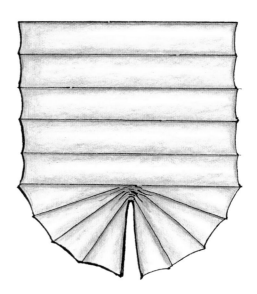

Center-Drawn Pleated
Roman Shade

Folded Roman Shade

Roman Shade

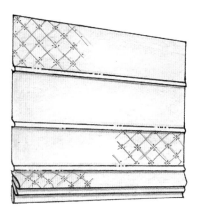

Doweled Roman Shades

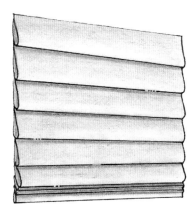

Hobbled Roman Shade

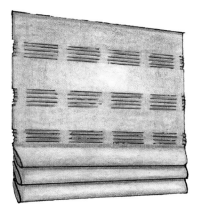

Pleated Roman Shade

Slouched Roman Shade

Embellishments

Embellishments

Embellishments are decorative elements used to provide the finishing touches necessary to complete your treatments. Use these tools to express your individuality and customize your designs.

APPLIQUÉS	MEDALLIONS
BANDING	PINS
BEADS	RIBBONS
BORDERS	ROSETTES
BOWS	RUFFLES
BRAID	SILK FLOWERS
BUTTONS	TAPE
CHANDELIER CRYSTALS	TIES
CORDING	TRIMS
EMBROIDERY	TASSELS
FRINGE	TIEBACKS
GIMP	WELTING
LACE	

Panel Toppers

Any panel heading, whether pleated or hung with ties, tabs, or rings, can be embellished with simple elements to enhance and customize its appearance. This is a great option to spruce up store-bought or existing panels.

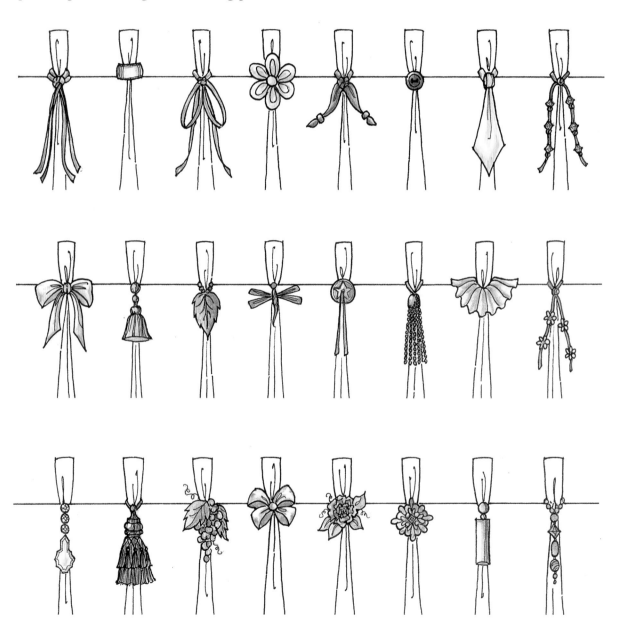

Welting

Welting is an important finishing detail that defines quality in window treatment design. It is an extra added touch that sets custom treatments apart from ready-mades. Welting is used to separate, define, or contain components of the treatment.

Cord Welting

A continuous narrow length of fabric that has been folded in half and into which a length of cording has been inserted. The fabric should be cut on the bias for optimal performance; however, fabric cut with the grain can be used if the pattern demands it.

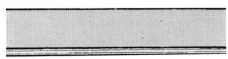

String Welt 1.8mm

Cord 4/32" – 6/32" – 10/32" – 12/32" – 16/32" – 22/32" Cord Welt

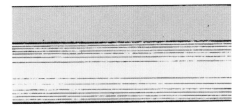

Jumbo Welt 1'–1 1/2"–2"

Ruched Cord Welt

Flat Welting

A narrow continuous length of fabric that has been folded in half and then folded, pleated, or gathered into a decorative trim.

Knife Edge Welt

Double Knife Edge Welt

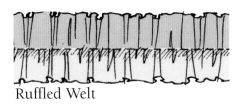

Ruffled Welt

Box-Pleated Welt

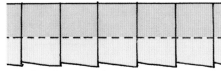

Knife Pleat Welt

Tying Back Side Panels

Drapery panels can be tied back or held back in many different ways. Each method produces its own unique look.

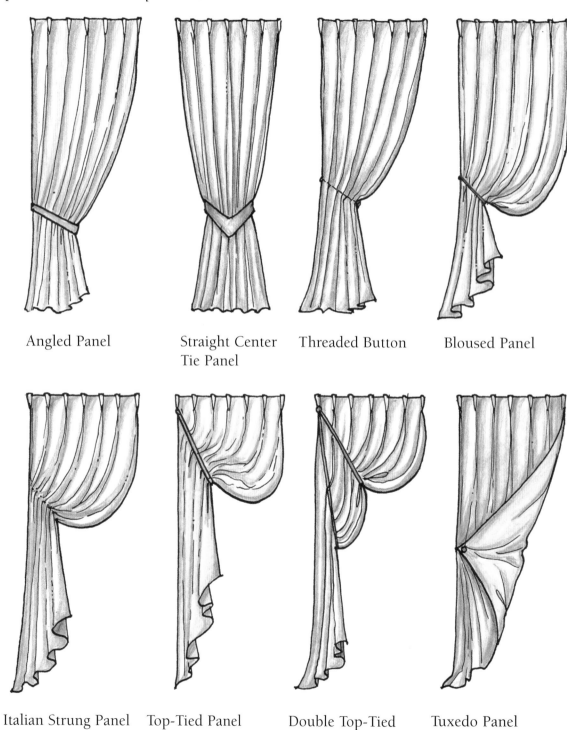

Angled Panel

Straight Center
Tie Panel

Threaded Button

Bloused Panel

Italian Strung Panel

Top-Tied Panel

Double Top-Tied
Panel

Tuxedo Panel

Tied-back side panels require some advance planning if they are meant to have a hem that lays flush with the floor or puddles.

- A straight bottom on the panel will result in a cascading bottom hem.

- Adding an angled section to the top or bottom of the panel will allow a straight hem.

- Add the angled section to the top of the panel when using a fabric with a horizontal pattern or stripe.

- When measuring for a straight hem, use string weight to plot the length required for the leading edge. Hold the string at the finished height of your panel and drape it according to your design to the floor. Measure the finished length of the string; add allowances for puddle and heading to calculate your cut length. Calculate the other side of the panel as you would for a straight panel. The difference between the two cut lengths will determine the angle needed.

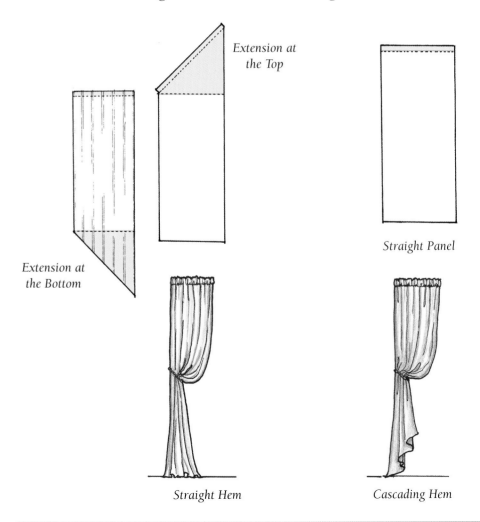

Extension at the Top

Extension at the Bottom

Straight Panel

Straight Hem

Cascading Hem

Tiebacks

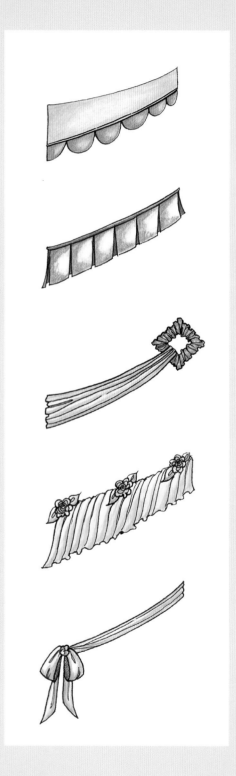

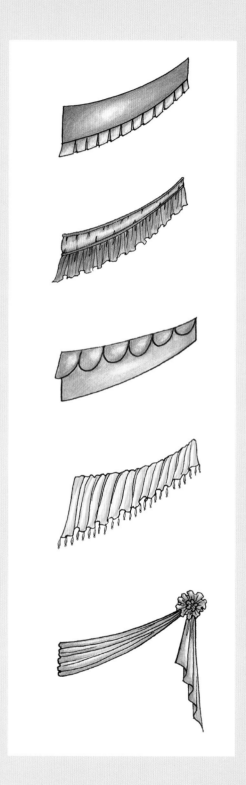

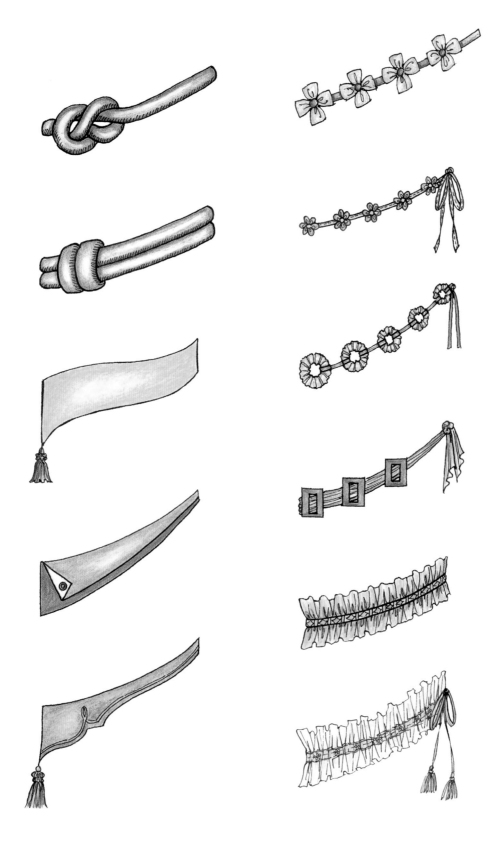

Banding, Borders, and Trims

Be creative with the placement of your banding, borders, and trims. Every variation creates a whole new look.

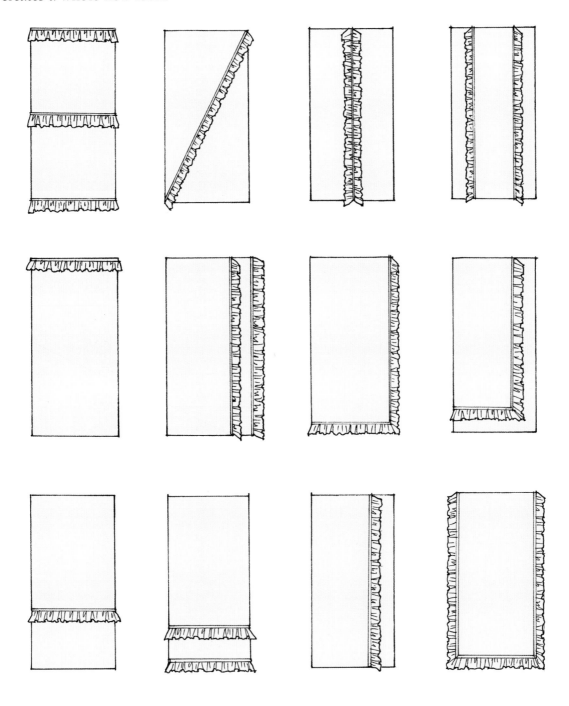

Borders

A border is a decorative embellishment applied to the hem or edge of a treatment. There are an infinite number of designs that can be used. Exercise your imagination and use borders as a way to create one-of-a-kind couture designs. Here are just a few combinations to consider:

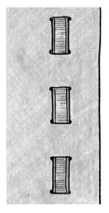

Grosgrain ribbon threaded through button holes

Alternating threaded ribbon and bows

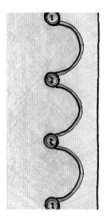

Inverted scallop overlay with buttons

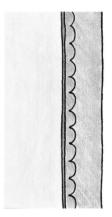

Contrasting band with scalloped overlay and welting

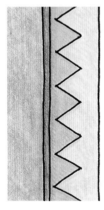

Contrasting banding with zigzag overlay and flat welt

Floral appliqués with round button centers

Contrast banding with lip cord insert

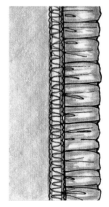

Ruched sleeve ruffle with decorative gimp

Hemmed edge
with blanket
stitching

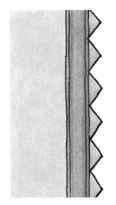

Zigzag edging with
a contrast band and
double welting

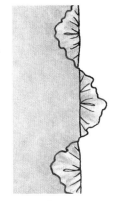

Accordion-
pleated scal-
loped ruffle

Flat tape or gimp
with ribbon
rosettes

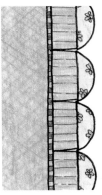

Scalloped edge with
contrasting inverted
box-pleated ruffle and
welting

Straight edge with
zigzag banding
and alternating
zigzag panel edge

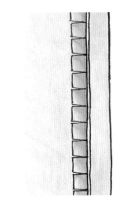

Back-facing inverted
box-pleated
ruffle with welting
and contrast banding

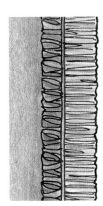

Ruched sleeve
ruffle with welt-
ing and ribbon
loop fringe

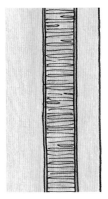

Shirred banding
with contrasting
welting

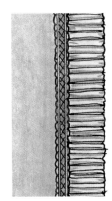

Ruched sleeve
ruffle with deco-
rative braid

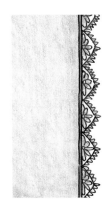

Flat lace trim
with welting

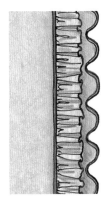

Scalloped banding
with welted edge
and contrasting
ruffle with welting

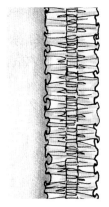

Double ruffle with
center shirring

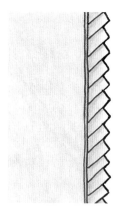

Zigzag angled
knife-pleated
edging with welt

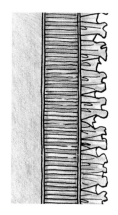

Ruffle with shirred
banding and
contrasting welt

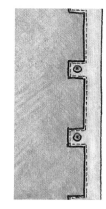

Shaped banding
with topstitching
and contrasting
buttons

Scalloped
knife-pleated ruffle

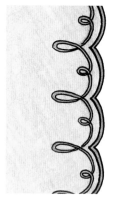

Scalloped wedge
with welting and
satouche braid
design

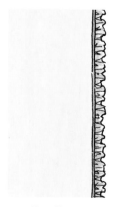

Small ruffle with
contrasting welt

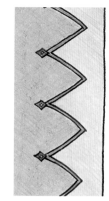

Shaped overlay
with contrasting
welted edge and
appliqués

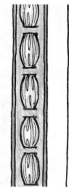

Inset contrasting
band with welting
and scarf threaded
through buttonholes

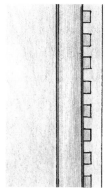

Scalloped banding
with welted edge
and single ruffle
with welting

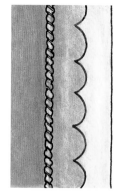

Contrast banding
with scalloped
overlay and cords
with lip insert

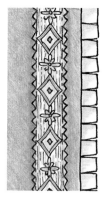

Tapestry ribbon
with inverted box
pleat ruffle

Rosettes, Bows, and Ties

Rosettes, bows, and ties are used to add visual interest, create rhythm, or provide a focal point to the treatment.

Knot	Twisted knot	Shirred pouf
Shirred rosette	Pleated rosette	Pleated double rosette
Choux	Double choux	Shirred spiral
Folded spiral with choux	Petal rosette	Daffodil rosette
Accordion fan	Peacock	Bunched fan

Maltese cross

Padded Maltese cross

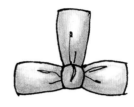

Trefoil

Pointed petal cross

Pointed petal rosette

Pointed trefoil

Flame trefoil

Pointed cross

Accordion bow

Maltese cross with
rosette

Double Maltese cross

Multi-ribbon bow

Ruched square

Ruched doughnut

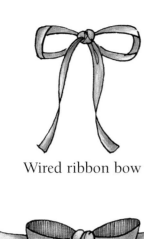

Wired ribbon bow

Knotted tie

Thin ribbon bow

Straight ribbon bow

Hanging ribbon bow

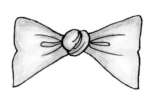

Bow tie

Triple petal bow

Bow with rosette

Shirred bow

Cinched bow

Double petal bow

Pointed tie

Double clipped tie

Double angled tie

Single-pointed tie

Passementerie

Passementerie is the historic French term for the vast category of decorative trims, tassels, and embellishments used to decorate window treatments and home furnishings.

Over the past few years there has been a resurgence and revitalization of the home décor trim industry, which has led to an unlimited range of styles and products to choose from. The main categories are:

Beaded Fringe	Gimps
Beaded Tapes	Pom-poms
Braids	Ribbons
Bullion	Rope
Cartouches	Rosettes
Cords	Tapes
Fringes	Tassels
Galons	Tiebacks

✦ Trim can be applied with adhesives, heat bonding tapes, by machine, or by hand.

✦ Be aware that most trim can be very delicate and is susceptible to fading and sun rot. Adjust your designs accordingly.

✦ Most trim is not washable and many styles are not dry cleanable. If using such trim on a treatment that must be washed or cleaned, apply the trim in a manner that makes it easily removed for cleaning such as hand tacking.

✦ Trim will create additional stiffness to the areas of fabric to which it is applied. Take the size, weight, and body of the trim you select into consideration and try to determine what effect it will have on your treatment.

✦ Trim can often shrink when taken off the bolt. Always order extra to avoid running short.

Braid

Gimp

Ribbon-wrapped cord with lip

Picot ribbon

Cord

Galon with scalloped brush

Cord with lip

Galon

Grosgrain ribbon

Moss fringe

Grosgrain-wrapped cord with lip

Jacquard looped fringe

Ribbon-Wrapped Cord with lip

Jacquard ribbon

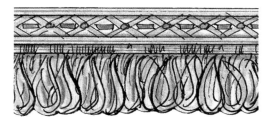

Brush fringe

Onion fringe

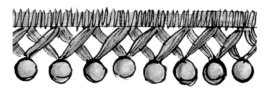

Ball fringe

Small tassel fringe

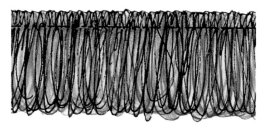

Loop fringe

Brush tassel fringe

Beaded gimp

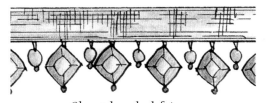

Short beaded fringe

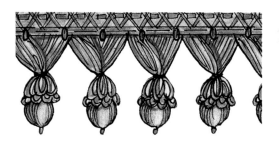

Ball and flower fringe

Long beaded fringe

Tassel fringe

Draped tassel fringe

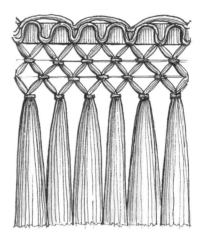

Tied tassel fringe

Graduated tassel fringe

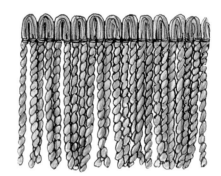

Bullion

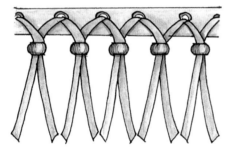

Faux leather tied fringe

Bell fringe

Brush and tassel fringe

Chainette tassel   Bell tassel   Beaded tassel   Key tassel

Beaded chair   Chair tie tassel   Beaded wire   Rosette tassel
tie tassel   tieback

Rosette   Button   Button rose

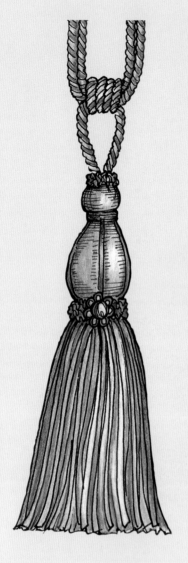

Single tassel tieback

Large key tassel

Double tassel tieback

Custom Ties and Tassels

Silk flower nose gay
with painted wooden
bead heading and
ribbon loop

Fabric circle tassel with
tassel fringe trim and
looped fringe top with
ribbon hanger

A bunch of silk grapes
with velvet leaves and a
looped fringe top

Bias-cut spiral
cascade tassel
with lace trim
headed with a
glass bead and
ribbon loop

Bias-cut spi-
ral cascade
tassel with
bullion trim
and ribbon
loop

Silk flower nose gay
embellished with
ribbons

Small embroidery
hoop covered with
wound ribbon with a
long bow

Looped ribbon bound
with a fabric-covered
wooden bead and
ribbon loop

Ghost tassel made with a
fabric circle cinched over
a wooden bead and tied
with a ribbon

Blown glass
beads threaded
on a ribbon tie

Drapery ring covered with
wound decorative cord
with a matching chair tie
looped over it

Drapery rings and
beads connected
with flat leather cord

Drapery ring with
ribbon ties looped
over it and secured
with beads

Drapery ring is used
to hang a necktie tail
with chandelier
crystals at the points

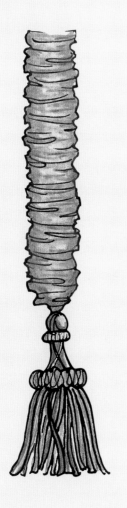

Shirred cord ended
with a key tassel

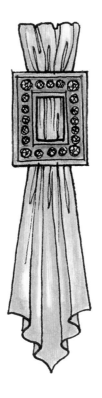

Small over-the-rod
cascade cinched with
an elaborate belt
buckle

Two simple velvet leaves
with silk flowers attached
to a ribbon

Hand-strung glass beads
with a cord tie

The Workroom

The Workroom

A workroom is a professional business specializing in the manufacturing of custom window treatments. Many workrooms provide services to designers and to the public, while some are exclusive to the design trade. The following are some tips to work effectively with your workroom to achieve your desired results.

- Always double check your yardage estimates with the workroom. Their methods of construction may require additional yardage that you are not aware of. Better to be safe than to run short of materials at the last minute.

- No two workrooms are the same. Find out what your workroom's individual standards are: hem and heading widths, fullness factors, product brands, etc. Be prepared to specify your preferred options if their standard option does not fit your requirements.

- Discuss your design ideas with your workroom professional. They may have great tips and cost-saving techniques that can be applied to your design. They may also prevent you from making some costly mistakes.

- Always sketch a scale drawing of the wall, the window, and your design to visualize its proportion and scale. It doesn't have to be a work of art! Just sketch it out on 4 x 4 square-inch graph paper at 1/4 inch scale.

- Always provide the workroom with a professional worksheet with a color-coded scale drawing of your design including complete specifications.

- Tag your COM (customers own material) and trims clearly, in at least two places with your contact information and job specifications to avoid your products being misplaced.

- Think about your lining choices before settling on "standard" lining. Find out which linings your workroom stocks and request samples to keep on hand.

- Have your workroom make small samples of your favorite pleats, headings, or panel styles to use as examples of their work to your clients.

✦ Identify your work. Order dressmaker labels with your name and contact information online and ask your workroom to sew them inside your treatments. This adds a couture touch and lets future owners of the home know who provided the treatments.

✦ Most workrooms are run in a very professional manner. Ask your workroom for a copy of their business license and proof of liability insurance and keep them on file. This will ensure you and your clients that you are using a legitimate business and that your products are insured while on their premises.

Worksheets

Once you have completed the design process and chosen all of the materials to be used in the construction of your treatment, you must be able to communicate your design clearly and effectively to your workroom.

- You can never provide too much information.

- Always use the same worksheet format so the workroom can become familiar with your system.

- Many workrooms will provide you with a worksheet system that they have found works well for them.

- Always go over each worksheet in person with your workroom and have them sign a copy.

- Always provide detailed, to-scale drawings showing key measurements.

- Always provide a separate color-coded drawing. Create a color system by choosing a different highlighter color for each fabric and trim to be used. Use the highlighter to color the areas on the drawing that correspond to fabric or trim for that color. This gives the workroom a quick visual reference that can cross language barriers and is easy to understand.

- Whenever possible, do not ship fabric or trim directly to your workroom. It is better to receive the goods yourself, make sure it is the correct product, and check it for flaws. Once the product is cut, it cannot be returned. The inconvenience of having to deliver it to your workroom yourself is well worth avoiding a costly mistake.

- Do not be afraid to visit your workroom periodically during construction of your treatments. Ask questions and take a good look at the work. Your workroom is just as invested as you are in producing an error-free product. Mistakes cost everyone time and money. Good communication is the key to avoiding them.

- Be prepared to make concessions. There are many times when a design looks great on paper but cannot be produced exactly as shown in reality. If your workroom tells you that a change in your design is necessary, there is usually a very good reason to do so.

Client Interview

CLIENT INTERVIEW SHEET

CLIENT	DATE
HOME PHONE	CEL PHONE
FAX	OFFICE PHONE
EMAIL	TYPE OF RES

HOME ADDRESS

	STATE	ZIP

BILLING ADDRESS

	STATE	ZIP

GATE CODE	ALARM CODE
SPOUSE	CHILDREN

SPECIAL INSTRUCTIONS

REFFERED BY	BIRTHDAY
BUDGET:	TIMELINE:

NOTES :

Workroom Service Request

Your Company Name Here

WORKROOM SERVICE REQUEST

Customer:					Phone:					Wrksht #:

Phone:			Room:		Window:		Workroom:			Drop Off:

	Finished Length	Finished Width	Return	IM / OM	L/R	Pair	Finial Length	Rod Diam		Pick Up:

Quantity: / Install:

Hardware:

Drawing:

Notes:

Fabric 1:   Yds.

Fabric 2:   Yds:

Trim 1:   Yds:

Trim 2:   Yds:

Lining:

Interlining:

C.O.M.

C.O.M. is an abbreviation for "customers own material" and is the term used to identify any fabric trim or hardware belonging to you or your customers that has not been provided by the workroom or manufacturer.

Always mark your fabric, or C.O.M., clearly and in multiple locations. Use a C.O.M. tag like the one shown below and staple a small cutting of the fabric to the tag in case it should come loose from the bolt. Make an extra tag with a cutting for your files.

Workrooms will always assume that the face of the fabric is rolled to the inside of the bolt, which is how fabric is usually shipped from the mill. If you are buying fabric from a fabric store, it may be rolled to the outside. In this case always mark the face clearly and note it on your worksheet and C.O.M. tag.

Trims such as braids, tapes, galloon, ribbon, and cord have a face side. If it is not clear which side is which, mark it clearly. Many times multicolored bullions and fringes can look very different from side to side. One color will dominate on one side more than the other. Mark the side you want to face up.

Always ask that your workroom save any un-used fabric and trim for you. It may come in handy later on, or it can be used for pillows or throws.

```
┌─────────────────────────────────┐
│          COM TAG                │
│                                 │
│  Designer:_____       │
│                                 │
│  Job:_____  │
│                                 │
│  _____          │
│                                 │
│  Room:_____         │
│                                 │
│  Work Order #:_____       │
│                                 │
│  PO#:_____         │
│                                 │
│  Vendor:_____        │
│                                 │
│  Pattern:_____        │
│                                 │
│  Notes:_____        │
│                                 │
└─────────────────────────────────┘
```

Window Treatment Product Worksheet

WINDOW TREATMENT PRODUCT WORKSHEET

CUSTOMER: _____ ORDER DATE: _____ INSTALL DATE: _____

ROOM: _____ WINDOW: _____ WORKROOM: _____

	MNFCT	FABRIC	COLOR	YDG.	PRICE	TOTAL	STATUS	X
FABRIC								
LINING								
INTERLINING								
TRIM								
HARDWARE								
LABOR								
INSTALLATION								
SUB TOTAL								
MARKUP								
TOTAL								

Cornice Treatment Worksheet

CORNICE WORKSHEET

Customer:	Room:	Window:	Workroom:	Worksheet #:
Phone:	Installer:		Installer Phone:	Drop Off:
Quantity:			Pick Up:	Install:

FAB 1 YDG: **FAB 2** YDG:

Drawing:

TRIM 1 YDG: **TRIM 2** YDG:

HDWR   **WOOD FINISH**

TUFTING   **MISC**

W	H	LONG PT	SHORT PT	RETURN

NOTES:

Soft Treatment Worksheet

SOFT TREATMENT WORKSHEET

								Phone:		Wrksht #:
Customer:			Room:		Window:					Drop Off:
Phone:	Length	Width	Return	IM / OM	L/R	# PLTS	Rod Diam	Rings	Tabs	Workroom:
Quantity:										Pick Up:
Scrf Hldr	Spcng	Extsn	Tie Back	Spcng	Extsn	Crown	Width	Extsn		Install:

Tabs | Ties | Pins

Drawing:

Hardware:

Notes:

Fabric 1:   Yds.   Fabric 2:   Yds:

Trim 1:   Yds: Trim 2:   Yds:

Lining: Yds: Interlining: Yds:

Copyright © 2007 The Design Directory of Window Treatments

Subcontractor Agreements

Working with subcontractors such as workrooms and installers should be approached in the same manner as with any business. You should always enter into a written agreement. It should identify the scope of services to be provided, as well as conditions of the relationship between yourself and the vendor.

Subcontractor Agreement

This agreement is made this _____ day of _____, 20____,
By and between _____ and _____
With it's principal place of business at _____
For a term of _____ months *from* the date above.

The parties above agree to as follows:

1. Work to be preformed. The subcontractor shall perform work and provide materials as set forth specifically on written purchase orders signed by the company. No other work shall be preformed unless in written change order.

2. Payment: Company shall remit payment within 30 days of receipt of payment from client for work preformed by subcontractor. If client objects to work preformed, or materials provided by subcontractor, and results in credit to customer, subcontractor's payment shall be accordingly adjusted.

3. Workmanship: All work preformed and materials provided by subcontractor shall be in a quality manner and as is standard to the trade. Company alone shall determine if work and materials comply with requirements.

4. Insurance: Subcontractor shall obtain and maintain insurance and hold harmless the company from any claims that may arise out of his/her or employer's work, for example:
   a. Any and all workman's compensation claims.
   b. Any personal Injury claims.
   c. Any claim arising from damages from injury or property damage.
   d. Any claims to damage of use of a vehicle.
   The above-required insurance shall be written for not less than limits of liability specified in a contract or required by company in the amount of 1 million dollars.

   Insurance Co: _____ Policy # _____

5. Independent Contractor, Subcontractor relationship with company shall be an independent contractor.

6. The Subcontractor is independently established in his/her own business of
   _____ persons other than the company.

7. The Subcontractor will not solicit or provide any services or product directly to the Company's clients. All bids must be presented by the Company only. This applies to any current and future bids or contracts.

In witness whereof, the parties have signed this agreement the day and year written above.

_____   _____
Contractor   Company

_____   _____
Address   Phone

_____   _____
License # (type)   Expiration / Renwal Date

Helpful Charts and Graphs

PLEAT TO FULLNESS CHART

(48" Fabric) 2-1/2x Fullness

Pleat-To	19	38	57	76	95	114	133	152	171	190	209	228	247	266	285
Widths	1	2	3	4	5	6	7	8	9	10	11	12	13	14	15

(48" Fabric) 3x Fullness

Pleat-To	15	30	45	60	75	90	105	120	135	150	165	180	195	210	225
Widths	1	2	3	4	5	6	7	8	9	10	11	12	13	14	15

(54" Fabric) 2-1/2x Fullness

Pleat-To	21	42	63	84	105	126	147	168	189	210	231	254	273	294	315
Widths	1	2	3	4	5	6	7	8	9	10	11	12	13	14	15

(54" Fabric) 3x Fullness

Pleat-To	17	34	51	68	85	102	119	136	153	170	187	204	221	238	255
Widths	1	2	3	4	5	6	7	8	9	10	11	12	13	14	15

STACKBACK CHART

Window Width	Total Stackback	Rod Face Width
38 inches	26 inches	64 inches
44	28	72
50	30	80
56	32	88
62	34	96
68	36	104
75	37	112
81	39	120
87	41	128
94	42	136
100	44	144
106	46	152
112	48	160
119	49	168
125	51	176
131	53	184
137	55	192
144	56	200
150	58	208
156	60	216
162	62	224
169	63	232
175	65	240
181	67	248
187	69	255

DRAPERY YARDAGE CHART

Finished Length	2	3	4	5	6	7	8	9	10	11	12	13	14	15
36"	3 ¼	4 ¾	6 ¼	7 ¾	9 ¼	10¾	12¼	13¾	15¼	16¾	18¼	19¾	21¼	22¼
40"	3 ½	5	6 ½	8	9 c	11	12 ½	14	15½	17	18½	20	21½	23
44"	3¾	5½	7¼	9	10¾	12 ½	14¼	16	17¾	19½	21¼	23	24¾	26½
48"	4	5¼	7 ½	9¼	11	12¾	14½	16¼	18	19¾	21½	23¼	25	26¾
52"	4	6	8	10	12	14	16	18	20	22	24	26	28	30
56"	4¼	6½	8½	10¾	12¾	15	16¾	19	21¼	23¼	25½	27½	29¾	31¾
60"	4¼	6¼	9	11¼	13½	15¾4	18	20	22¼	24½	26¾	29	31¼	33½
64"	4¾	7	9½	11¾	14	16½	18¾	21	23½	25¾	28	30½	32¾	35
68"	5	7½	10	12¼	14¾	17¼	19¾	22	24½	27	29½	32	34¼	36¾
72"	5¼	7¾	10¼	13	15½	18	20½	23	25¾	28¼	30¾	33¼	36	38½
76"	5½	8	10¾	13½	16	18¾	21½	24	26¾	29½	32	34¾	37½	40
80"	5¼	8½	11¼	14	16¾	19½	22¼	25	28	30¾	33½	36¼	39	41¾
84"	6	8¾	11¾	14½	17½	20¼	23¼	26	29	32	34¾	37¾	40½	43½
88"	6	9	12	15	18	21	24	27	30	33	36	39	42	45
92"	6¼	9½	12½	15¾	18¾	22	25	28	31¼	34¼	37½	40½	43¾	46¾
96"	6½	9¾	13	16¼	19½	22¾	26	29	32¼	35½	38¾	42	45¼	48½
100"	6¼	10	13½	16¼	20	23½	26¾	30	33½	36¾	40	43½	46¾	50
104"	7	10½	14	17¼	20¾	24¼	27¾	31	34 ½	38	41½	45	48¼	51¾
108"	7¼	10¾	14¼	18	21½	25	28½	32	35¾	39¼	42¾	46¼	50	53½

Window Treatment Measurement Form

WINDOW MEASUREMENT WORKSHEET

CUSTOMER: _____ PHONE: _____

ROOM: _____ WALL: _____ WINDOW: _____

Your Company Name Here

DATE: _____ WRKRM: _____

INSIDE HEIGHT																							
INSIDE WIDTH																							
OUTSIDE HEIGHT																							
OUTSIDE WIDTH																							
INSIDE DEPTH																							
OUTSIDE CASING DEPTH																							
TOP OF WDW TO CLNG																							
BTM OF WDW TO FLOOR																							
LFT EDGE TO WALL / WNDW																							
RT EDGE TO WALL / WNDW																							
WALL TO WALL																							
FLOOR TO CEILING																							
FLOOR TO CROWN HEIGHT																							
BASEBOARD HEIGHT																							
WAINSCOATING HEIGHT																							
MULTIPLE WDWS																							
OUTLETS																							
SWITCHES																							
AIR REGISTERS																							

www.designdirectory4.com

Copyright © 2007 The Design Directory of Window Treatments

Installer Checklist

INSTALLER CHECKLIST	Installer		Installer Phone	
Client	**Address**		**Client Phone**	
Install Date	**Time**		**Room**	
Window			**Ladder Height**	
Top Treatment			Install Height	
Stationary Side panels			Install Height	Puddle
Functional Sheers			Install Height	Draw
Functional Draperies			Install Height	Draw
Shades		IM / OM	Cord	Draw
Blinds		IM / OM	Cord	Draw
Other			**Weight**	**Oversize**
Decorative Hardware	Rod Diam		Rod Width	
Finials	Rings		Brackets	
Hold Backs	Scarf Holders		Medallions	
Crown	Hooks		Other	
Functional Hardware			Install Height	
Traverse Rod Width	# of Carriers		Projection	
Cord Length	Cord Position		Draw	
Sash Rods	Brackets		Wall Construction	
Floor Clearance				

Special Instructions:

Workroom Product Receipt

Your Company Name Here

WORKROOM PRODUCT RECEIPT

Designer:

Customer :

Workroom:

Date :

Worksheet #:

Item	Vendor	Description	Color	Ydg

Received By

Time / Date

www.designdirectory4u.com

Glossary and Resources

Glossary

Allowance: A customary variation from an "exact" measurement, taken for the purpose of anticipated needs.

Apron: The wood-trim molding below the windowsill.

Appliqué: To sew or fuse a piece of cutout cloth to another piece of cloth. Also the term used for the piece of cloth applied.

Arch window: A window in the shape of a half-circle. Often placed over a door or other windows for decoration and additional light.

Arched valance: A valance treatment that is arched along the lower edge.

Austrian shade: A fabric shade known for its formal appearance and vertical shirring between the scallops. Usually made of sheer fabric and classified as a sheer under treatment.

Austrian valance: A soft, stationary valance fabricated like the Austrian shade, with a vertical row of shirred fabric that forms a scalloped bottom edge.

Awning window: Windows that are hinged on top and swing outward to open; usually rectangular and wider than they are long.

Back tack (aka backstitch): Stitching at the beginning or the end of the seam done by stitching backwards and forwards in order to lock and secure the seam.

Balloon shade: a type of fabric shade known for the permanent poufs that form at the bottom of the shade as it is raised. The shade has permanent poufs in it when it is down as well. The heading may be any type as long as the fabric has the correct fullness. Some examples are box pleated, gathered, and smocked.

Balloon valance: A soft, stationary valance fabricated like the balloon shade that is known for the poufs at the bottom edge.

Banding: Strips of fabric sewn to the edge of drapery and curtains. Banding is made with a fabric complementary to the fabric of the main portion of the window treatment.

Banner valance: A series of fabric triangles attached to a mounting board or threaded on a rod. Also called a handkerchief valance.

Bar-tack: A sewing machine operation of repeated stitches concentrated to secure the lowest portion of drapery pleats.

Baton: A rod or wand used to hand draw traverse draperies.

Bay window: A group of windows set at angles to each other.

Bed skirt (aka dust ruffle): A skirt that covers the box springs of the mattress and the bed frame.

Bendable lauan (aka wiggle board): Bendable plywood usually ripped into return sizes and used for arched treatments. It can also be used to form a curved face on cornices and coronas.

Bias cut: Fabric cut at a 45-degree angle of the fabric weave. This cut of fabric will have give to it, allowing swags to drape better and cording to hug curves better. Prints should be checked before cutting on the bias. Some upright prints can be cut on the bias and look great; others cannot.

Board line: The line drawn on the pattern pieces to indicate where the treatment will be placed at the front edge of the board.

Bishop's sleeve: A drapery in which each side panel can be tied back in one or more places in order to create a poufy appearance above the tieback. Allow extra length for poufing over the tieback.

Blackout drapery or shade: Drapery or shade made with room-darkening fabric. The lining of a window treatment is usually made of the blackout material.

Bottom hem: The turned part that forms a finished edge at the bottom of drapery.

Boston edge (aka micro cord): 1.8mm welt cord.

Bowed cornice: A cornice with convex or concave curves on the face.

Bow window: A type of window that is curved or semicircular.

Box pleats: Pleats formed by two folded edges facing each other. Box pleats are evenly spaced and stitched.
1) Closed box pleats: Pleats of fabric pressed flat so the edges of the pleats touch each other all the way across the front and all the way across the back of the treatment (three times the fullness).
2) Open box pleats: Pleats of fabric taken on the front of the treatment and pressed flat against the front but leaving a space between the edges of the pleats on the front.
3) Inverted box pleats: Pleats of fabric taken in the back of the treatment and pressed flat against the back but the sides do not touch.

Braid: A flat decorative trim that can be used to embellish curtain window treatments. Gimps and woven ribbons can fall in this category.

Break: The extra length added to draperies so they lay on the floor just 1 inch to a few inches.

Breaking the buckram: The practice of creasing the buckram between pleats in order to make the pleats fall properly when draperies are opened. Usually done at installation.

Bracket: Metal piece attached to the wall or casing to support a drapery or curtain rod, blinds, or shade.

Brighton shades (aka London shades): Similar to balloon shades but without the pleats, rings, and cords along the sides. This allows the sides to fall in relaxed tails. The center section is usually wider than the sides.

Brocade: A rich fabric with an embossed design, usually gold or silver.

Bullion fringe: A long, thick fringe of individual cords or twisted cords.

Bump: Cotton lining added to curtain panels to add body to a curtain.

Buckram (aka crinoline): See "crinoline" for definition.

Buckram: A coarse cotton, hemp, or linen cloth stiffened with glue or a glue-like substance used in the header of pleated curtains. Buckram can give lasting shape to a valance.

Butterfly pleat: Pleat with two rather than three folds.

Café curtain: A traversing or non-traversing short drapery, designed as a tier, with various heading styles.

Café rings: Clip-on or sew-on rings used to hang café curtains.

Café rod: A small, round decorative rod used to mount café curtains that do not have a rod pocket. Café rods are meant to be seen and add a decorative touch to the window treatment.

Calico: A plain-weave fabric made from raw, unbleached cotton.

Canopy: A fabric bed treatment that goes over the top of a specialty bed frame.

Cantonniere: A three-sided shaped or straight cornice that "frames" the window across the top and to the floor on both sides. It is usually made of hardboard then padded and covered with fabric.

Cape Cod curtain: A café curtain with a ruffle around each edge.

Carriers (aka slides): Small runners installed in the traverse rod, which hold a drapery pin or hook.

Cartridge pleat: A fold of cloth sewn into place to create fullness in a drapery. This is a round pleat 2 to 2 1/2 inches in depth. Stuffing the pleat with buckram that may be removed for cleaning creates a round shape.

Cascade (aka tails): Often used with swags, a fall of knife-pleated fabric that descends in a zigzag line from the drapery heading or top treatment. They should be self- or contrast lined.

Casement: 1) Fabric casement: A cloth drapery that is an open-weave material but more opaque than a sheer. **2)** Window casement: A type of vertically hinged window, whose panes open by sliding sideways or cranking outward.

Casing: 1) Drapery casing: A pocket made in fabric for a curtain rod, weight board, or drawstring. **2)** Window casing: A wooden frame around the window.

Cathedral window: Slanted window often found with cathedral ceilings; top of window follows the slope of the ceiling.

Center draw (aka split draw): A traversing pair of draperies that draw open from and close to a window's center point.

Center support: A piece of hardware that supports a traverse rod from above to prevent the rod form sagging, yet does not interfere with the rod operation. A wood or metal support is used for poles and metal rods that do not traverse; they are supported from underneath the rod.

Chain weights: A continuous chain of small heavy beads covered in a casing; used to prevent billowing in lightweight fabric.

Chenille: Chenille fabric is woven with fuzzy yarns. It is soft to the touch like velour. Chenille can be plain or patterned.

Chintz: A cotton fabric, often floral, that is coated with resin to give it shine.

Clearance: Distance from the back of the rod/pole to the wall.

Cleat: A metal or plastic hook placed at the side of the window to hold the cords of a shade or curtain.

Clerestory windows: A series of small windows that let in light and air, usually high up on the wall to allow privacy.

Cloud shade: Similar to a balloon shade; forms poufs at the bottom of the treatment as the shade is raised, but the bottom is straight across when it is down.

Cloud valance: A stationary top treatment similar to the cloud shade that cannot be raised or lowered.

C.O.M. (aka COM): Customer's own material. (MB fix this in previous)

Combination rods: Two or three rods on one pair of brackets; used to create layered window treatments. Combination sets can include traverse only, both traverse and curtain rods, or several curtain rods.

Comforter: A bed covering without a pillow tuck that is usually a throw style and does not cover the entire bedside. It covers the mattress plus 3 or 4 inches on the sides and foot of the bed.

Concave curve: An inward curve (a bow window has an inward curve).

Continental rod: Flat curtain rods that protrude from the wall to add depth and interest to rod pocket treatments. The most common widths are 2 1/2 inches and 4 1/2 inches.

Contrast lining: A decorative fabric used as a lining or decking when parts of it may show from the front of the top treatment.

Conventional traverse rod: A cord-controlled drapery rod. Both length and the distance it projects from the wall are adjustable. Available in one- or two-way draw.

Convex curve: An outward curve.

Cording (aka welt cord): A rope that is covered with fabric, also referred to as piping or welting.

Cord cleat: A piece of hardware attached to the wall around which window treatment cords can be secured. (For safety, use cleats to keep the cords out of children's reach.)

Cord lock: A piece of hardware mounted to the head rail of a shade through which the operating cords run. When the cords are pulled up, they secure the shade at the desired location.

Corner windows: Windows that meet at right angles at the corner of a room.

Cornice: A box treatment usually constructed of wood that can be padded and upholstered and usually installed across the top of a window to conceal the drapery, shade, or blind hardware.

Cottage curtains: Treatment combining café curtains over the lower part of the window, with tieback curtains or a valance over them.

Cotton: A natural-fiber fabric made from fibers in the boll of the cotton plant.

Coverlet: A bedcovering with a pillow tuck and a short drop that covers the mattress but not the box springs. This is usually used in conjunction with a bed skirt.

Crinoline (aka buckram): A heavily sized or stiff fabric used as a foundation for pleats in draperies.

Crosswise grain (aka fillers, woof, weft): The threads of a woven fabric that run perpendicular to the selvage. The fabric has a slight give in the crosswise grain.

Curtain: Usually unlined, a curtain is a panel of hemmed fabric hung from a rod at the top of a window. Panels can be floor length or end at the windowsill.

Curtain drop: The length of a curtain window treatment from the hanging system to the bottom edge.

Custom-made draperies: Draperies made to order in a workroom or decorator shop.

Custom-made treatments: products made to exactly fit window dimensions. They include draperies, pleated shades, vertical blinds, and mini-blinds.

Cut length: The length of fabric needed to construct a window treatment. The cut length includes the length of the window treatment, as well as the extra amount needed for headers and hems.

Cuts: The number of widths of fabric needed to construct a window treatment.

Cut allowance: The amount of fabric added to finished measurements for hems and headings.

Cut drop: The finished bottom of curtain window treatments, plus allowances for hems and headings.

Cut length (aka cut): The length of the fabric cut after allowances have been added for heading, hem, and repeats.

Cutout return: A buttonhole or rectangular cutout at the top return of the panel or top treatment to allow the return to go back to the wall in a pole-mounted treatment.

Cut width: The complete amount of fabric needed for treatment width, including hems and/or any other allowances.

Damask: A woven fabric made from wool, silk, or cotton. The special weave gives the fabric a raised appearance.

Decking: 1) Top treatment: A contrast or self-fabric sewn to the bottom of the top treatment and pressed to the back to form a hem. This should be used when parts of the back side of the treatment may show from the front view. 1) Bed skirt: The fabric that covers the box springs on a dust ruffle or bed skirt and to which the bed skirt is attached.

Decorative hardware: Hardware (such as swag holders, rods, poles, tiebacks, and rings) that can add aesthetic appeal to a window fashion, as well as serve functional purposes.

Decorative holdbacks: Decorative hardware mounted to the side of the window to hold a swag or to hold back drapery panels.

Decorative traverse rod: A cord-operated rod designed so draperies ride below it on decorative rings, allowing the rod to show whether the draperies are open or closed.

Dormer window: An upright window that breaks the surface of a sloping roof.

Double fullness: Using fabric twice the measured width of the window.

Double hem: Folding the fabric over twice in equal amounts. A 4-inch double hem would utilize 8 inches of fabric.

Double-hung draperies: Two sets of draperies, usually a sheer fabric under an opaque fabric, both operating separately.

Double-hung window: The most common style of window; two sashes move up and down.

Double top heading: This heading is commonly used for both pinch pleat and rod pocket draperies where the heading has another full layer of fabric under the visible layer on the back side.

Dowel: An unfinished, round wooden rod in various diameters and lengths.

Dowel rod: A slender rod placed inside the fabric pocket to raise or lower a shade.

Drapability: The ability of a fabric to hang in pleasing folds.

Drapery: Proper name for a long window covering; e.g., pinch-pleated drapery.

Drapery hardware: Functional hardware that is either used to support hard or soft window fashions (such as traverse rods, rings, hooks, etc.) or to support other hardware (such as end brackets, angle irons, pulleys, etc.)

Drapery hooks: Pin-on and slip-on hardware used to hang drapery from the rods.

Draping: Technique of looping and securing fabric in graceful curves and folds.

Draw draperies: Panels of fabric that will open and close, usually on a traverse rod.

Draw-up (aka take-up): The loss in measurement as a result of the method of mounting and/or fabrication. This usually happens when gathering fabric on a rod.

Drop: A term for length commonly used in reference to valances.

Drop match: A drop match is one in which when the width is cut straight across by the print. The pattern will not line up perfectly to be seamed at the selvage. The pattern repeat does not match until down 1/2 of the vertical pattern repeat. Therefore, additional yardage is required. Add 1/2 pattern repeat per cut. This is commonly found in fabrics that coordinate with wallpaper. It is usually designated in the sample books (but not always) as a drop match.

Dropped dust board cornice: A cornice with a decorative that sometimes requires the dust board to be lower than usual. (Some workrooms use this method with arched top cornices.)

Dust board: The portion of the mount board or cornice to which the legs and/or the face are attached.

Duvet: A non-decorative throw-style comforter designed to be used with a decorative removable cover.

Duvet cover: A slipcover for a removable comforter or duvet.

Dye lots: A batch of fabric printed at the same time. Each time a new printing is done, the fabric is classified with a new die lot. Fabrics from different die lots can vary in color. If color matching is important for your project, always get a cutting of the die lot you will order from.

Elbow ends (aka elbow bracket): Added to a wood pole, metal or PVC, this section is a continuation of the same shape that will turn the corner, providing the return and support.

End brackets: The two supporting pieces of hardware that hold a drapery rod to the wall or ceiling. They control the amount of projection.

End housing: Refers to the box parts at the extreme ends of a traverse drapery rod. They enclose the pulleys through which the cords run.

Envelope fold: A method of folding banding for application. The 1/2-inch seam allowance is pressed down on one side only. The remainder of the band is then folded double with the remaining raw edge going under the 1/2-inch seam allowance to meet the fold to create the finished width.

Envelope shades: Curtains attached to a mounting board and hung as a pair of flat panels. The bottom inside corners are then pulled out to the sides and hooked to the wall.

Euro pleat: A free-flowing drapery pleat, with or without crinoline, that has either two or three folds and is tacked within 1/2 inch from the top.

Eyebrow window: Arched top window with elongated width. Not a true half-circle.

Extender curtain rod: Piece of curtain rod that fits onto another rod to lengthen it.

Fabrication: The process of manufacturing raw goods into a finished product.

Fabric panel: The result of all fabric widths sewn together to make curtain window treatments.

Face fabric: The decorative fabric on a treatment that "faces" into the room. The lining is behind it.

Fascia: A vertical board that covers the curtain heading.

Facing: A piece of fabric stitched to a raw edge and turned to the back side to form a finished edge. The diagonals of jabots or cascades are sometimes faced to show a contrast in the angles.

False cord (aka flat welt or flat trim): A flat, folded fabric stitched in the seam the same as a welt cord, minus the cord. This gives the look of welt without the bulk.

Fan curtains: The same as the fan shade, but used on half-circle windows with the fan facing up. A curved curtain rod is required to install fan curtains.

Fan folded: A back-and-forth fold, like an accordion. Pinch-pleated draperies are folded this way by folding pleat to pleat. This helps to train the folds of the drapery and makes handling the drapery easier and neater for installation.

Fan shades: Arcs of fabric pulled together in the center by cords and rings fastened to the back of the shades. The arc, or fan, faces down. When lowered, the shade becomes a flat panel.

Festoon: A decorative valance made of folded fabric that hangs in a graceful curve over the window.

Flat roman shade: A tailored fabric shade that hangs flat at the window. Soft pleats form at the bottom as the shade is raised.

Finial: Decorative end of a pole, usually ornamental and affixed to the end of a rod, serving to keep drapery rings from falling off the rod.

Finish: Product applied to fabric as a protection against watermarks and fading.

Finished drop line: The place where the curtain stops.

Finished length: The length after draperies have been made.

Finished width: The actual width after the treatment is finished.

Flame-retardant fabric: Fabric that will not burn. It can be inherently flame retardant, which means the actual fiber from which it was made is a flame-retardant fiber, e.g., polyester, or be treated to become flame retardant, which usually changes the fibers and makes the fabric stiff.

Flat fell seam: A seam that gives extra strength to a seam.

French doors: Usually used in pairs, the doors are made almost entirely of glass panes and open outward. They often open onto a porch or patio.

French pleat: See pinch pleat.

French seam: A way of stitching fabric together with the seam hidden from view. Used on sheer fabrics.

Fringe: Decorative trim used on the edges/hem of curtains, pillows, lampshades, and rugs.

Front width: The width of the valance board without returns.

Fullness: The amount of extra fabric added to a finished measurement to create the desired "full" effect. Standard custom fullness is 2 1/2 to 3 times the total width of a treatment.

Gather: Bringing fabric into a tighter position to add fullness.

Gathered roman shade: Shade made by shirring fabric onto horizontal ribs before assembling as a working Roman shade.

Gathering tape: A heading tape that creates a ruffling effect.

Gingham: Plain-weave cotton cloth with a checked pattern.

Glass curtains: An old term for the draperies underneath draw draperies or stationary panels, known today as sheers.

Goblet pleat (aka cartridge pleat with bottom tack): A fold of cloth sewn into place to create fullness in a drapery. This is a round pleat 2 to 2 1/2 inches in depth and tacked or pinched at the bottom. Stiffing made from tissue, Dacron, or similar material that can be removed for cleaning may be inserted into the pleat in order to maintain the round or "goblet" shape.

Grain: The direction of threads in a fabric. Can be crosswise or lengthwise.

Griege goods: Fabrics, regardless of color, that have been woven on a loom and have received no wet or dry finishing applications. Some griege goods have names such as "print cloth" and "soft-filled sheeting," which are used only for the griege goods. Other griege goods' names, such as "lawn," "broadcloth," and "sateen," are also used for the finished cloth.

Grommet: Brass or chrome hole reinforcements at the top of a curtain.

Half-drop match: One in which the pattern itself drops down 1/2 the repeat on the horizontal but does match at the selvage. It is a concern when planning cuts for horns, pelmets, empire swags, box pleats, etc., when the same design or motif is needed on each piece. It is usually designated in the sample books as a half drop.

Hand-draw draperies: A drapery treatment pulled open or closed by hand or with a baton.

Header: The ruffle edge that extends above a rod pocket.

Heading: The way a treatment is finished at the top; e.g., rod pocket draperies can have single or double tops. Also a decorative element, e.g., smocked heading.

Headrail: The "board" to which shades are attached. The size is given according to the measurement of the return.

Hem: The finished sides and bottom edge of a drapery.

Hidden single top (aka pillow-cased): A type of buckram heading for pinch pleat draperies where the lining goes all the way to the top of the heading. There are 4 inches of face fabric and lining covering the buckram inside the panel.

Hopper windows: Hinged from the bottom of the window and opened inward from the top. The reverse of awning windows.

Hobbled (aka soft fold): A roman shade with permanent soft folds all the way up the shade.

Holdback: A decorative piece of hardware used to hold back draperies or hold up swags.

Hook and loop tape fastener (Velcro): Composed of two tape strips, one with a hook nap and the other with a loop nap. When pressed together, they grip firmly to each other.

Horn: Smooth, tapered portion of a top treatment that resembles a horn or bell shape. It can be made and attached separately or sewn in.

Hourglass curtain: A curtain panel anchored top and bottom and pulled tight in the middle with a tieback to reveal a triangular area of light on each side.

Inside measurement: Measurement for a treatment so the window facing would be exposed after the treatment is installed.

Inside mount (aka IM): Location of hardware and treatment are inside a structure, usually a window frame or cornice board. Mounting a treatment wall to wall is also treated as an inside mount.

Interfacing: A stiffener fabric that is either sewn or fused on to give body to fabrics.

Interlining: A soft, flannel-like fabric put between the face fabric and lining of a drapery to add luxurious body. Interlinings add to a quality look, give weight, protect from fading, and help to insulate. Interlining also comes in heavier weights called bump and table felt.

Jabots (aka pelmets): Additional optional pieces of a top treatment, often shaped like a tie, cone, cylinder, or mini-cascade, that are generally used between and over swags as decoration and hide seams.

Jalousie: A type of window or storm door featuring a series of moveable glass slats.

Jamb: Interior side of a door or window frame.

Kerf (kerfs, kerfing, kerfed): A channel created by a saw. These cuts are usually about 1/2 to 1 inch apart and halfway through the thickness of the board. They allow the board to be bent to desired shapes.

Kick pleat: An inverted pleat used at the corner of a cascade or return. The center of this pleat "kicks out" as it turns the corner and hangs to give the effect of an additional pleat.

Knotting: A technique used when looping and arranging fabric panels.

Lambrequin: A top treatment that is constructed on a wood frame, padded and covered with fabric.

Lath: The top of a shade is fitted to this piece of wood, which is usually 2 inches x 1 inch. The lath can be attached to the wall, ceiling, or window frame.

L bracket (aka angle irons): A metal bracket in the shape of an L, used to install a valance and cornices.

Leading edge: Opposite of return edge. The leading edges of a pair of pinch pleat draperies are the two edges that overlap. On stationary panels, they frame the glass.

Lengthwise grain (aka warp): The threads in a woven fabric that run parallel to the selvages. Fabrics are stronger along the lengthwise grain.

Lining: A fabric that is used for the back of the window treatment. This fabric should be compatible with the face fabric.

Lip: The twill tape attached to ready-made twisted rope cord used as a seam allowance; also refers to the seam allowance of a self-welt cord.

London shades: Similar to balloon shades but without the pleats, rings, and cords along the sides. This allows the sides to fall in relaxed tails. The center section is usually wider than the sides.

Long point (aka deep point): The measurement of a treatment at its deepest area.

Master carrier: Two arms that overlap in the center of a rod when draperies are closed, allowing draperies to overlap and close completely.

Memory stitch (aka flagging): A stitch usually done by hand in the back of the drapery, used to keep the lining and face in even folds.

Mending plate: A flat metal strip with holes for screws; used to join two pieces of lumber.

Micro cord (aka Boston edge): 1.8mm shade cord (normally used for stringing roman and balloon shades) that is covered with fabric and used in the same manner as standard fabric cord.

Millennium tape: A double-sided bonding tape made by 3M that is used by burnishing or rubbing it in. The longer this tape is on the fabric, the stronger the bond becomes.

Mitering: The joining of two surfaces evenly in an angle.

Mounting board: A wooden board installed inside or out of the window frame to which curtains are attached.

Mullion: The vertical wood or masonry sections between two window frames.

Multi-draw: A simultaneous opening and closing of several draperies on one rod at one time.

Muntin: The horizontal and vertical wood strips that separate panes of glass in a window.

Nap: A fabric with a texture or design that runs in one direction, such as corduroy and velvet. A fabric with a nap will often look different when viewed from various directions. When using a fabric with a nap, all pieces must be cut and sewn together so the nap runs in only one direction.

Nominal lumber: The actual measurement of stock boards differs from the nominal measurement. A 1 x 2 board is actually 3/4 inch x 1/2 inch; a 1 x 4 board is actually 3/4 inch x 3 1/2 inches; a 1 x 6 board is actually 3/4 inches x 5 1/2 inches; and a 1 x 8 board is actually 3/4 inch x 7 1/4 inches. Be sure to measure the board for accuracy.

Off-center-draw: Draperies that traverse to a non-centered point.

One-way-draw: One panel of drapery designed to draw one way.

Opera draperies: Draperies that, when raised, form scallops at the bottom, with the highest point in the middle and progressively lower scallops to each side, forming and inside arch.

Outside measurement: Measurements taken of the outside perimeter of the window frame so that the treatment will cover all window facings.

Outside mount (aka OSM): The hardware for treatment is mounted on the outside of the window on the frame or wall, and the treatment is not against any structure on the ends.

Over draperies: the topmost draperies in a double or combination drapery treatment.

Overlap: The portion of fabric that overlaps (crosses over) in the middle of a pair of draperies when they are closed. When two swags crossover each other on a board or pole, that is the crossover, or overlap, area. The standard overlap for Kirsch and Graber traverse rods is 3 1/2 inches.

Pagoda cornice: A cornice with face and sides that flare outward and/or upward.

Pair width: Rod width plus one overlap and two returns. This is a measurement you would get if you took two panels of a pair of pinch pleat draperies and you laid them down end to end widthwise, not overlapping. When closed, the draperies should hug the traverse rod.

Palladian window: A series of windows with an arch on top.

Panel: One half of a pair of draperies or curtains, even though it may consist of several widths of fabric.

Panel width: The pair width divided by 2. This is the finished width of a panel of draperies.

Passementerie (aka trims): The French term for a range of decorative cords, bands, and tassels used on window fashions and furnishings to give definition or add decorative detail.

Pattern repeat (aka repeat): The distance between any given point in a design and where that exact point first appears again. Repeats can be horizontal or vertical.

Pelmet: A panel that covers the top of a curtain. Also called a cornice.

Pencil pleats: Pleats created using a special tape sewn to the heading of a valance or curtain. When the tape is drawn up, it creates a narrow row of folds resembling a row of pencils laid side by side.

Picture window: A type of window with a large center glass area with usually two smaller glass areas on each side.

Pillowcase (aka pillowslip): The technique where face fabric and lining fabric are seamed together, usually with a 1/2-inch seam, and then turned and pressed so the seam becomes the very edge of the item.

Pillowcase heading: The heading of a pinch pleat drapery is pillowcased with the buckram stitched in the seam and may have a seam allowance from 1/2 inch to 1 inch.

Pin-on-hook: A metal pin to fasten draperies to a rod. It pins into the drapery pleat and hooks onto the traverse carrier, café rod, or to a ring.

Pinch pleat (aka French pleat): A drapery heading where the basic pleat is on the right side of the fabric and is divided into three smaller, equal folds sewn together at the bottom edge.

Piping: A term used in the apparel industry for cording.

Pleat: A fold of cloth sewn in place to create fullness.

Pleated balloon shade: A balloon shade made with box pleats.

Pleated roman shade: A roman shade with horizontal pleats, usually 4 to 8 inches deep, accented by stitching at the front and back of each crisp pleat; sometimes referred to as a Venetian (aka tucked) roman or a stitched roman.

Pleat to: A finished width of the fabric after it has been pleated.

Pleat to pleat: The measurement from the first pleat to the last pleat.

Pleater tape: Pocketed heading material designed to be used with slip-in pleating hooks.

Pleater tape: A stiffened drapery heading that makes it easier to create pinch pleats. Space between pleats is pre-measured, and woven-in pockets hold pleating hooks that fasten onto the drapery rod.

Plinth: A square of decorative wood installed at the corners of a window frame.

Poplin: Cotton fabric with corded surface.

Pouf: The three-dimensional informal scallop created by the way the treatment hangs; e.g., balloon valances and shades.

Pouf valance: A top treatment similar to the cloud, but the effect is one continuous pouf rather that separate poufs, and the pouf valance does not have a skirt.

Pressing: Lifting and lowering an iron set at an appropriate temperature in an overlapping pattern to avoid stretching fabric while ironing, as sliding the iron up and down over the fabric) would.

Priscilla curtains: A pair of extra-wide, ruffled, tieback curtains hung on crisscross curtain rods so the panels crisscross in the center. Often used with an attached valance.

Projection (aka return): The distance from the front of the window treatment to the wall.

Proportion: The size relationship of one part of an object to other parts of the object.

Puddle: Formed by drapery panels that are long enough to literally lie on the floor. Extra length must be added, from 1 to 18 inches, depending upon the effect desired.

Pull: The knob on the end of the cord used to operate shades or draperies. It also refers to the side from which a shade is pulled, whether right pull or left pull.

PVC pole: A strong but lightweight plastic plumbing pipe. This can be found at plumbing supply and home improvement stores. Must be covered with fabric or painted.

Railroad: To turn fabric so the selvage runs across the treatment instead of up and down. A 118-inch sheer is made to be used this way so that pinch pleats are put in across the selvage end instead of across the cut end. This can eliminate seams on some treatments.

Ready-mades: Standard-size draperies, factory made and available at local stores or through mail-order houses.

Repeat: See pattern repeat.

Return: The distance from the face of the rod to the wall or casing where the bracket or board is attached.

Right side: The printed side of the fabric that is used as the finished side of an item. The right side generally has the most color and the most finished look to it.

Rings: Rings of wood or plastic are hooked or sewn to the top edge of a curtain; the rings are then threaded through the curtain rod.

Rod: A metal fixture that holds curtain window treatments instead of a pole.

Rod pocket: A hollow sleeve in the top, and sometimes in the bottom, of a curtain or drapery through which a rod is inserted. The rod is then attached to the wall.

Rod-pocket curtains: Flat-panel curtains with a pocket or casing sewn into them to receive the curtain rod. The rod pocket is generally 2" larger than the size of the rod.

Roller shades: Made of vinyl or fabric attached to spring rollers that are mounted to the inside of the window frame/casing.

Roman shade (aka flat roman shade): A tailored fabric shade that hangs flat at the window; soft pleats form at the bottom as the shade is raised.

Roman valance: A soft, stationary valance fabricated similarly to a roman shade, with stationary horizontal folds.

Rosette: A fabric accent constructed to resemble an open rose. It is often used to accessorize a window fashion or disguise an area of construction.

Ruching: Extremely tight gathers used as a decorative top finish to a panel.

Ruched header: A method of gathering by incorporating extra fabric; this can be done by using shirring tape or adding extra fullness into rod pocket headers.

Running foot (aka RF): the same as linear foot. A method of measuring by counting the length or width by the number of feet in the treatment.

Sash: The part of a window that opens and closes. It includes a frame and one or more panes of glass. Also the frame and glass of an inoperable window.

Sash curtain: Any sheer material hung close to the window glass. Usually hung from spring-tension rods or sash rods mounted inside the window casing.

Sash rod: A small rod, either decorative or plain.

Scab: A thin strip of fiberboard or lumber glued over a seam that joins two pieces of lumber.

Scale: Relationship between an object's size and the size of the space in which it is located.

Scalloped heading: A popular top treatment for café curtains featuring semicircular spaces between pleats.

Sconce: A wall-mounted fixture that is great for draping fabric through.

Seam: The join where two pieces of fabrics are sewn together.

Seam allowance: An extra amount of fabric used when joining fabric.

Self-lined: The face of the fabric is also used as the lining.

Self-pelmet: A piece of fabric stitched to the top curtain window treatment to make it appear to be separate.

Self-styling tape: A stiff tape with woven-in cords used to create pleated and shirred curtains.

Selvage (aka selvedge): The tightly woven edge on the length of the fabric to hold the fabric together.

Shade: An operational device used to reduce or screen light or heat.

Shade cord: Strong left cord used to string through rings, screw eyes, pulleys, and locks on roman, Austrian and balloon shades.

Sheers: Curtains or draperies made of translucent fabric to filter light and provide minimal privacy; often used under another drapery.

Shirred: Gathered.

Shirred curtains: Any curtain gathered onto a curtain rod, but the term is frequently used for curtains gathered onto rods at both the top and bottom edges.

Shirred roman shade: Fabric is shirred onto horizontal ribs and operates as a roman shade.

Shirring tapes: Heading material used to create pleats, gathers, smocking, and other decorative headings.

Short point: The measurement a treatment will hang at its shortest area.

Sidelight: A glass panel adjacent to a door; often used at entries for appearance and to provide more light.

Side hem: The hem of the treatment has only 1/2 to 1 inch turned down inside to make a fold for sewing to the body fabric.

Single top: Heading in which the fabric is turned down the back and is finished either by turning 1/2 to 1 inch under the bottom of it or by serging the bottom along the edge of the buckram.

Sill: The horizontal, ledge-like portion of a window casing.

Sleeve: A decorative casing made to cover a rod without a panel hanging below. It may or may not have a header or skirt.

Slides (aka carriers): Small runners installed in a traverse rod, which hold a drapery pin or hook.

Slouch drapery panel: A type of drapery panel generally made without traditional pleats. It is a more casual style where the fabric along the heading is wavy to very loose, and the fabrication method for the heading can be any type, depending on desired look. For example, pleats of any type, tabs, tucks, or none at all, with or without buckram or crinoline.

Slot heading: See rod pocket.

Smocked pleats: A heading that resembles a hand-worked smocked pattern.

Soft cornice: A flat, stiffened fabric valance attached to a mount board with or without legs.

Spacing: Refers to the flat space between the pleats.

Spring tension rod: A curtain rod designed to compress snugly inside a window frame. Used when permanent fastening of a curtain rod is not desired.

Stack back (aka stack up): The amount of space taken up by a drapery or shade when they are completely open.

Stacking: The area required for draperies when they are completely opened.

Stagecoach valance: Used on narrow windows, this is a panel of fabric mounted on a board and attached to the inside frame of the window. It is rolled up and tied in the center with a ribbon.

Stationary panels: Purely decorative drapery panels that do not open or close.

Stay stitch: A row of long stitching, just inside the seam line, to prevent stretching and to protect the grain line.

Straight grain: The lengthwise threads of the fabric, running parallel to the selvages.

Sunburst: A semicircular window fashion used in the arch-top windows or above rectangular window to give the appearance of an arch-top window. Fabric is shirred around the circumference of the circle and gathered at the lower center.

Support: A pole or track that holds a curtain window treatment or shade.

Swag: A fabric top treatment that drapes into soft semicircular folds of fabric. Swags can be used with draperies or as a top treatment only.

Swag holder: Provides support for loosely draped treatments such as a throw swag. The harp shape allows fabric to be secured in a pouf fashion.

Swing arm: A hinged metal curtain rod that swings away to uncover a window fully.

Tabling: Measuring a treatment and marking it to the finished length before the final finishing.

Tab-top curtain: A curtain with fabric loops sewn to its top so it can loop around a drapery rod or pole.

Tail: The fabric that hangs from the end of a swag.

Tack strip: (Window treatments) A piece of fabric attached to a valance at the top to finish the raw edges and to allow for it to be mounted on the board. (Upholstery) A thin cardboard strip, 3/8 or 1/2 inch wide, used to prevent fabric from puckering between staples and giving a sharp, even edge.

Tapestry: Machine-woven fabric that looks hand-woven.

Tension pulley: The pulley attachment through which the traverse cords move when the drapery is drawn. Insures one smooth, continuous operation. May be mounted on baseboard, casing, or wall, on one or both sides.

Tension rod: See spring tension rod.

Thermal lining: Fabric that is layered with aluminum on one side for insulation.

Tieback: A decorative element used to gather drapery panels to the center or sides of a window opening to allow light and ventilation. It is also for aesthetic purposes.

Tiered curtains: Usually café curtains hung in two or more tiers with top curtains slightly overlapping lower ones.

Tie-tab curtains: Similar to tab-top curtains but with ribbons or fabric bands tied onto the rod.

Top treatment: Any decorative design at the top of a window. Top treatments can either stand alone or be incorporated as part of a larger window treatment design. Includes cornices, valances, and swags, etc.

Total width: The width of the board or rod, end to end, plus two returns.

Traverse: To draw across. A traverse drapery is one that opens and closes across a window by means of a traverse rod from which it is hung.

Traverse drapery: Treatment that opens or closes easily across a window by way of a traverse rod which it hangs from.

Traverse rod: Adjustable drapery rods that open and close the window treatment by pulling a cord.

Trims: Decorative braids, fringes, tassels, cords, gimps, and other fabric trims used as accent on curtains, draperies, or tiebacks.

Triple fullness: A fabric panel that is three times the width of the window. Often sheers and lightweight curtains are made in triple fullness.

T-square: An instrument consisting of two pieces used for testing the accuracy of square work and for making right angles.

Tuft: Clusters of thread drawn tightly through a pillow or cushion or furniture that holds the fabric and padding in place.

Turn of cloth: The minute ease of fabric that is lost from making a fold.

Twill tape: A strong (sew-on) tape that has a diagonal weave.

Two-way draw: A traverse rod that allows the draperies hung from it to pull closed from both sides to the center.

Under-drapery: A lightweight drapery, usually a sheer, closest to the window glass. It hangs beneath a heavier over drapery.

Upson board: A type of fiberboard that is made from 100 percent recycled components. Sometimes used to construct cornice boards. It is light-

weight, comes in 1/4 inch and 3/8 inch thickness, and is easy to work with.

Valance: A horizontal decorative fabric treatment used at the top of draperies to screen hardware and cords or as a stand-alone decorative element.

Valance board (aka mount board or dust board): The flat board without a front or sides from which a valance is hung.

Valance board with legs: A flat board with boards extending down each return end. It looks like a cornice without the front. This board is used when it is necessary to anchor the sides of the valance.

Velcro: Hook and loop tape used for attaching fabric to a mounting board. Sometimes used for lightweight fabrics and valances.

Venetian blinds: Made of wood or metal slats, attached to cloth tape, and worked by a cord pulley system.

Vertical blinds: Similar to Venetian blinds except that slats run vertical and are on a traverse track.

Wall mounting: Mounting a treatment on the wall beyond the window frame.

Waste: Any fabric that is left over or not used in the finished produce; e.g., excess parts of the repeats.

Warp and weft: Refers to the direction of threads in a fabric. Warp threads run the length of the fabric. They are crossed by the weft threads that run from selvage to selvage across the width of the fabric.

Weights (chain and lead): Lead weights are sewn in at the vertical seams and each corner of drapery panel. Chain weights are small heavy beads strung in a line along the bottom hemline of sheers to ensure an even hemline and straight hanging.

Welting: See cording.

Width: A word to describe a single width of fabric (from selvage to selvage). Several widths of fabric are sewn together to make a panel of drapery.

Wiggle board: Flexible board used to make soft or rounded edges and shapes in cornices.

Window jewelry: Small pieces of decorative hardware used as accents on fabric, usually serving no functional purpose but to add interest.

Window scarf: A long piece of fabric casually draped or swagged over a pole or rod at the top of a window.

Wrong side: The back side of the fabric that is the non-printed or less finished side; it may have stray threads or a rougher look to it.

Resources

Fabric Companies and Suppliers

Ado Corporation
adoservice@ado-usa.com
www.ado-usa.com

Arc-Com Fabrics, Inc.
Orangeburg, NY
914.365.1100

Artmark Fabrics Co., Inc.
Frazer, PA
610.647.3220

Ashbourne Fabrics, Inc.
Ivy Land, PA
215.364.6915

Barrow Industries
8260 N.W. 27th St.
Miami, FL 33122
800.624.9034
www.barrowindustries.com

Beacon Fabrics Web site
www.beaconfabric.com

Beacon Hill
225 Foxboro Blvd.
Foxboro, MA 02035
800.343.1470
www.beaconhilldesign.com

Bead Industries
mmeyer@beadindustries.com
www.beadindustries.com

Benartex, Inc.
1359 Broadway, Ste. 1100,
8th Fl.
New York, NY 10018
212.840.3250
www.benartex.com

Blonder
216.433.560

Brewster Wallcovering Company
781.963.4800

Brimar
28250 Ballard Dr.
Lake Forest, IL 60045
800.274.1205
www.brimarinc.com

Brocton Court
Los Alamitos, CA
714.236.8636

Brunschwig and Fils
75 Virginia Rd.
North White Plains, NY 10603
914.872.1100
www.brunschwig.com

Calvin Fabrics
2046 Lars Wy.
Medford, OR 97501
541.732.1996
www.henrycalvin.com

Carole Fabric
P.O. Box 1436
Augusta, GA 30903
800.241.2700
www.carolefabrics.com

Christopher Norman Collection, Inc.
11 Pen Plaza, Fifth Fl.
New York, NY 10001
877.846.0845
www.christophernorman.com

Clarence House Fabric
800.803.2850
www.clarencehouse.com

CMC Industries
Birmingham, AL
205.322.4546

Corry Textiles
Brooklyn, NY
718.858.4296

Covington Fabrics
New York, NY
212.689.2200

Creative Fabrics, Inc.
Hewitt, TX
254.666.1001

Creative Treatments
Parry Hall, MD
410.529.0342

Crestmont Fabrics, Ltd.
Hauppauge, NY
516.851.0950

Curtain and Drapery
Fashion, Inc.
704.861.8416

Custom Designs
Wilmington, NC
877.569.9025

Cyrus Clark Co., Inc.
New York, NY
212.684.5312

Decorator Land
Roseville, MI
810.293.0010

Decorators Supply Co.
888.218.5571
207.782.1392

Decorators Walk
Plainview, NY
516.249.3100

Delta Fabrics, Inc.
Atlanta, GA
770.458.7659

Distinctive Shades and Coverings (DSC)
303.423.5151

Diversified Fabrics, Inc.
Kings Mountain, NC
704.739.0708

Dixie Designers Resource Center
Orlando, FL
407.578.0000

Donghia Furniture/Textiles, Ltd.
New York, NY
212.925.2777

Duralee
1775 Fifth Ave.
Bay Shore, NY 11706
631.273.8800
www.duralee.com

Elite Textile, Inc.
Los Angeles, CA
213.689.3247

EMDEC Industries
Ozone Park, NY
718.848.8800

Expressive Design Systems, Inc.
Miami, FL
305.265.3700

Fabricade, Inc.
P.O. Box 438
Bohemia, NY 11716
800.645.5540

Fabrications International, Inc.
954.971.1462

Fabrics 21, Inc.
Montebello, CA
323.726.1266

Fabricut Fabrics
9303 E. 46th St.
Tulsa, OK 74145
800.999.8200
www.fabricut.com

Fabtex, Inc.
Danville, PA
570.275.7500

Fame Fabrics
New York, NY
212.679.6868

Fantagraph
Cincinnati, OH
513.761.9255

Franklin Corporation
Grandview, MO
816.763.1092

Garotex International, Inc.
Sandy Springs, SC
800.522.1209

Golding Fabrics
7097 Mendenhall Rd.
Archdale, NC 27263
336.883.9171
www.goldingfabrics.com

Gretchen Bellinger, Inc.
Cohoes, NY
518.235.2828

H. Lynn White, Inc.
Lenexa, KS
913.492.4100

Hampshire Printed Fabrics, Inc.
Lawrence, MA
978.683.9910

Hart-Lines by Valerie
Pompano, FL
954.783.7473

Heritage House Fabrics, Inc.
New York, NY
212.685.5556

Highland Court
A division of Duralee
1775 Fifth Ave.
P.O. Box 9179
Bay Shore, NY 11706
631.273.8800
www.highlandcourtfabrics.com

Interior Designers Supply, Inc.
405.235.8238

Interior Installations International
410.674.7097

Interspec Fabrics
Allenwood, NJ
732.938.4114

J. Ennis Fabrics, Ltd.
780.474.5721

J. F. Fabrics
Tonawanda, NY
905.624.5744

J. R. Burrows and Co.
P.O. Box 522
Rockland, MA 02370
800.347.1795
www.burrows.com

J. Robert Scott
500 N. Oak St.
Inglewood, CA 90302
800.322.4910
www.jrobertscott.com

JAB
A division of Stroheim and Romann
155 E. 56th St.
New York, NY 10022
212.486.1500
www.jab.de

Kaslen Fabrics
5899 Downey Rd.
Vernon, CA 90058
800.777.5789
www.kaslentextiles.com

Kasmir Fabric
2051 Alpine Wy.
Hayward, CA 94545
800.765.3284
www.kasmirfabrics.com

Kast Fabric
Preston Rd.
P.O. Box 1660
Pasadena, TX 77501
800.733.5278
www.kastfabrics.com

Kay & L Draperies, Inc.
Waverly, IA
319.352.1934

Kenfair Manufacturing Co.
Alexandria, VA
703.751.5900

Kenney Designer Resources, Inc.
314.576.6140

Kirsch Fabric Corp.
Minneapolis, MN
612.544.9111

Kravet Fabrics, Inc.
Bethpage, NY
516.293.2000
www.kravet.com

Lady Ann Fabrics, Inc.
St. Petersburg, FL
727.344.1819

Lafayette Venetian Blind, Inc.
765.742.8418

Laurco Fabrics, Inc.
Wichita, KS
316.262.5022

Lee Jofa
201 Central Ave. S.
Bethpage, NY 11714
800.453.3563
www.leejofa.com

Libas Silk
4400 Soto St.
Vermon, CA 90058
213.747.2406
www.libassilk.com

LoomCo Fabrics Int'l., Inc.
Tampa, FL
813.247.3611

Lord Jay, Inc.
Miami, FL
305.576.0157

Louver-Lite (Canada), Ltd.
905.684.0123

Lubotex, Inc.
St. Laurent, QB, Canada
514.335.1070

M. G. and Associates
Tampa, FL
813.974060

Maen Line Fabrics, Inc.
Philadelphia, PA
215.925.5537

Malitex Textil GmbH
Auerbach, Germany
49.3744.8270.0

Maxwell Fabric, Inc.
925 B. Boblett St.
Blaine, WA 98230
800.663.1159
www.maxwellfabrics.com

Met Fabrics
Birmingham, AL
205.322.5497

Metro Mills, Inc.
Paterson, NJ
973.942.8885

**Meyer Drapery
Services, Inc.**
Champaign, IL
217.352.5318

Michael Jon Designs
P.O. Box 59243
Los Angeles, CA 90058
323.582.0166
www.michaeljondesigns.com

Michaels Textile Co., Inc.
Petersburg, VA
804.732.0420

Mitchell Fabrics
810 SW Adams St.
Peoria, IL 61602
800.447.0952
www.mitchellfabrics.com

Motif Design
718 S. Fulton Ave.
Mount Vernon, NY 10550
800.431.2424
www.motif-designs.com

MW Canada
Cambridge, ON, Canada
519.621.5460

Oilcloth International
Los Angeles, CA
323.344.3967

On Track, Inc.
Columbus, OH
614.486.0348

Onthank Co.
Des Moines, IA
515.265.9801

P. Collins, Ltd.
High Point, NC
336.887.3086

Panoramic Shades
Concord, ON, Canada
905.669.6009

Park Wylie Distributors
Baltimore, MD
410.944.0082

**Payne
Westgate Fabrics, LLC**
905 Ave. T, Ste. 310
Grand Prairie, TX 75050
800.527.2517
www.paynefabrics.com

Pep-Tex, Inc.
Laval, PQ, Canada
450.622.0449

**Philip Graf
Wallpapers, Inc.**
Sarasota, FL
941.922.3452

Pillow Parlor
Dania, FL
954.925.6111

Pindler & Pindler, Inc.
Moorpark, CA
805.531.9090

Plumridge Silks
kitplum@earthlink.net
www.plumridge.com

Posh Limited
Albuquerque, NM
505.889.8880

Rackley's Rods, Inc.
Savannah, GA
912.354.0521

Ralph Lauren Home
867 Madison Ave.
New York, NY 10021
888.475.7674
www.rlhome.polo.com

Rapier-Cambridge Mills
High Point, NC
336.883.4141

Ray-Shel Enterprises
Chicago, IL
312.467.0891

Reliable Fabrics
Everette, MA
617.387.5321

Richard Bernard Fabrics
1810 John Towers Ave.
El Cajon, CA 92020
800.366.9800

**Richard Felber Designs,
Inc.**
Cleveland, OH
216.491.0900

Richloom Fabrics Group
New York, NY
212.685.5400

Rick Ackerman Associates
888.638.0364

Riftex Corp
South River, NJ
888.638.0364

RM Coco
P.O. Box 1270
Cape Girardeau, MO 63702
573.334.0517
www.rmcoco.com

Robert Allen Fabrics
55 Cabot Blvd.
Mansfield, MA 02048
800.295.3776
www.robertallendesign.com

Rockland Mills Div.
Rockland Ind., Inc.
410.522.2505

S & D Fabrics
Los Angeles, CA
213.748.9200

S. Harris
9303 E. 46th
Tulsa, OK 74145
800.999.5600
www.sharris.com

S. L. Textile Corp.
Yonkers, NY
914.375.0800

S & S Fabrics
Miami, FL
305.371.6684

Sanderson
285 Grand Ave.
3 Patriot Centre
Englewood, NJ 07631
800.894.6185
www.sanderson-online.co.uk

Sandi Distributors
Uniondale, NY
516.486.6220

Sani Line Sales
Carrollton, GA
770.832.2587

Scalamandré Fabrics
37-24 – 24th St.
Long Island City, NY 11101
718.361.8311
www.scalamandre.com

Schumacher and Co.
1325 Old Cooches Bridge Rd.
P.O. Box 6002
Newark, DE 19714
302.454.3200
www.fschumacher.com

Scroll Fabrics
770.432.7228
800.3.SCROLL

Sebring & Co.
Lenexa, KS
913.888.8141

Sheer Supply Corporation
Sarasota, FL
941.925.8787

Sidney Davis Fabrics, Inc.
San Francisco, CA
415.864.4400

Sierra Textile Company
San Diego, CA
619.550.3880

Silver State Fabrics
4343 Moreno Blvd., Ste. 4
San Diego, CA 92117
858.273.8349
www.silverstatefabrics.com

Soletex Fabrics, Inc.
Weston, ON, Canada
416.747.6797

Spectrum Fabrics
New York, NY
212.684.7100

Spring St. Designs, Inc.
Sarasota, FL
941.922.3452

Steven Fabrics
1400 Van Buren St. NE
Minneapolis, MN 55413
800.328.2558
www.stevenfabrics.com

Stout Fabric
3050 Trewigton Rd.
Colmar, PA 18915
800.523.2592

Stroheim and Romann
311 Thomson Ave.
Long Island, NY 11101
718.706.7000
www.stroheim.com

The Thomas Collection
Houston, TX
713.864.8086

Tietex International, Ltd.
Spartanburg, SC
864.574.0500

Travers
979 Third Ave.
New York, NY 10022
212.888.7900
www.traversinc.com

Trimland USA
60 E. Jefryn Blvd.
Deer Park , NY 11729
631.420.0814
Fax: 631.420.0832
TrimlandUSA@oz-is.com
www.trimland.com

Tritex Fabrics, Ltd.
Vancouver, BC, Canada
604.255.4242

**Unique Custom
Drapery & Upholstery**
501.751.2557

Urkov Mfg. Co.
Chicago, IL
312.633.0900

Vertilux, Ltd.
Miami, FL
305.591.1719

The Warner Co.
Chicago, IL
312.372.3540

Warren Shade Co.
Minneapolis, MN
612.331.5939

Waverly Fabric
800.523.1200
www.waverly.com

Wesco Fabric, Inc.
4001 Forest St.
Denver, CO 80126
303.388.4101
www.wescofabric.com

Westgate Fabrics
905 Ave. T, Ste. 310
Grand Prairie, TX 75050
800.527.6666
www.westgatefabrics.com

**Williamson Supply
Co., Inc.**
Houston, TX
713.660.0762

Window World, Inc.
Honolulu, HI
808.834.1114

The Wonderly Co., Inc.
Kingston, NY
914.331.0148

Passementerie

Brimar
28250 Ballard Dr.
Lake Forest, IL 60045
800.274.1205
www.brimarinc.com

British Trimmings
Stockport, UK
01614 806122
www.britishtrimmings.com

Conso
8701 Red Oak Blvd., Ste. 250
Charlotte, NC 28217
800.628.9362
www.conso.com

D'kei, Inc.
P.O. Box 1570
Council Bluffs, IA 51502
712.328.1800
www.dkei.net

Fabricut
9303 E. 46th St.
Tulsa, OK 74145
800.999.8200
www.fabricut.com

Kasmir
2051 Alpine Wy.
Hayward, CA 94545
800.765.3284
www.kasmirfabric.com

Kast
P.O.Box 1660
Pasadena, TX 77501
800.733.5278
www.kastfabric.com

Kenneth Meyer Company
1504 Bryant St., 3rd Fl.
San Francisco, CA 94103
415.861.0118

Kirsch
P.O. Box 0370
Sturgis, MI 49091
800.528.1407
www.kirsch.com

**Leslie Hannon Custom
Trimmings**
4018 E. 5th St.
Long Beach, CA 90814
562.433.0161

Lina's
525 S. Main St.
Greenville, MS 38701
800.459.5462

Maxwell
188 Victoria Dr.
Vancouver, BC, Canada
V5L4C3
604.253.7744
www.maxwellfabric.com

Pierre Frey
Paris, France
www.pierrefrey.com

Renaissance Ribbons
P.O. Box 699
Oregon House, CA 95961
530.692.0842
www.renaissanceribbons.com

RM Coco
P.O. Box 1270
Cape Garardeau, MO 63702
573.334.0517
www.rmcoco.com

Robert Allen
55 Cabolt Blvd.
Mansfield, MA 02048
800.295.3776
www.robertallendesign.com

Rue De France
78 Thomas St.
Newport, RI 02840
800.777.0998
www.ruedefrance.com

**San Francisco
Pleating Co.**
425 2nd St., 5th Fl.
San Francisco, CA
415.982.3003

Springs Window Fashions
7549 Graber Rd.
Middleton, WI 53562
800.521.8071

Stroheim and Romann
311 Thomson Ave.
Long Island City, NY 11101
718.706.7000
www.stroheim.com

Wendy Cushing Trimmings
Chelsea Harbour
Design Center
London, UK
020.7351.5796

Wesco
188 Victoria Dr.
Vancouver, BC, Canada
V5L 4C3
604.253.7744
www.maxwellfabric.com

**West Coast
Trimming Corp.**
7100 Wilson Ave.
Los Angeles, CA 90001
323.587.0701

Drapery Hardware

Amore
12121 Veteran's Memorial
Dr., Ste. 2
Houston, TX 77067
281.440.0123
www.amoredrapery
hardware.com

**Antique Drapery Rod
Company**
140 Glass St.
Dallas, TX 75207
214.653.1733
www.antiquedraperyrod.com

**Blaine Window
Hardware, Inc.**
17319 Blaine Dr.
Hagerstown, MD 21740
301.797.6500

Brimar
28250 Ballard Dr.
Lake Forest, IL 60045
847.247.0100
www.brimarinc.com

Cassidy West, Inc.
3151 Scott St.
Vista, CA 92081
800.755.2748
www.cassidywest.com

**Connecticut Curtain
& Linen Company**
Commerce Plaza, Rt. 6
Danbury, CT 06810
800.732.4549
sales@curtainrods.com
www.curtainrods.com

Conso Products
P.O.Box 326
Union, SC 29379
864.427.9004

Country Curtains
800.456.0321
www.countrycurtains.com

The Curzon Collection
680–8th St., Ste. 166
San Francisco, CA 94103
415.626.9038
www.curzon.co.za

D'Kei, Inc.
P.O. Box 1570
Council Bluffs, IA 51502
800.535.3534
www.dkei.net

Dorra Accents, Ltd.
310 Davenport Rd., Ste. 202
Toronto, ON, Canada M5R 1K6
416.977.9967
www.decoraccents.com

The Finial Company
8939 Directors Row
Dallas, TX 75247
214.678.0805
www.finialco.com

Gaby's Shoppe
1311 Dragon St.
Dallas, TX 75207
800.299.4229
www.gabys.com

Graber
877.792.0002
www.graberblinds.com

Helser Brothers, Inc.
3294 N. Nevada St.
Chandler, AZ 85225
888.FINIALS
www.4drapery.com

Highland Forge
Atlanta, GA
866.716.7555
Fax: 866.748.7557
www.highlandforge.com

**JL Anthony Custom
Drapery Hardware**
10420 Markison Rd.
Dallas, TX 75238
214.340.3108
www.jlanthony.com

K-Blair Finials
2870 N. Berkeley Lake Rd.,
Ste. 3
Duluth, GA 30096
770.622.1972
www.k-blairfinials.com

Kirsch
524 W. Stevenson St.
Freeport, IL 61032
800.528.1407
www.kirsch.com

Le Fer Forge Drapery
4629 SW 74th Ave.
Miami, FL 33155
305.266.1984
www.leferforge.com

Lundy's Ornamental Iron
34 Boston St.
Lynn, MA 01904
781.595.8639
www.lundysiron.com

M&T Drapes
523 S. 5th St.
Montrose, Co. 81401
970.240.8494
www.mtdrapes.com

Ona Drapery Co., Inc.
5320 Arapahoe Ave.
Boulder, CO 80303
800.231.4025
Fax: 303.786.7159
www.onadrapery.com

Orion Ornamental Iron, Inc.
6918 Tujunga Ave.
North Hollywood, CA 91605
877.476.6278
www.artbyorion.com

Paris Texas Hardware
5151 Mercantile Row
Dallas, TX 75247
800.540.7637
www.paristexashardware.com

Premier Window Wear
255 Ottley Dr. NE
Atlanta, GA 30324
800.251.5800
www.premierwindowwear.com

Pottery Barn
600 Broadway
New York, NY 10012
800.922.5507
www.potterybarn.com

Renovators Supply
P.O. Box 2515
Conway, NH 03818
800.659.0203
www.renovatorssupply.com

Restoration Hardware
104 Challenger Dr.
Portland, TN 37148
800.762.1005
www.restorationhardware.com

RM Co.
P.O. Box 1270
Cape Girardeau, MO 63702
573.334.0517
www.rmcoco.com

Robert Allen Fabrics
55 Cabot Blvd.
Mansfield, MA 02048
800.295.3776
www.robertallendesign.com

Sarkis Studio
306 Westfield St.
Greenville, SC 29601
800.793.0337
www.sarkisstudio.com

Stroheim and Romann
311 Thomson Ave.
Long Island City, NY 11101
718.706.7000
www.stroheim.com

Umbra
www.umbra.com

**Vesta Decorative
Home Accents**
109 Welpine Ridge Rd.
Pendleton, SC 29670
800.638.3782
www.ivesta.com

Drapery Pattern Companies

Decorate Now
P.O. Box 0168
Milledgeville, GA 31059
Fax: 478.453.3185
www.decoratenow.net

Home Dec In A Sec
866.466.3352
customerservice@homedeci-
nasec.com
www.homedecinasec.com

McCall
Patterns/Vogue/Butterick
Consumer Order Processing
Dept.
P.O. Box 3755
Manhattan, KS 66505
www.mccall.com

M'Fay Patterns
P.O. Box 2650
Matthews, NC 28106
704.847.1464
www.mfay.com

Pate Meadows Designs
1904 2nd Ave. N.
Bessemer, AL 35020
205.424.1770
www.patemeadows.com

Patterns Plus
P.O. Box 4338
N. Fort Myers, FL 33918
239.543.2355
www.patternsplus.com

Simplicity Patterns
www.simplicity.com

WCB Distributors
520.877.7908
www.windowcrowns.com

Drapery Workrooms

Carole Fabrics, Inc.
P.O. Box 1436
Augusta, GA 30903
706.863.4742
www.carolefabrics.com

Carol's Roman Shades
489 N. 1st St.
Grover Beach, CA 93433
800.422.1210
www.carolsromanshades.com

Home Dec In A Sec
866.466.3352
customerservice@homedeci-
nasec.com
www.homedecinasec.com

Kasmir
Attn.: Warehouse #2
3191 Commonwealth Dr.
Dallas, TX 75247
800.527.4630
www.kasmirfabrics.com

Robert Allen
Attn.: Soft Home Dept.
225 Foxboro Blvd.
Foxboro, MA 02035
800.333.3777
www.robertallendesign.com

Wesco Fabrics, Inc.
4001 Forest St.
Denver, CO 80216
303.388.4101
www.wescofabrics.com

Workroom Professionals
15680 Croaker Rd.
Jacksonville, FL 32226
904.714.2350
www.workroomprofessionals.com

Professional Organizations and Industry Resources

American Sewing Guild ("ASG")
www.asg.org

American Society of Interior Designers (ASID)
608 Massachusetts Ave., NE
Washington, DC 20002
202.546.3480
Fax: 202.546.3240
asid@asid.org
http://www.asid.org

Council for Interior Design Accreditation (formerly FIDER)
146 Monroe Center NW,
Ste. 1318
Grand Rapids, MI 49503
616.458.0400
Fax: 616.458.0460
info@accredit-id.org
http://www.accredit-id.org

Draperies and Window Coverings Magazine
840 U.S. Hwy. 1, Ste. 330
North Palm Beach, FL 33408
561.627.3393
561.694.6578
www.dwconline

Drapery Pro
27281 Las Nieves
Mission Viejo, CA 92691
949.916.9372
Fax: 949.916.9374
www.draperypro.com

Grace McNamara, Inc.
4215 White Bear Pkwy,
Ste. 100
St. Paul, MN 55110
651.293.1544
Fax: 651.653.4308
www.gracemcnamarainc.com

IFDA
International Furnishings and
Design Association
International Headquarters
191 Clarksville Rd.
Princeton Junction, NJ 08550
609.799.3423
Fax: 609.799.7032
info@ifda.com
www.ifda.com

Interior Design Educators Council (IDEC)
7150 Winton Dr., Ste. 300
Indianapolis, IN 46268
317.328.4421
Fax: 317.280.8527
info@idec.org
http://www.idec.org

International Interior Design Association (IIDA)
13-500 Merchandise Mart
Chicago, IL 60654
312.467.1950
Fax: 312.467.0779
iidahq@iida.org
http://www.iida.org

Window Covering Association of America (WCAA)
2646 Hwy. 109, Ste. 205
Grover, MO 63040
636.273.4090
Fax: 636.273.4439
www.wcaa.org

Window Fashions Certified Professionals Program (WFCP)
4215 White Bear Pkwy.,
Ste. 100
St. Paul, MN 55110
651.293.1544
Fax: 651.653.4308
www.wfcppro.com

Schools and Training

Cheryl Strickland
800.222.1415
828.686.3185
Fax: 828.686.3186

Custom Home Furnishings School
13900 South Lakes Dr., Ste. F
Charlotte, NC 28273
800.222.1415
704.333.4636
Fax: 704.333.4639
info@CHFschool.com
www.draperyschool.com

**HKH Design,
San Francisco, CA**
(Interlining training)
415.564.2385

LaVelle Pinder Decorating Professional Workroom & Design School Window Coverings Network
512.282.0717

Maureen Whitemore
British author and instructor
Enquires@maureenwhitmore.
co.uk

Merv's Upholstery Training
Videos, Merv's Videos
715.258.8785
www.mervstrainingvideos.com
info@ProfessionalDrapery.com
www.ProfessionalDrapery.com

Slipcover America, Inc.
Specializing in 1 and 2 days
slipcover workshops for
groups and associations. Also
individual consultations
for workrooms.
914 Repetto Dr.
St Louis, MO 63122
800.267.4958
karen@slipcoveramerica.com
www.slipcoveramerica.com

WCAA
2646 Hwy. 109, Ste. 205
Grover, MO 63040
636.273.4090
888.298.9222
Fax: 636.273.4439
www.wcaa.org

WFCP
Window Fashions
Certification Program
Grace McNamara, Inc.
4215 White Bear Pkwy., Ste. 100
St. Paul, MN 55110
651.293.1544
Fax: 651.653.4308
www.wfcppro.com

**Workroom Concepts/
Kitty Stein**
877.304.4939
Fax: 540.667.3170
kstein@WorkroomConcepts.com
www.WorkroomConcepts.com

Trade Shows and Seminars

**Custom Home Furnishings
Educational Conference
& Trade Show**
406 Christian Creek Rd.
Swannanoa, NC 28778
888.993.7273
Fax: 828.686.3186
bknorr@chfconferences.com
www.chfconferences.com

**International Window
Coverings Expo**
Grace McNamara, Inc.
www.windowcoveringexpo.com

**Las Vegas
World Market Center**
495 S. Grand Central Pkwy.
Las Vegas, NV 89106
866.229.3574
info@lasvegasmarket.com
www.lasvegasmarket.com

High Point Market
High Point International Home
Furnishings
Market Authority
P.O. BOX 5243
High Point, NC 27262
800.874.6492
www.highpointmarket.org

BORDERS.

BORDERS
BOOKS AND MUSIC
12055 METCALF AVE.
OVERLAND PARK KS 66213
(913) 663-2356

STORE: 0109   REG: 06/46   TRAN#: 3679
SALE   06/24/2010 EMP: 00411

DESIGN DIRECTORY OF WINDOW TRE
        9014996   CL T   60.00

            Subtotal   60.00
BR: 8241258691   S

            Subtotal   60.00
            KANSAS 7.65%   4.59
1 Item   Total   64.59
            VISA   64.59
ACCT # /S XXXXXXXXXXXXX2572
                AUTH: 024571
NAME: MURRAY/SAMANTHA

CUSTOMER COPY

06/24/2010 12:12PM
TRANS BARCODE: 01090636790041106240

BORDERS.

Returns

Returns of merchandise purchased from a Borders, Borders Express or Waldenbooks retail store will be permitted only if presented in saleable condition accompanied by the original sales receipt or Borders gift receipt within the time periods specified below. Returns accompanied by the original sales receipt must be made within 30 days of purchase and the purchase price will be refunded in the same form as the original purchase. Returns accompanied by the original Borders gift receipt must be made within 60 days of purchase and the purchase price will be refunded in the form of a return gift card.

Exchanges of opened audio books, music, videos, video games, software and electronics will be permitted subject to the same time periods and receipt requirements as above and can be made for the same item only.

Periodicals, newspapers, comic books, food and drink, digital downloads, gift cards, return gift cards, items marked "non-returnable," "final sale" or the like and out-of-print, collectible or pre-owned items cannot be returned or exchanged.

Returns and exchanges to a Borders, Borders Express or Waldenbooks retail store of merchandise purchased from Borders.com may be permitted in certain circumstances. See Borders.com for details.

BORDERS.

Returns

Returns of merchandise purchased from a Borders, Borders Express or Waldenbooks retail store will be permitted only if presented in saleable condition accompanied by the original sales receipt or Borders gift receipt within the time periods specified below. Returns accompanied by the original sales receipt must be made within 30 days of purchase and the purchase price will be refunded in the same form as the original purchase. Returns accompanied by the original Borders gift receipt must be made within 60 days of purchase and the purchase price will be refunded in the form of a return gift